Implementing Modern DevOps

Enabling IT organizations to deliver faster and smarter

David Gonzalez

BIRMINGHAM - MUMBAI

Implementing Modern DevOps

First published: October 2017

Production reference: 1290917

Published by Packt Publishing Ltd.
Livery Place
35 Livery Street
Birmingham
B3 2PB, UK.
ISBN 978-1-78646-687-7

www.packtpub.com

Credits

Author
David Gonzalez

Reviewer
Joakim Verona

Commissioning Editor
Kartikey Pandey

Acquisition Editor
Divya Poojari

Content Development Editor
Sharon Raj

Technical Editor
Prashant Chaudhari

Copy Editor
Stuti Srivastava

Project Coordinator
Virginia Dias

Proofreader
Safis Editing

Indexer
Pratik Shirodkar

Graphics
Kirk D'Penha

Production Coordinator
Deepika Naik

About the Author

David Gonzalez is an enthusiastic engineer and author of a book called *Developing Microservices with Node.js*; as microservices don't work without platform automation, he wrote this book to deliver the best possible deal to the readers of both books.

He is a Google Developer Expert (a nomination from Google to certain experts in several areas) in Kubernetes (GKE), who enjoys being pushed out of his comfort zone in order to sharpen his skills. Java, Node.js, Python, and DevOps--as well as a holistic approach to security--are part of the skill set that has helped him deliver value across different start-ups and corporations.

Nowadays, he is a consultant at nearForm, enabling companies to deliver the best possible solution to their IT problems or proposals, as well as an avid speaker at conferences, such as RebelCon and Google I/O Extended, among others.

About the Reviewer

Joakim Verona is a consultant with expertise in continuous delivery and DevOps. He has worked with all aspects of systems development since 1994. He has actively contributed as the lead implementer of complex multilayered systems, such as web systems, multimedia systems, and mixed software/hardware systems. His wide-ranging technical interests led him to the emerging field of DevOps in 2004, where he has stayed ever since. Joakim completed his master's in computer science at Linköping Institute of Technology. He has also worked as a consultant in a wide range of assignments in various industries, such as banking and finance, telecom, industrial engineering, press and publishing, and game development. He is also interested in the Agile field and is a certified Scrum master, Scrum product owner, and Java professional.

He has also technically reviewed *Practical DevOps*.

www.PacktPub.com

For support files and downloads related to your book, please visit www.PacktPub.com. Did you know that Packt offers eBook versions of every book published, with PDF and ePub files available? You can upgrade to the eBook version at www.PacktPub.com and as a print book customer, you are entitled to a discount on the eBook copy. Get in touch with us at service@packtpub.com for more details. At www.PacktPub.com, you can also read a collection of free technical articles, sign up for a range of free newsletters and receive exclusive discounts and offers on Packt books and eBooks.

https://www.packtpub.com/mapt

Get the most in-demand software skills with Mapt. Mapt gives you full access to all Packt books and video courses, as well as industry-leading tools to help you plan your personal development and advance your career.

Why subscribe?

- Fully searchable across every book published by Packt
- Copy and paste, print, and bookmark content
- On demand and accessible via a web browser

Customer Feedback

Thanks for purchasing this Packt book. At Packt, quality is at the heart of our editorial process. To help us improve, please leave us an honest review on this book's Amazon page at https://www.amazon.com/dp/1786466872.

If you'd like to join our team of regular reviewers, you can email us at customerreviews@packtpub.com. We award our regular reviewers with free eBooks and videos in exchange for their valuable feedback. Help us be relentless in improving our products!

To my wife, Ester. No matter how many crazy ideas I have, you are always there to support and push me forward. This book wouldn't have been possible without you.

To our daughter, Elena. Always remember, we raised you to be happy, not perfect. No matter what path you follow, we will be there, helping you.

Table of Contents

Preface

DevOps is the newest revolution in deploying software quickly and efficiently. With a set of automation tools, an orchestration platform, and a few processes, companies can speed up the release cycle of their IT systems by enabling the engineers to do more with fewer resources and become more engaged in the business process.

What this book covers

Chapter 1, *DevOps in the Real World*, shows the place of DevOps in the current engineering department of IT companies and how to align resources to maximize delivery potential.

Chapter 2, *Cloud Data Centers*, compares the different cloud solutions for managing resources (VMs, networks, disks, and so on) on the cloud and on demand.

Chapter 3, *Docker*, teaches about Docker and some of its internals in order to better understand how containerization technologies work.

Chapter 4, *Continuous Integration*, talks about continuous integration technologies that can be used to execute tests across your applications as well as many other actions, as we will see in Chapter 8, *Release Management – Continuous Delivery*.

Chapter 5, *Infrastructure as Code*, shows how to describe our infrastructure in a way that can be managed as code and apply the SDLC best practices to it in order to ensure its integrity.

Chapter 6, *Server Provisioning*, shows how to use Ansible to manage the configuration of remote servers in order to facilitate the maintenance of a large number of servers that, even though we are going to focus on Kubernetes, are good to know.

Chapter 7, *Docker Swarm and Kubernetes - Clustering Infrastructure*, briefly visits Docker Swarm and then points your attention toward Kubernetes, the most modern container orchestration technology, which is used across the biggest corporations in the world, such as Google.

Chapter 8, *Release Management – Continuous Delivery,* shows how to set up a continuous delivery pipeline on Google Cloud Platform with Kubernetes and Jenkins.

Chapter 9, *Monitoring,* shows how to monitor our software and servers to be the first ones to know about a potential outage very quickly and fix it (potentially) before impacting our customers.

What you need for this book

In order to follow this book and its contents, you will need a trial account on Google Cloud Platform and an editor (I used Atom but any other editor will work) as well as Node.js installed on your local machine. You will also need to install Docker locally in order to test the different examples. We will use **Google Container Engine** (**GKE**)for the Kubernetes examples but if you want to play locally with Kubernetes, Minikube can also be used, although you need a fairly powerful computer.

Who this book is for

This book is for engineers who want to step up in the DevOps ladder, particularly if they want to master Kubernetes and containers. People of mid-level skills are ideal readers.

Conventions

In this book, you will find a number of text styles that distinguish between different kinds of information. Here are some examples of these styles and an explanation of their meaning. Code words in text, database table names, folder names, filenames, file extensions, pathnames, dummy URLs, user input, and Twitter handles are shown as follows: "The next lines of code read the link and assign it to the BeautifulSoup function." A block of code is set as follows:

```
resource "google_compute_address" "my-first-ip" {
 name = "static-ip-address"
}
```

When we wish to draw your attention to a particular part of a code block, the relevant lines or items are set in bold:

```
resource "google_compute_address" "my-first-ip" {
 name = "static-ip-address"
}
```

Any command-line input or output is written as follows:

```
docker commit 329b2f9332d5 my-ubuntu
```

New terms and **important words** are shown in bold. Words that you see on the screen, for example, in menus or dialog boxes, appear in the text like this: "In order to download new modules, we will go to **Files** | **Settings** | **Project Name** | **Project Interpreter**."

Warnings or important notes appear like this.

Tips and tricks appear like this.

Reader feedback

Feedback from our readers is always welcome. Let us know what you think about this book-what you liked or disliked. Reader feedback is important for us as it helps us develop titles that you will really get the most out of. To send us general feedback, simply email feedback@packtpub.com, and mention the book's title in the subject of your message. If there is a topic that you have expertise in and you are interested in either writing or contributing to a book, see our author guide at www.packtpub.com/authors.

Customer support

Now that you are the proud owner of a Packt book, we have a number of things to help you to get the most from your purchase.

Downloading the example code

You can download the example code files for this book from your account at http://www.packtpub.com. If you purchased this book elsewhere, you can visit http://www.packtpub.com/support and register to have the files emailed directly to you. You can download the code files by following these steps:

1. Log in or register to our website using your email address and password.
2. Hover the mouse pointer on the **SUPPORT** tab at the top.

3. Click on **Code Downloads & Errata**.
4. Enter the name of the book in the **Search** box.
5. Select the book for which you're looking to download the code files.
6. Choose from the drop-down menu where you purchased this book from.
7. Click on **Code Download**.

Once the file is downloaded, please make sure that you unzip or extract the folder using the latest version of:

- WinRAR / 7-Zip for Windows
- Zipeg / iZip / UnRarX for Mac
- 7-Zip / PeaZip for Linux

The code bundle for the book is also hosted on GitHub at `https://github.com/PacktPublishing/Implementing-Modern-DevOps`. We also have other code bundles from our rich catalog of books and videos available at `https://github.com/PacktPublishing/`. Check them out!

Downloading the color images of this book

We also provide you with a PDF file that has color images of the screenshots/diagrams used in this book. The color images will help you better understand the changes in the output. You can download this file from `https://www.packtpub.com/sites/default/files/downloads/ImplementingModernDevOps_ColorImages.pdf`.

Errata

Although we have taken every care to ensure the accuracy of our content, mistakes do happen. If you find a mistake in one of our books-maybe a mistake in the text or the code- we would be grateful if you could report this to us. By doing so, you can save other readers from frustration and help us improve subsequent versions of this book. If you find any errata, please report them by visiting `http://www.packtpub.com/submit-errata`, selecting your book, clicking on the **Errata Submission Form** link, and entering the details of your errata. Once your errata are verified, your submission will be accepted and the errata will be uploaded to our website or added to any list of existing errata under the Errata section of that title.

To view the previously submitted errata, go to https://www.packtpub.com/books/content/support and enter the name of the book in the search field. The required information will appear under the **Errata** section.

Piracy

Piracy of copyrighted material on the internet is an ongoing problem across all media. At Packt, we take the protection of our copyright and licenses very seriously. If you come across any illegal copies of our works in any form on the internet, please provide us with the location address or website name immediately so that we can pursue a remedy. Please contact us at copyright@packtpub.com with a link to the suspected pirated material.

We appreciate your help in protecting our authors and our ability to bring you valuable content.

Questions

If you have a problem with any aspect of this book, you can contact us at questions@packtpub.com, and we will do our best to address the problem.

1
DevOps in the Real World

In the past few years, the software world has evolved at a very high pace. One of my favorite examples of evolution is FinTech, a new field whose name comes from the fusion of finance and technology. In this field, companies tend to build financial products in a disruptive way up to a point that they are threatening the big traditional banks and putting them in jeopardy.

This happens mainly due to the fact that big companies lose the ability to be cost-effective in their IT systems and banks are fairly big companies. It is not strange that banks still run their systems in an IBM mainframe and are reluctant to move to the cloud, and it is also not strange that the core components of the banks are still COBOL applications that haven't been renewed since the 90s. This wouldn't be bad if it wasn't because a small number of talented engineers with an AWS or Google Cloud Platform account can actually build a service that could virtually replace some bank products such as currency exchange or even a broker.

This has become a norm in the last few years, and one of the keys for the success of small companies in FinTech is partially due to DevOps and partially due to its scale. Usually, big companies commoditize the IT systems over time, outsourcing them to third parties that work on price, pushing the quality aside. This is a very effective cost-cutting measure, but it has a downside: you lose the ability to deliver value quickly.

In this chapter, we are going to put DevOps into perspective and see how it can help us create cost-effective work units that can deliver a lot of value in a very short period of time.

What is DevOps?

There is a famous quote by Henry Ford, the creator of Ford (the popular car-maker brand):

> *"If I had asked people what they wanted, they would have said faster horses."*

This is what happened with the traditional system administrator role: people were trying to solve the wrong problem.

By the wrong problem, I mean the lack of proper tools to automate the intervention in production systems, avoiding the human error (which is more common than you may think) and leading to a lack of communication continuity in the processes of your company.

Initially, DevOps was the intersection of development and operations as well as QA. The DevOps engineer is supposed to do everything and be totally involved in the SDLC (software development life cycle), solving the communication problems that are present in the traditional release management. This is ideal and, in my opinion, is what a full stack engineer should do: end-to-end software development, from requirement capture to deployments and maintenance.

Nowadays, this definition has been bent up to a point where a DevOps engineer is basically a systems engineer using a set of tools to automate the infrastructure of any company. There is nothing wrong with this definition of DevOps, but keep in mind that we are losing a very competitive advantage: the end-to-end view of the system. In general, I would not call this actor a DevOps engineer but an **Site reliability engineering** (SRE). This was a term introduced by Google few years back, as sometimes (prominently in big companies), is not possible to provide a single engineer with the level of access required to execute DevOps. We will talk more about this role in the next section, SRE model.

In my opinion, DevOps is a philosophy more than a set of tools or a procedure: having your engineers exposed to the full life cycle of your product requires a lot of discipline but gives you an enormous amount of control over what is being built. If the engineers understand the problem, they will solve it; it is what they are good at.

DevOps origins

In the last few years, we have gone through a revolution in IT: it sparkled from pure IT companies to all the sectors: retail, banking, finance, and so on. This has led to a number of small companies called start-ups, which are basically a number of individuals who had an idea, executed it, and went to the market in order to sell the product or the service to a global market (usually). Companies such as Amazon or Alibaba, not to mention Google, Apple, Stripe or even Spotify, have gone from the garage of one of the owners to big companies employing thousands of people.

One thing in common in the initial spark with these companies has always been corporate inefficiency: the bigger the company, the longer it takes to complete simple tasks.

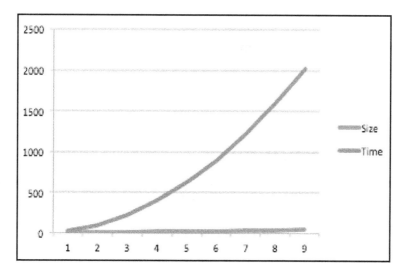

Example of corporate inefficiency graph

This phenomenon creates a market on its own, with a demand that cannot be satisfied with traditional products. In order to provide a more agile service, these start-ups need to be cost-effective. It is okay for a big bank to spend millions on its currency exchange platform, but if you are a small company making your way through, your only possibility against a big bank is to cut costs by automation and better processes. This is a big drive for small companies to adopt better ways of doing things, as every day that passes is one day closer to running out of cash, but there is a bigger drive for adopting DevOps tools: failure.

Failure is a natural factor for the development of any system. No matter how much effort we put in, failure is always there, and at some point, it is going to happen.

Usually, companies are quite focused on removing failure, but there is a unwritten rule that is keeping them from succeeding: the 80-20 rule:

- It takes 20% of time to achieve 80% of your goals. The remaining 20% will take 80% of your time.

Spending a huge amount of time on avoiding failure is bound to fail, but luckily, there is another solution: quick recovery.

Up until now, in my work experience, I have only seen one company asking "what can we do if this fails at 4 A.M. in the morning?" instead of "what else can we do to avoid this system from failing?", and believe me, it is a lot easier (especially with the modern tools) to create a recovery system than to make sure that our systems won't go down.

All these events (automation and failure management) led to the development of modern automation tools that enabled our engineers to:

- Automate infrastructure and software
- Recover from errors quickly

DevOps and corporations

DevOps fits perfectly into the small company world (start-ups): some individuals that can access everything and execute the commands that they need to make the changes in the system quickly. Within these ecosystems is where DevOps shines.

This level of access in traditional development models in big companies is a no-go. It can be an impediment even at a legal level if your system is dealing with highly confidential data, where you need to get your employees security clearance from the government in order to grant them access to the data.

It can also be convenient for the company to keep a traditional development team that delivers products to a group of engineers that runs it but works closely with the developers so that the communication is not an issue.

SREs also use DevOps tools, but usually, they focus more on building and running a middleware cluster (Kubernetes, Docker Swarm, and so on) that provides uniformity and a common language for the developers to be abstracted from the infrastructure: they don't even need to know in which hardware the cluster is deployed; they just need to create the descriptors for the applications that they will deploy (the developers) in the cluster in an access-controlled and automated manner in a way that the security policies are followed up.

SRE is a discipline on its own, and Google has published a free ebook about it, which can be found at `https://landing.google.com/sre/book.html`.

I would recommend that you read it as it is a fairly interesting point of view.

Traditional release management

Through the years, companies have pushed the development of their IT systems out of their business core processes: retail shop business was retail and not software but reality has kicked in very quickly with companies such as Amazon or Alibaba, which can partially attribute their success to keeping their IT systems in the core of the business.

A few years ago, companies used to outsource their entire IT systems, trying to push the complexity aside from the main business in the same way that companies outsource the maintenance of the offices where they are. This has been successful for quite a long time as the release cycles of the same applications or systems were long enough (a couple of times a year) to be able to articulate a complex chain of change management as a release was a big bang style event where everything was measured to the millimeter with little to no tolerance for failure.

Usually, the life cycle for such projects is very similar to what is shown in the following diagram:

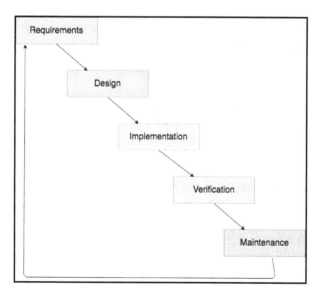

This model is traditionally known as **waterfall** (you can see its shape), and it is borrowed from traditional industrial pipelines where things happen in very well-defined order and stages. In the very beginning of the software industry, engineers tried to retrofit the practices from the traditional industry to software, which, while a good idea, has some drawbacks:

- Old problems are brought to a new field
- The advantages of software being intangible are negated

With waterfall, we have a big problem: nothing moves quickly. No matter how much effort is put into the process, it is designed for enormous software components that are released few times a year or even once a year. If you try to apply this model to smaller software components, it is going to fail due to the number of actors involved in it. It is more than likely that the person who captures the requirements won't be involved in the development of the application and, for sure, won't know anything about the deployment.

Chain of communication

I remember that when I was a kid, we used to play a game called the crazy phone. Someone would make up a story with plenty of details and write it down on paper. This person read the story to another person, who had to capture as much as possible and do the same to the next person, up until we reached the end of the number of people playing this game. After four people, it was almost guaranteed that the story wouldn't look anywhere close to the initial one, but there was a more worrying detail: after the first person, the story would never be the same. Details would be removed and invented, but things would surely be different.

This exact game is what we are trying to replicate in the waterfall model: people who are working on the requirements are creating a story that is going to be told to developers, who are creating another story that is going to be told to QA so that they can test that the software product delivered matches with a story that was in two hands (at the very least) before reaching them.

As you can see, this is bound to be a disaster but hold on, what can we do to fix it? If we look at the traditional industry, we'll see that they never get their designs wrong or, at least, the error rate is very small. The reason for that (in my opinion) is that they are building tangible things, such as a car or a nuclear reactor, which can easily be inspected and believe me or not, they are usually simpler than a software project. If you drive a car, after a few minutes, you will be able to spot problems with the engine, but if you start using a new version of some software, it might take a few years to spot security problems or even functional problems.

In software, we tried to ease this problem by creating very concise and complex diagrams using **Unified Modeling Language** (**UML**) so that we capture the single source of truth and we can always go back to it to solve problems or validate our artifacts. Even though this is a better approach, it is not exempt from problems:

- Some details are hard to capture in diagrams
- People in the business stakeholders do not understand UML
- Creating diagrams requires time

Particularly, the fact that the business stakeholders do not understand UML is the big problem here. After the capture of requirements, changing them or even raising questions on lower levels (development, operations, and so on) requires involving some people, and at least one of them (the business stakeholder) does not understand the language of where the requirements were captured. This wouldn't be a problem if the project requirements were spot on since the first iteration, but in how many projects have you been involved where the requirements were static? The answer is none.

The cost of fixing a bug

Once we have made it clear that we have a communication problem, bugs are expected to arise during our process. Either a misalignment with the requirements or even the requirements being wrong usually leads to a defect that could prevent us from deploying the application to production and delay everything.

In waterfall, fixing a bug is increasingly possible in every step we take. For example, fixing a bug in the requirements phase is very straightforward: just update the diagrams/documentation, and we are done. If the same bug is captured by a QA engineer in the verification phase, we need to:

- Update the documents/diagrams
- Create a new version of the application

- Deploy the new version to the QA environment

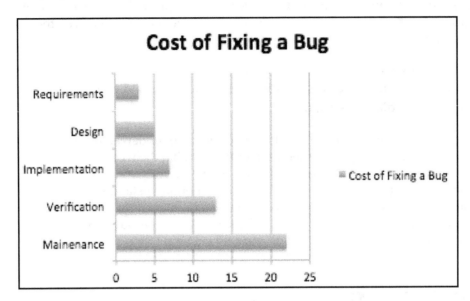

If the bug is caught in production, you can imagine how many steps are involved in fixing it, not to mention the stress, particularly if the bug compromises the revenue of your company.

Releasing new versions

A few years ago, I used to work in a company where the production rollouts steps were written in a Microsoft Word document command by command along with the explanation:

- Copy this file there: `cp a.tar b.tar`
- Restart the server `xyz` with the command: `sudo service my-server restart`

This was in addition to a long list of actions to take to release a new version. This happened because it was a fairly big company that had commoditized its IT department, and even though their business was based on an IT product, they did not embed IT in the core of their business.

As you can see, this is a very risky situation. Even though the developer who created the version and the deployment document was there, someone was deploying a new WAR (a Java web application packed in a file) in a production machine, following the instructions blindly. I remember asking one day: if this guy is executing the commands without questioning them, why don't we just write a script that we run in production? It was too risky, they said.

They were right about it: risk is something that we want to reduce when deploying a new version of the software that is being used by some hundred thousand people on a single day. In fairness, risk is what pushed us to do the deployment at 4 A.M. instead of doing it during business hours.

The problem I see with this is that the way to mitigate the risks (deploy at 4 A.M in the morning when no one is buying our product) creates what we call, in IT, a single point of failure: the deployment is some sort of all or nothing event that is massively constrained by the time, as at 8 A.M., the traffic in the app usually went from two visits per hour to thousands per minute, around 9 A.M. being the busiest period of the day.

That said, there were two possible outcomes from the rollout: either the new software gets deployed or not. This causes stress to the people involved, and the last thing you want to have is stressed people playing with the systems of a multi-million business.

Let's take a look at the maths behind a manual deployment, such as the one from earlier:

Description	Success Rate
Detach `server 1` from the cluster	99.5%
Stop `Tomcat` on `server 1`	99.5%
Remove the old version of the app (the WAR file)	98%
Copy the new version of the app (the WAR file)	98%
Update properties in configuration files	95%
Start `Tomcat`	95%
Attach `server 1` to the cluster	99.5%

This describes the steps involved in releasing a new version of the software in a single machine. The full company system had a few machines, so the process would have to be repeated a number of times, but let's keep it simple; assume that we are only rolling out to a single server.

Now a simple question: what is the overall failure rate in the process?

We naturally tend to think that the probability of a failure in a chained process such as the preceding list of instructions is the biggest in any step of the chain: 5%. That is not true. In fairness, it is a very dangerous, cognitive bias. We usually take very risky decisions due to the false perception of low risk.

Let's use the math to calculate the probability of failure:

The preceding list is a list of dependent events. We cannot execute step number 6 if step 4 failed, so the formula that we are going to apply is the following one:

```
P(T) = P(A1)*P(A2)...*P(An)
```

This leads to the following calculation:

```
P(T) = (99.5/100) * (99.5/100) * (98/100) * (98/100) * (95/100) * (95/100)
* (99.5/100) = 0.8538
```

We are going to be successful only 85.38% of the times. This translated to deployments, which means that we are going to have problems 1 out of 6 times that we wake up at 4 A.M. to release a new version of our application, but there is a bigger problem: what if we have a bug that no one noticed during the production testing that happened just after the release? The answer to this question is simple and painful: the company would need to take down the full system to roll back to a previous version, which could lead to loss of revenue and customers.

Modern release management

A few years ago, when I was in the middle of a manual deployment at 4 A.M., I remember asking myself "there has to be a better way". Tools were not mature enough, and the majority of the companies did not consider IT the core of their business. Then, a change happened: DevOps tools started to do well in the open source community and companies started to create continuous delivery pipelines. Some of them were successful, but a big majority of them failed for two reasons:

- Release management process
- Failure in the organizational alignment

We will talk about organizational alignment later on in this chapter. For now, we are going to focus on the release management process as it needs to be completely different from the traditional release management in order to facilitate the software life cycle.

In the preceding section, we talked about different phases:

- Requirements
- Design
- Implementation
- Verification
- Maintenance

We also explained how it works well with gigantic software where we group features into big releases that get executed in a big bang style with all or nothing deployments.

The first try to fit this process into smaller software components was what everyone calls agile, but no one really knew what it was.

Agile development and communication

In the traditional release management, one of the big problems was the communication: chains of people passing on messages and information, as we've seen, never ends well.

Agile encourages shorter communication strings: the stakeholders are supposed to be involved in the software development management, from the definition of requirements to the verification (testing) of the same software. This has an enormous advantage: teams never build features that are not required. If deadlines need to be met, the engineering team sizes down the final product sacrificing functionality but not quality.

Deliver early and deliver often is the mantra of agile, which basically means defining an **Minimum Viable Product** (**MVP**) and delivering it as soon as it is ready in order to deliver value to the customers of your application and then delivering new features as required. With this method, we are delivering value since the first release and getting feedback very early on in the product life.

In order to articulate this way of working, a new concept was introduced: the sprint. A sprint is a period of time (usually 2 weeks) with a set of functionalities that are supposed to be delivered at the end of it into production so that we achieve different effects:

- Customers are able to get value very often

- Feedback reaches the development team every 2 weeks so that corrective actions can be carried on
- The team becomes predictable and savvy with estimates

This last point is very important: if our estimates are off by 10% in a quarter release, it means that we are off by two weeks, whereas in a two weeks sprint, we are off only by 1 day, which, over time, with the knowledge gained sprint after sprint, means the team will be able to adjust due to the fact that the team builds a database of features and time spent on them so that we are able to compare new features against the already developed ones.

These features aren't called features. They are called stories. A story is, by definition, a well-defined functionality with all the info for the development team captured before the sprint starts, so once we start the development of the sprint, developers can focus on technical activities instead of focusing on resolving unknowns in these features.

Not all the stories have the same size, so we need a measurement unit: the story points. Usually, story points do not relate to a time-frame but to the complexity of it. This allows the team to calculate how many story points can be delivered at the end of the sprint, so with time, they get better at the estimates and everybody gets their expectations satisfied.

At the end of every sprint, the team is supposed to release the features developed, tested, and integrated into production in order to move to the next sprint.

The content of the sprints are selected from a backlog that the team is also maintaining and preparing as they go.

The main goal is to meet everyone's expectations by keeping the communication open and be able to predict what is being delivered and when and what is needed for it.

There are several ways of implementing the agile methodologies in our software product. The one explained earlier is called **Scrum**, but if you look into other development methodologies, you'll see that they all focus on the same concept: improving the communication across different actors of the same team.

If you are interested in **Scrum**, there is more info at `https://en.wikipedia.org/wiki/Scrum_(software_development)`.

Releasing new versions

As explained earlier, if we follow the Scrum methodology, we are supposed to deliver a new version every 2 weeks (the duration of a sprint in the majority of the cases), which has a dramatic impact on the resources consumed. Let's do the maths: quarter versus bi-weekly releases:

- In quarter releases, we release only four times a year in addition to emergency releases to fix problems found in production.
- In bi-weekly releases, we release once every 2 weeks in addition to emergency releases. This means 26 releases a year (52 weeks roughly) in addition to emergency releases.

For the sake of simplicity, let's ignore the emergency releases and focus on business as usual in our application. Let's assume this takes us 10 hours to prepare and release our software:

- Quarter releases: *10 x 4 = 40* hours a year
- Bi-weekly releases: *10 x 26 = 260* hours a year

As of now, releasing software is always the same activity, no matter whether we do it every quarter or every day. The implication is the same (roughly), so we have a big problem: our bi-weekly release is consuming a lot of time and it gets worse if we need to release fixes for problems that have been overlooked in QA.

There is only one solution for this: automation. As mentioned earlier, up until 2 years ago (around 2015) the tools to orchestrate automatic deployments weren't mature enough. Bash scripts were common but weren't ideal as bash is not designed to alter the state of production servers.

The first few tools to automate deployments were frameworks to manage the state of servers: Capistrano or Fabric wrapped `ssh` access and state management in a set of commands on Ruby and Python, which allowed the developers to create scripts that, depending on the state of the servers, were executing different steps to achieve a goal: deploying a new version.

These frameworks were a good step forward, but there were bigger problems with them: a solution across different companies usually solves the same problem in different ways, which implies that DevOps (developers + ops) engineers need to learn how to handle this in every single company.

The real change came with Docker and orchestration platforms, such as Kubernetes or Docker Swarm. In this book, we will look at how to use them, particularly Kubernetes, to reduce the deployment time from 10 hours (or hours in general) to a simple click, so our 260 hours a year become a few minutes for every release.

This also has a side-effect, which is related to what we explained earlier in this chapter: from a very risky release (remember, 85.38% of success) with a lot of stress, we are moving toward a release that can be patched in minutes, so releasing a bug, even though it is bad, has a reduced impact due to the fact that we can fix it within minutes or even roll back within seconds. We will look at how to do this in Chapter 8, *Release Management – Continuous Delivery*.

Once we are aligned with these practices, we can even release individual items to production: once a feature is ready, if the deployment is automated and it gets reduced to a single click, why not just roll out the stories as they are completed?

DevOps and microservices

Microservices are a big trend nowadays: small software components that allow companies to manage their systems on vertical slices of functionality, deploying features individually instead of bundling them in a big application, which can be problematic in big teams as the interaction across functionalities often leads to collisions and bugs being released into production without anyone noticing.

An example of quite a successful company using microservices is Spotify. Not only at the technical level but at the business level, they have organized things to be able to orchestrate a large number of services to provide a top class music streaming service that pretty much never fails, and if it does, it is a partial failure:

- Playlists are managed by a microservice; therefore, if it goes down, only playlists are unavailable.
- If the recommendations are not working, the users usually don't even notice it.

This comes at a huge cost: operational overhead. Splitting an application into many requires a proportional amount of operations to keep it running, which can be exponential if it is not handled well. Let's look at an example:

- Our system is composed of five applications: A, B, C, D, and E.

- Each of them is a microservice that is deployed individually and requires around 5 hours a month of operations (deployments, capacity planning, maintenance, and so on)

If we bundle all five applications together into a single big application, our maintenance cost goes down drastically to pretty much the same as any of the previously mentioned microservices. The numbers are clear:

- 25 hours a month for a microservices-based system
- 5 hours a month for a monolithic application

This leads to a problem: if our system grows up to hundreds (yes, hundreds) microservices, the situation becomes hard to manage as it consumes all our time.

The only solution to this is automation. There will always be an operational overhead, but with automation, instead of adding 5 hours a month per service, this time will decrease with time, as once we have automated our interventions, there is pretty much no time consumed by new services as everything happens as a chain of events.

In Chapter 8, *Release Management – Continuous Delivery*, we are going to set up a continuous delivery pipeline to demonstrate how this is possible, and even though we will have some manual steps for sanity, it is possible to fully automate the operations on a microservices environment running in a cluster such as Kubernetes.

In general, I would not advise any company to start a project based on microservices without proper automation in place and more specifically, if you are convinced that the system will grow over time, Kubernetes would be a very interesting option: it gives you the language that other platforms lack, such as load balancers, routing, ingress, and more. We will dive deep into Kubernetes in the upcoming chapters.

All these activities are supposed to be part of the DevOps engineer's day-to-day work (among many others), but first, there is a problem that we need to solve: how to align our company resources to be able to get the most from the DevOps engineer figure.

DevOps: Organizational alignment

Up until now, we have looked at how the modern and traditional release life cycle works. We have also defined what a DevOps engineer is and also how they can help with Microservices, which, as explained, are not viable without the right level of automation.

Apart from technicalities, there is something that is extremely important for the DevOps culture to succeed: organizational alignment.

The traditional software development used to divide teams into different roles:

- Business analysts
- Developers
- System administrators
- QA engineers

This is what we call horizontal slices: a team of system administrators has a few contact points with the developers so that they get enough information to deploy and maintain software.

In the modern release life cycle, this simply does not work. Instead of horizontal slices of our company, we need to get vertical slices: a team should be composed of at least one member of every horizontal team. This means having developers, business analysts, system administrators, and QA engineers together...well, not 100%.

With the DevOps philosophy, some of these roles become irrelevant or need to evolve. The idea is that a single team is able to build, deploy, and run an application on its own without anything external: this is called cross-functional autonomous team.

In my professional experience, cross-functional teams are the best organization for delivering high-quality reliable products. The product is run by people who build; therefore, they know it inside out. A combination of analysts (depending on the nature of the business), developers, and DevOps engineers is all you need to deliver high-quality software into production. Some teams might as well include a QA engineer, but in general, automated testing created by DevOps and developers should be the holy grail: it is impossible to release software in a continuous delivery manner without having good code coverage. I am a big fan of the analyst being the one that tests the software as he/she is the person who knows the best the requirements and is, therefore, the most indicated to validating them.

The DevOps engineer plays a cross-cutting role: they need to know how the application is built (and possibly be part of its development), but their focus is related to the operation of the app: security, operational readiness, infrastructure, and testing should be their day-to-day job.

I have also seen teams built entirely by DevOps engineers and analysts without any pure developers or QAs. In this variant, the DevOps engineers are responsible for the infrastructure part as well as the application development, which can be very challenging depending on the complexity of the system. In general, every case needs to be studied in isolation as DevOps is not a one size fits all product.

What to expect from this book

Now that we have introduced DevOps, it is time to specify what are we going to learn in this book. It will be mainly focused on the Google Cloud Platform and the DevOps tools around it. There are several reasons for this:

- The trial period of GCP is more than enough to go through the entire book
- It is a very mature product
- Kubernetes is a big part of GCP

You will learn the fundamentals of the DevOps tools and practices, which provide enough detail to allow you to search for extra information when needed but up to a point where you can use the learnings straight away in your company.

It will be strongly focused on the ops part of DevOps as there is enough literacy in application development, and that hasn't changed in the DevOps world. Needless to say, we are not going to show how to write tests for your application, which is a fundamental activity to ensure the stability of our systems: DevOps does not work without good code coverage and automated testing.

In general, the examples are simple enough to be followed by people at the entry level of DevOps, but if you want to go deeper into some aspects of GCP, there is a good collection of tutorials available at `https://cloud.google.com/docs/tutorials`.

The book is structured in an incremental way: first, the Docker fundamentals will be shown just after a walkthrough of the different cloud providers but before going deep into configuration management tools (specifically, Ansible) and containers' orchestration platform (mainly Kubernetes).

We will end up setting up a continuous delivery pipeline for a system that manages timezoned timestamps called Chronos, which I use for talks for several reasons:

- It has pretty much no business logic
- It is based on microservices
- It pretty much covers all the required infrastructure

You can find the code for Chronos on the following GitHub repository at `https://github.com/dgonzalez/chronos`.

The majority of the examples can be repeated in your local machine using a virtualization provider such as VirtualBox and MiniKube for the Kubernetes examples, but I'd encourage you to sign up for the trial on Google Cloud Platform as it provides you (at the time of writing this) with $300 or 1 year of resources to spend freely.

Summary

On this chapter we have seen how we should align our resources (engineers) to deliver low cost and high impact IT systems. We have seen how a poor communication can lead into a defective release process deadlocking our rollouts and making the system quite inefficient from the business point of view. Through the rest of the book, we are going to look at tools that can help us not only to improve this communication but also enable our engineers to deliver more top quality functionality with lower costs.

The first of these set of tools are described on the next chapter: the cloud data centers. These data centers allow us to create resources (VMs, networks, load balancers...) from their pool of resources in order to satisfy our needs of specific hardware, at a very reasonable price and flexibility. These type of cloud data centers are being adopted more and more by the modern (and not so modern) IT companies, which is leading to the creation of a set of tools to automate pretty much everything around the infrastructure.

2
Cloud Data Centers - The New Reality

In the last few years, there has been a shift toward cloud systems, which enable the companies to scale in an easy and cheap way depending on the needs. They also enable companies to take advantage of something called **Infrastructure as Code** (**IAC**), which basically allows you to treat your physical resources (servers and routers) that previously had to be bought according to the needs as code that you can review, run, and re-run to adapt the infrastructure to your requirements.

In this chapter, we are going to walk through the main cloud providers, taking a look at their main strengths and weak points in order to form a clear picture of what they offer and how we can, as engineers, take advantage of it.

Out of all the providers in the market, we are going to focus on these two:

- **Amazon Web Services** (**AWS**)
- Google Cloud Platform

We are also going to talk a bit about these:

- Heroku
- Azure
- DigitalOcean

We should have an open minded attitude, as all of them can offer a different and valuable set of features, something that should not be overlooked.

We are going to introduce **Kubernetes**, which is, in my humble opinion, the answer to many problems in the modern DevOps world.

Amazon Web Services

Amazon is by far the biggest online retailer with an almost worldwide presence. Everyone has heard about Amazon and the possibilities that this type of store present to the busy society of the 21st century: they offer home delivery of pretty much anything that can be bought in a conventional store.

Amazon was founded in 1994 by Jeff Bezos, and since then, it has grown consistently every year, offering more and more products and services, but at some point, they got into the cloud computing business. It makes sense that a big company such as Amazon needs a lot of processing power, is reliable, and is able to adapt to the necessities of the business quickly.

Initially, the cloud services were an internal solution to satisfy the high availability needs of the business as well as have the capacity to grow in a uniform way. This created a lot of expertise within the company in building a top notch **Infrastructure as a Service (IaaS)** that, at some point, they realized could be sold to customers.

By 2006, there was nothing in the market to compete with them, so they were in the sweet spot for a successful start.

I remember I was only in college when the first two services, EC2 and EC3, were introduced in a conference.

EC2 allowed you to create virtual machines on the cloud with an API that was manipulated through a command-line interface as well as a web interface that would act as a monitor of your resources.

S3 was a key value (kind of) storage that allowed you to store immense sets of data at a very low price manipulated through the command-line interfaceas well.

It really was a revolution. It was a complete paradigm shift: now you could ask for more resources as you need. This was as simple as an API call, and there you go: three new machines ready to be used in 2 minutes. The following screenshot is a list of services on AWS:

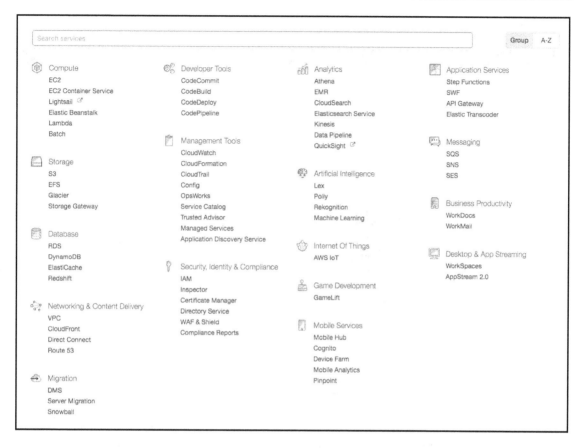

Catalog of services in AWS at January 2017

In the last few years, Amazon has been adding services very often, up until a point where it is hard to keep up with the pace. In this chapter, we are going to walk through the main services (or what I consider the most useful), showing their features and areas of application.

EC2 - computing service

The first element that a cloud system has to provide to the users is computing power. **EC2** stands for **Elastic Compute Cloud**, and it allows you to create machines on the cloud with a few clicks.

This is what the EC2 interface looks like:

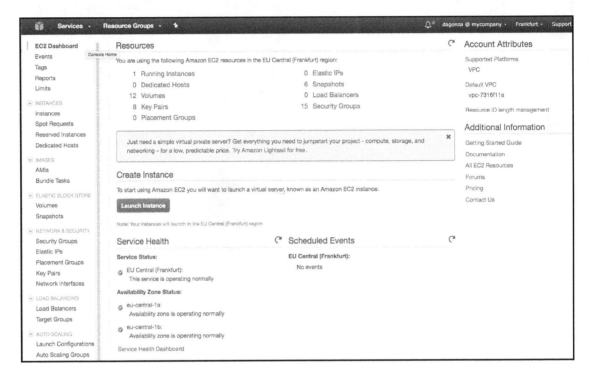

EC2 interface

EC2 was launched on August 25, 2006 (beta version), and it has evolved a lot since then. It provides the user with different sizes of machines and is available across the globe (11 different regions as of today). This means that the user can spin up machines in different parts of the globe for high availability and latency purposes, enabling the engineers of your company to build multi-zone applications without coordinating teams across the globe.

They also provide different types of instances optimized for different tasks so that the users can tailor the infrastructure to their needs. In total, there are 24 different type of instances, but they are also grouped by type, which we will walk through later on in this chapter.

Let's look at an example of how to launch an instance.

Launching an instance

The first thing you need to do is go to the AWS EC2 interface.

1. Now click on the **Launch Instance** button, which will bring you to the following screen:

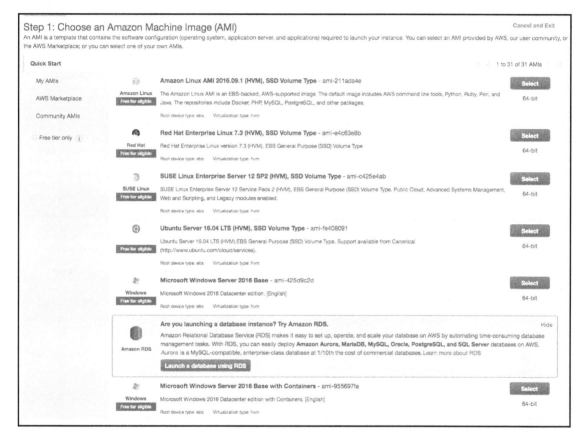

2. This is where you can choose the image to run. As you can see, the image is the operating system that will run on top of the EC2 Instance. In Amazon jargon, this image is called **Amazon Machine Image**(**AMI**), and you can create your own ones and save them for later usage, allowing you to ship prebuilt software. For now, choose Ubuntu Server 16.04 by clicking on **Select**.

3. The next screen is about the size of the image. AWS offers quite a big variety of sizes and types of images. This parameter drastically affectsthe performance of the application regarding the network, memory, and CPU performance as well as the I/O of the machine.

4. Let's look at the different types:

Type	Description
Bursting instances	T2 are general-purpose instances for burst processing. They provide a baseline level of CPU for peaks of processing power, but these peaks are available on an accumulative basis: while idle, the CPU accumulates credits that can be used during high demand periods, but once these credits are used, the performance goes back to the baseline level.
General purpose	M3 is a general-purpose instance with dedicated resources (no burst credits). It provides a good balance between CPU, memory, and network resources, and it is the minimum instance for production applications that need solid performance. M4 follows the same philosophy as M3 but with an updated hardware: **Amazon Elastic Block Store(AmazonEBS)**optimized and a better CPU as well as enhanced networking are the highlights of this instance type.
Compute Optimized	The compute optimized instances in AWS are C3 and C4. In the same way as the M instances, C4 is a hardware upgrade of the C3. These types of instances are prepared for intensive CPU work, such as data processing and analysis or demanding servers. C4 also comes with an enhanced network system, which is very helpful for high networking traffic applications.
Memory Optimized	As you can guess, AWS also provides memory optimized instances that can be used for applications that need high memory usage. Applications based on Apache Spark (or big data in general), in memory databases and similar, benefit the most from these type of instances. In this case, the memory optimized instances are divided into two sub-families:X1: These are large scale enterprise grade instances. X1 can be used for the most demanding applications in the enterprise ecosystem and it is the flagship of the memory intensive instances and is only used for very large applications.R3/R4: Even though are more modest than X1, R instances are well capable of handling the majority of day-to-day memory intensive applications. Cache systems, in memory databases, and similar systems are the best use cases for X and R instances.
Accelerated Computing Instances	Some applications, such as**Artificial Intelligence (AI)**,have specific computing requirements, such as**Graphical Processing Unit (GPU)**processing or reconfigurable hardware. These instances are divided into three families:P2: GPU compute instances. These are optimized to carry specificprocessing tasks, such as breaking passwords through brute force as well as machine learning applications (they usually rely on GPU power).G2: Graphical processing instances. Rendering videos as well as ray tracing or video streaming are the best use cases for these instances.

5. As you can see, there is an instance for every necessity that the user can have. For now, we are going to choose a small instance first because we are just testing AWS and second because AWS has a free tier, which enables you to use the `t2.micro` instances for up to 1 year without any charge, as shown in the following screenshot:

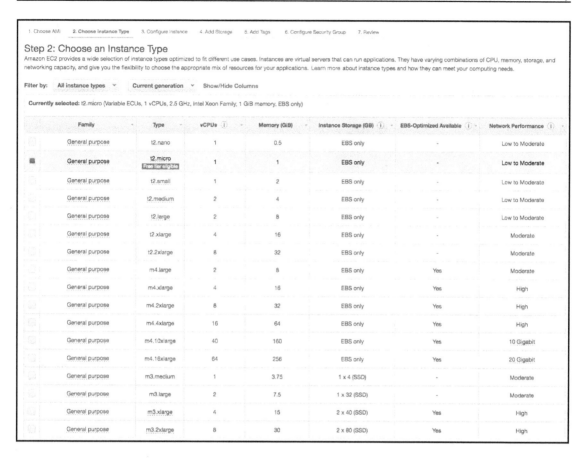

6. Now we have two options. Click on **Review Instance Launch** or **Configure Instance Details**. In this case, we are going to click on **Review Instance Launch**, but by clicking on **Configure Instance Details**, we can configure several elements of the instance, such as networking, storage, and so on.

7. Once you click on**Review Instance Launch**, the review screen shows up. Click on**Launch** and you should get presented with something similar to what is shown in the following screenshot:

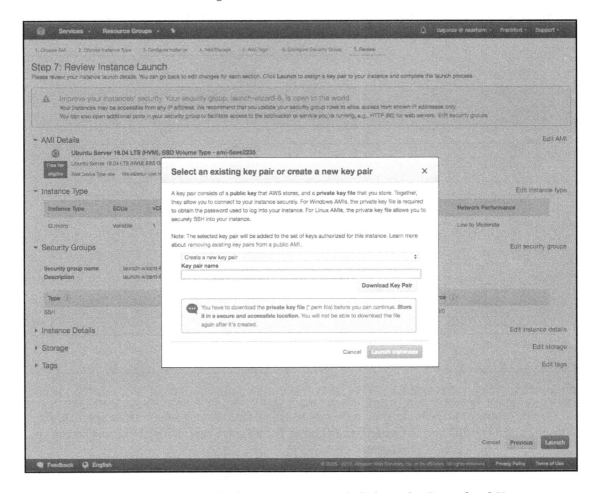

8. Just assign a name to the key-pair name and click on the **Download Key Pair**button,which will download a `.pem` file that we will use later on to access via `ssh` to the instance.

9. Once you have specified the key pair, click on **Launch Instance**, as shown in the preceding screenshot, and that's all. After a few checks, your image will be ready for installing the required software (this usually takes a couple of minutes).

This is the bare minimum needed to create a running instance in AWS. As you can see, the full process is very well explained on the screen and in general, if you know the basics of DevOps (`ssh`, networking, and device management), you don't really need much help creating instances.

Relational Database Service

What we have shown in the previous section are EC2 machines that can be used to install the required software. There is another service that allows you to administer high availability databases (MySQL, PostgreSQL, Maria DB, and Aurora as well as Oracle and SQL Server) across regions. This service is called RDS and it stands for Relational Database Service.

One of the big headaches with relational databases is the high availability configuration: master-master configuration is something that is usuallyexpensive and out of reach of small companies. AWS has raised the bar with RDS offering multi-region high availability databases with a few clicks.

Networking in AWS and EC2

AWS provides fine-grain control at the networking level. As with any physical data center, you can define your own networks, but AWS has a higher-level abstraction concept: The Virtual Private Cloud.

Amazon**Virtual Private Cloud**(Amazon **VPC**) is asegment of the AWS cloud that allows you to group and segregate your resources in subnetworks to organize and plan your infrastructure matching your requirements. It also allows you to create a VPN between AWS and your physical data center to extend the latter one, adding more resources from AWS. Also, when you create a resource in EC2, you have the possibility of creating the resource in your custom defined subnet within your VPC.

Before jumping into what a VPC looks like, let's first explainhow AWS works regarding the geographical distribution of resources. AWS provides you with different data centers in different regions such as Europe, Asia, and the US. As an example, let's take EU West, which has three different availability zones:

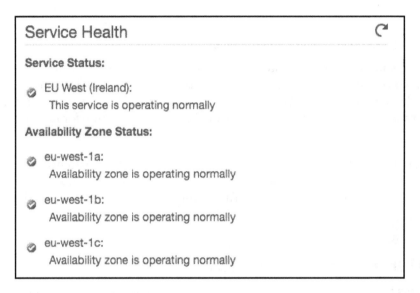

The concept of region in AWS is basically a geographical area where the AWS data center lives. Knowing this information enables us to build global scale applications that serve the traffic from the closest data center in order to improve latency. Another very good reason for this geographical distribution is the data protection laws in several countries. By being able to choose where our data lives, we can enforce the compliance with the laws.

Inside of these geographical regions, sometimes, we can find availability zones. One availability zone is basically a physically separated data center that ensures the high availability of our system, as in the case of a catastrophe in one of the data centers, we can always fall back on the other availability zones.

Let's see how the regions and availability zones look:

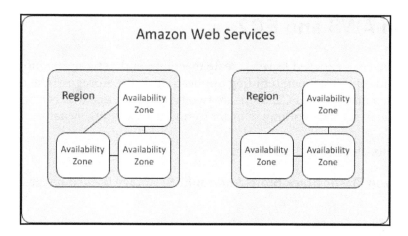

Now that we understand how AWS works from the geographical perspective, let's dig deeper into what a VPC is in terms of regions and availability zones.

A VPC is a logically separated segment of the AWS cloud that is private to the user, can hold resources, and spans across all the availability regions in an AWS zone. Inside of this VPC, we can define different subnets (public and privates in different availability zones) and define which machines are reachable from the Internet: AWS allows you to create routing tables, Internet gateways, and NAT gateways among other common networking resources that enable the user to build anything that they can build in a physical data center.

It would take a full book just to talk about the networking in AWS. We will go deeper into some concepts in the rest of the chapters of this book, but if you really want to dive deepinto the networking side of AWS, you can find more data and examples at`http://docs.aws.amazon.com/AmazonVPC/latest/UserGuide/VPC_Introduction.html`.

AWS also provides a very powerful element: **Elastic Load Balancing(ELB)**. An ELB is a modern version of the classic hardware load balancer. It enables us to health-check resources and only get the healthy onesinto the pool. Also, AWS comes in two flavors: classic load balancer and application load balancer. The first version is, as the name suggests, an application load balancer that distributes the traffic depending on health checks and does not understand the data being transmitted, whereas the application load balancer can route the traffic based on advanced policies dependent on the information of the request. ELBs can alsohandle the full HTTPS flow so that we can carry the SSL termination in the load balancer and allow our applications to offload the encryption/decryption to them.

Storage in AWS and EC2

Up until now, we have exposed how to create machines and networking infrastructure in AWS. One important thing when building applications is the storage of the data. By default, when we launch a machine in EC2, there are two types of storage that can be associated with the machine in the root volume in order to run the operating system:

- Instance storage backed images

- **Amazon Elastic Block Store(AmazonEBS)** storage backed images

The first one, instance storage backed images, relies on the storage associated with the image to mount and run the root volume. This means that the data stored in the image will be lost once the machine is terminated (these type of images do not support the stop action; they just support termination).

The second type of instances are the ones backed by EBS. Elastic Block Store is the name that AWS gives to its storage capabilities. With EBS, the user can create and destroy volumes (block devices) as needed as well as snapshots: we can create a copy of a running image before carrying a risky operation so we can restore it if something goes wrong.

The type of storage can vary depending on our needs: you can create things from magnetic block devices to SSD drives as well as general-purpose units that can cover a lot of the use cases in all the applications.

In general, all the instances are backed by EBS as the fact that the storage is a logically segregated from compute enables us to do things such as resizing an instance (for example, creating a more powerful instance) without losing the data.

Several volumes can be mounted into the same EC2 instance that gets exposed to it as if a physical device were attached to it, so if we are using a Linux-based image (such as Ubuntu), we can use the mount command to mount the devices into folders.

Amazon S3

Amazon **Simple Storage Service**(Amazon **S3**) is, as described by its name, a simple way of storing a large amount of data on the cloud at a very low cost with a nice set of features. Unlike EC2 storage based on devices with predefined size, Amazon S3 is practically a key value storage that enables us to identify data with a key. Unlike other key value storage technologies, S3 is prepared to store from tiny to very large objects (up to 5 terabytes) with very low response times and that are accessible anywhere.

In the same way as EC2, Amazon S3 is a feature that has the concept of regions, but S3 does not understand availability zones: the S3 service itself manages to get the objects stored on different devices, so you don't need to worry about it. The data is stored in an abstraction called buckets that, if we try to compare S3 with a filesystem, would be the equivalent to a folder but with one catch: the bucket name has to be unique across all the regions on your AWS account so we can't create one bucket called `Documents` in two different regions.

Another advantage of S3 is that AWS provides a REST API to access objects in a very simple way, which makes it fairly easy to use it as storage for the modern web.

One of the best use cases that I've come across in my professional life for S3 is the management of a large number of documents in a financial institution. Usually, when companies are dealing with money, they have to onboard the customers to a process called **Customer Due Diligence** (**CDD**). This process ensures that the customers are who they claim to be and that the money is coming from a valid source. The company also has to keep the documents for a minimum of 6 years due to financial regulations.

In order to carry on this investigation, the users need to send documents to the company, and Amazon S3 is the perfect match for it: the customer uploads the documents to the website of the company, which in reality is pushing the documents to S3 buckets (one per customer) and replicating them across regions with the Amazon S3 replication feature. Also, S3 provides another interesting feature for this model: links to objects that expire within a time frame. Basically, this enables you to create a link that is valid onlyfor a period of time so that if the person reviewing documents exposes the link to a third party, S3 will reply with an error, making it really hard to leak documents accidentally (the user could always download it).

Another interesting feature of S3 is the possibility of integrating it with Amazon **Key Management System** (Amazon**KMS**), another feature provided by AWS), so all our objects in S3 are encrypted by a key stored in KMS that can be transparently rotated periodically.

Amazon ECR and ECS

Containers are the new norm. Every single company that I've come across in the last few years is using or considering using containers for their software. This enables us to build software with the microservices principles in mind (small individual software components running independently) as it provides a decent level of abstraction from the configuration and deployment of different apps: basically, the entire configuration is stored in a container and we only need to worry about how to run it.

Amazon, as one of the pioneers of the microservices architectures, has created its own image registry and cluster (service).

As we will see in depth in `Chapter 3`, *Docker,* is built around two concepts: images and containers. An image is a definition of an application (configuration + software), whereas a container is an instance of the running image. The image is built through a Dockerfile (a description of the image with a very basic script language) and stored in a registry, in this case, Amazon**EC2 Container Registry**(**ECR**), our private registry in the AWS infrastructure. We don't need to worry about availability or managing resources; we just choose the region where our containers are going to run and push our images into that repository.

Then, from our host running Docker, the image is pulled and the container is instantiated. This is simple and effective, but there are a few considerations:

- What happens when our host does not have enough resources to run as many containers as we want?
- What happens if we want to ensure the high availability of our containers?
- How do we ensure that the containers are restarted when they fail (for some reason)?
- How can we add more hardware resources to our system without downtime?

All those questions were trickier a few years ago but are simple now: Amazon**EC2 Container Service**(Amazon **ECS**) will take care of it for us. ECS is basically a cluster of resources (EC2 machines) that work together to provide a runtime for our containers to be executed.

Within ECS, when creating a new service, we specify parameters such as how many replicas of our container should be running at the same time as well as what configuration (image) our container is supposed to use. Let's see how it works.

Creating a cluster

First, we are going to create a cluster in the AWS console and see how it works.

1. Go to the Amazon ECS page and click on **Get started** button (the only button in the screen as you haven't created any resources yet):

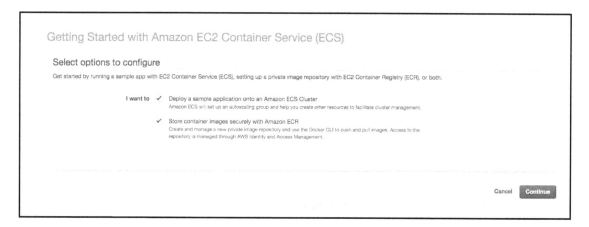

2. Make sure that the two checkboxes are ticked before continuing. We want to deploy a sample application to ECS but also we want to store the images in ECR.

3. The next screen is key: this is where we define the repository of our image, which will determine the repository URI that will be used for pushing images from our local machine using Docker.

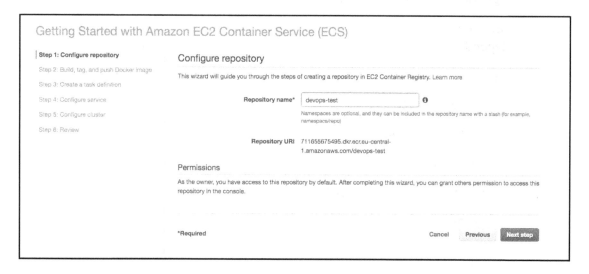

4. Just use `devops-test` as the repository name, and our repository URI will look very similar to the one shown in the preceding screenshot.

5. Step number 2 (out of 6) is a series of commands provided by AWS to log in into ECR and push the images of our project. In this case, we are going to use a very simple application in `Node.js`:

```
var express = require('express');
var app = express();

app.get('/', function (req, res) {
  res.send('Hello World!');
});

  app.listen(3000, function () {
    console.log('Example app listening on port 3000!');
  });
```

6. Save the code from earlier in a file called `index.js` within a folder called `devops-test` on your local machine. As we are using express, we need to install the required dependency. Just execute the following command:

```
npm init
```

7. After a few questions (just press Enter a few times and it should work), a file called `package.json` should be created. Now we need to install express for our program to run:

```
npm install --save express
```

8. And voila! Our `package.json` file should have a line describing the required dependency:

```
{
      "name": "code",
      "version": "1.0.0",
      "description": "",
      "main": "index.js",
  "scripts": {
  "test": "echo "Error: no test specified"
&& exit 1",
   "start": "node index.js"
  },
  "author": "",
  "license": "ISC",
  "dependencies": {
  "express": "^4.14.1"
```

```
        }
    }
```

9. This file allows us to reinstall the dependencies whenever required without having to do it manually; it also allows us to specify a command that will be run when we execute `npm start` (a standard way of running a Node app using npm). Add the line and highlight it, as shown in the preceding code, as we will need it later (don't forget the semicolon from the previous line).

10. Now we need to write our Dockerfile. A Dockerfile, as we will see in `Chapter 3, Docker`, is a file that describes what our Docker image looks like. In this case, we are going to reconstruct the steps needed to run the node application in a Docker container:

```
FROM node:latest

RUN mkdir -p /usr/src/app
WORKDIR /usr/src/app

COPY package.json /usr/src/app/
RUN npm install

COPY . /usr/src/app

EXPOSE 3000
CMD [ "npm", "start" ]
```

11. Don't try to understand the file; we will go deeper into this later on this book. Just save it with the name `Dockerfile` in the folder mentioned previously, `devops-test`. By now, your `devops-test` folder should look like this:

```
➜ devops-test ls
Dockerfile    index.js        node_modules package.json
➜ devops-test
```

12. Now we are ready to follow step 2 in the ECS setup. Be aware that the following image is regarding my user in AWS; your user will have different parameters, so use yours instead of copying from the preceding screenshot:

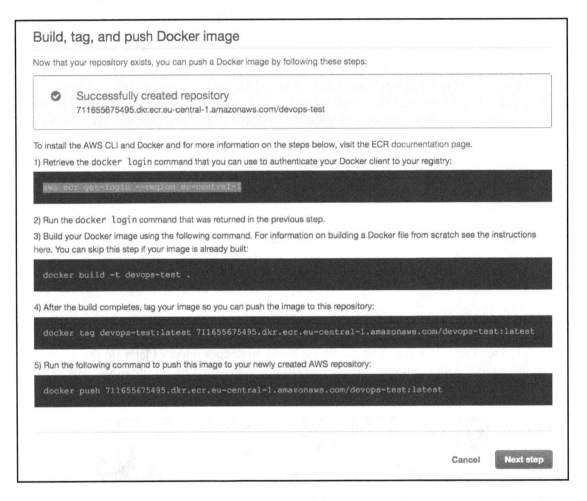

Once you finish it, a new version of the image with your app image should be installed in your private ECR.

14. The next step (step 3) is creating what AWS calls a task definition, which is basically the configuration for one instance of our containers: how much memory we are going to use, which image we are going to run, and what ports we are going to expose in the container. Just leave the default memory but change the port to `3000`, as it is the port that we used in the preceding example (the node application). This is typical docker parameter and we will learn more about it in the next chapter, where we will dive deeperinto docker.

15. Once you are ready, click on next and we will be with step 4. This step is where we are going to configure a service. By service, we mean the number of instances of our container are we going to keep alive and how are we going to expose them: using a load balancer or just in the EC2 instances that are part of the cluster. We will also be able to specify which IAM (AWS credential system) is going to be used for registering and deregistering running instances:

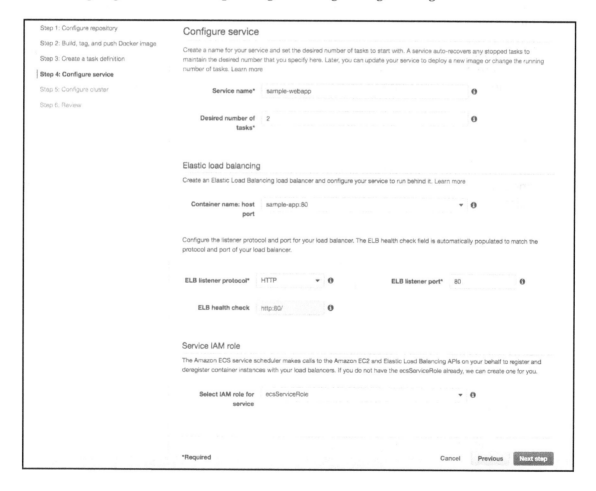

16. We just leave everything by default except two parameters:
    - The desired number of tasks: set to 2
    - In the ELB section, we just select sample-app: 80 (or the option that isn't **No ELB** so AWS provisions an ELB for us)

17. Click on the **Next step**, where we are going to define what our cluster is going to look like:
    - The number of nodes
    - The size of the nodes

18. Once we are ready, just review and launch the instance. After a few minutes, our cluster should be up and running and ready to work with our deployed task.

You can access the instance of the task that we created in the load balancer provisioned by the cluster itself on the port 3000. As you can see, ECS makes the task of setting up a container cluster simple.

In this book, we are going to give special attention to Kubernetes and Docker Swarm mainly because they are platform agnostic technologies, but I believe that Amazon ECS is a very valid technology to be considered when building a new container-based system.

Other services

As you can see, the list of services in AWS is pretty much endless. We have visited the ones that I consider the most important, and in the following chapters, we will visit some of them that are also interesting, but unfortunately, we cannot go in deep through all of them. However, AWS is pretty good in terms of the documentation, and every service always comes with quite acomprehensive explanation on how to use it.

In this section, we are going to touch base with some services that, even though are quite important, are not core to the development of this book.

Route 53

Route 53 is the DNS service in AWS. It is a global and scalable DNS service that allows you to perform some advanced operations:

- Register domain names
- Transfer domain names from other registrars
- Create traffic routing policies (such as failovers across regions)

- Monitor the availability of your applications (and reroute the traffic to healthy instances).

With Route 53, we can link domain names to AWS resources, such as load balancers, S3 buckets, and other resources, enabling us to expose a human-readable name for our resources (mainly VMs) created within our AWS instance.

CloudFront

CloudFront solves one of the biggest problems that low traffic websites experience when a spike in visits happens: it provides a cache in a way that makes us wonder whether AWS is the one that serves the data and not our server. Basically, CloudFront intercepts the request to our host, renders the page, and keeps it for up to 24 hours so our site offloads the traffic to AWS. It is designed for serving static content, as the second time that the user hits the same URL, the cached version will be served instead of hitting your server again.

It is highly recommended that you use CloudFront for the brochure site of your company so that you can serve all the traffic with a very small machine, saving some money in resources but also being able to improve your uptime when a traffic spike hits your site.

Amazon ElasticCache

Amazon ElasticCache, as the name suggests, is a distributed and scalable in-memory cache system that can be used to store cached data within our applications.

It solves one of the biggest problems that we can face when building an application that relies on a cache for storing and retrieving data: high availability and a consistent temporary datastore.

Amazon RDS

RDS stands for **Relational Database Service**. With RDS, you can provision DB instances with a few clicks that could be used to store data: Oracle, MySQL, and MariaDB are some of the options that we have for RDS. It leverages the high availability to the underlying DB system, which might be a problem if we are looking to rely on AWS for it, but it is usually acceptable as high availability in SQL databases is a complicated subject.

DynamoDB

DynamoDB is a fine piece of engineering. It is a NoSQL database that is fine-tuned down to the millisecond of latency at any scale. It stores objects instead of rows (SQL cannot be used) and is a good candidate for storing a big amount of data in a schema-less fashion. DynamoDB, in essence, is very similar to MongoDB, but there is a basic difference: DynamoDB is a service provided by AWS and can run onlywithin AWS, whereas MongoDB is a software that can be installed anywhere, including AWS. From the functional point of view, the majority of use cases for MongoDB are valid for modeling DynamoDB databases.

Google Cloud Platform

Google has always been at the top of the hill when it comes to technology. Surprisingly, Google didn't have a federated layer of services; instead, it offered every service separately, which was far from ideal in providing a solid platform for developers to build applications on top of it. In order to solve that, they released Google Cloud Platform, which is a collection of services (infrastructure as a service, platform as a service, containers and big data, as well as many other features) that enables developers and companies to build highly reliable and scalable systems with some of the most up-to-date features, such as Kubernetes and a set of unique machine learning APIs.

The interface is also one of the main points in Google Cloud: it offers you a web console where you basically have an available ssh Terminal that is connected to all your services, and you can operate from there without the need for any configuration on your local machine. Another good point in the interface is the fact that they use the terminology in the traditional sysadmin world, making the learning curve easy for the majority of the services.

In the same way as AWS, Google Cloud Platform allows engineers to create resources across the globe in regions and zones in order to ensure the high availability of our systems as well as the compliance with local laws.

But the real jewel in the crown is their container engine. I am a big fan of container orchestration. Nowadays, everyone is gravitating toward microservices-based systems, and it is not strange to see companies hitting the wall of the operational reality of a microservices-based system: this is impossible to manage without orchestration tools. From all the potential choices on the market (Amazon ECS, Docker Swarm, and DCOS), there is one in particular that has been a game changer in my life: Kubernetes.

Kubernetes is the answer to the question that I raised during the writing of my first book (*Developling Microservices with Node.js*): how can we efficiently automate the operations in a microservices environment by providing a common ground between development and operations? Kubernetes has incorporated all the expertise from working with containers that Google has accumulated through the years in order to create a product that provides all the necessary components for the efficient management of deployment pipelines.

In this book, we are going to place a special emphasis on Kubernetes, as in my opinion, it is the solution to many of the problems that teams have today when scaling up in members and resources.

In order to start working with GCP, Google offers a trial version of 300 USD credit or 60 days free of charge test, which is more than enough to get your head around the majority of the services and, of course, more than enough to follow the examples of this book and play around with the majority of the concepts that we are going to be exposing. I would recommend that you activate your trial period and start playing around: once the credit is used or the 60 days are over, Google requires explicit confirmation to activate the billing so there is not going to be any extra charge in your account (this is the case at the time of writing this).

Google Compute Engine

Google Compute Engine is the equivalent of EC2 in Amazon Web Services. It allows you to manage instances of machines, networks, and storage with a simplicity that I have never seen before. One of the downsides that I found when ramping up with AWS is the fact that they have created abstractions with names that are not very intuitive: Virtual Private Cloud, Elastic Block Storage, and many more. This is not a big deal as AWS is well known in the market, but Google got the message and has named its resources in a very intuitive way, facilitating the onboarding of new people into the platform with little to no effort.

Regarding the machine types, Google Cloud Platform provides a simplified and limited set of machines when compared to AWS but enough variety to satisfy our needs. One of the features to keep in mind with Google Cloud Platform is the fact that the hardware improves with the size of the instance, which means that the 64 cores machines get a better CPU than the two core machines.

Google Cloud Platform also provides a CLI tool to interact with the resources in GCP from a Terminal. In order to install it, just access this URL:`https://cloud.google.com/sdk/`.

Then, follow the instructions depending on your operating system.

Standard machine types

The standard machines are the most common to be used by any application. They offer a balance between CPU and memory that suits the majority of the tasks in all the projects that you can possibly imagine. These types of machines offer 3.75 GB of RAM for every single virtual CPU. Let's look at a few examples:

Name	CPUs	Memory
n1-standard-1	1	3.75 GB

n1-standard-2	2	7.50 GB
n1-standard-64	64	240 GB

As you can see, the naming convention is fairly straightforward and is easy in order to guess the machine RAM and the number of CPUs out of the canonical name.

High-memory machine types

These machines are optimized for memory-intensive applications. They come with an extra amount of RAM for every virtual CPU that allows you to go the extra mile regarding memory power.

Every machine of the high-memory type comes with 6.5 GB of RAM for every single virtual CPU, and here are a few examples:

Name	CPUs	Memory
n1-highmem-2	2	13
n1-highmem-8	8	52
n1-highmem-64	64	416

These machines come with a massive amount of RAM and are well suited for distributed caches, databases, and many other types of applications that require a high memory consumption relative to the CPU power.

High-CPU machine types

As the name states, high-CPU machines are instances that hold a high CPU/memory ratio with only 0.9 GB of RAM for every virtual CPU, which indicates that they are well suited for saving some money on high-intensive CPU tasks (as we cut down on a lot of memory). Here are some examples of these machines:

Name	CPUs	Memory
n1-highcpu-2	2	1.8 GB
n1-highcpu-8	8	7.2 GB
n1-highcpu-64	64	57.6 GB

As you can see, the only difference between the standard or high memory machines is that these machines are built with less amount of RAM, which allows us to save money on a resource that won't be used in some applications that are able to create machines with more CPUs at the same price. High-CPU machines are well suited for applications that require high CPU and low memory consumption, such as mathematical processing or other types of calculations.

Shared-core machine types

Sometimes, we really don't need a dedicated machine for our process, so Google Cloud offers shared machines that you can use for it. In my opinion, the shared-core machines are not suited for production usage, but they could well serve a prototype or experimenting with different resources. Here are the two types of machines:

Name	CPUs	Memory
f1-micro	0.2	0.6
g1-small	0.5	1.7

As you can see, there are only two options with different RAM and CPU power. I personally use these machines when I want to experiment with new software or new products of the Google Cloud Platform.

Don't forget that these are bursting machines that are only suited for short burst of intensive processing and not for sustained resource consumption as the CPU is shared across different applications.

Custom machines and GPU processing

Sometimes, we need an extra amount of something on our machines, which is usually not in the predefined machine instances of other providers, but in this case, Google Cloud Platform comes to the rescue with an amazing feature: custom machine types.

With custom machine types in Google Cloud Platform, we can get the benefit of the upgraded hardware of the large machines in a resource-modest machine or create specific configurations that suit our needs.

One of the best examples that we can find for custom machines is when we want to add some GPU processing to our mix. In Google Cloud, GPUs can be attached to any non-shared (f1 or g1) machine on demand. With the ability to create our custom machine types, we can define how many GPUs we want to burst our processing power in.

In general, when I design a system, I try to stick to the standard typesas much as possible in order to simplify my setup, but there is nothing wrong in creating custom machine types aside from the fact that we can easily fall in the premature optimization of our system, which is probably one of the biggest problems that you can find when working in IT.

Launching an instance

In Google Cloud Platform, everything is grouped in projects. In order to create resources, you need to associate them with projects, so the first step to launch an instance is to create a project. In order to do that, just select the new project button when entering the Google Cloud Platform interfacethe first timeor in the drop-down in the top bar when you have already created one project:

1. For the examples of this book, I am going to create a project called `Implementing Modern DevOps`, which I will to be using for running all the examples:

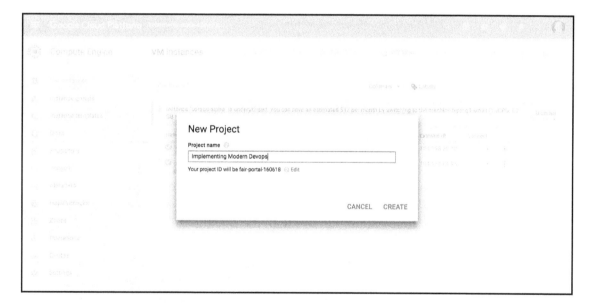

2. Once we have created our project, we proceed to create a new VM instance. Even though it is possible to create instances with more than 64 cores (with the custom machine types), we are going to stick to the standard ones in order to save costs. Proceed to create the instance with the default values (just change the name):

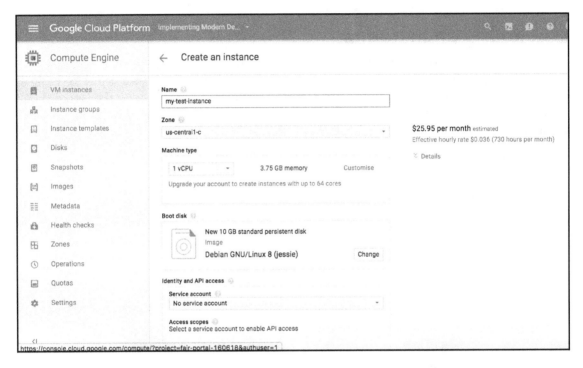

3. There are two details that I really like from Google Cloud Platform:
    - How easy they name their resources and make everything clear to understand
    - How transparent they are with the pricing

4. While creating a virtual machine in Google Cloud Platform, these two characteristics are present: the form to create a machine has only a few fields, and it gives you the cost of the machine per month (so there are no surprises).

5. In the same way as AWS, Google Cloud Platform allows you to select the region and the zone (remember, a physically separated data center) where your instance is going to live in order to ensure the high availability of the overall system.

6. Also, this (not in the preceding figure) allows you a couple of clicks in two checkboxes in order to allow the `http` and `https` traffic into the instance from the outer world. This is just as simple and effective.

7. You can also configure other things, such as networking, ssh keys, and other parameters that we are going to skip for now. Just click on the **Create**button (at the bottom of the form) and wait until the machine is fully provisioned (it might take up to few minutes), and you should see something similar to what is shown in the following screenshot:

8. One of the most appealing features of Google Cloud Platform is how curated their usability is. In this case, you can see a column in your machine description called **Connect** that allows you to connect to the machine in a few different ways:
   - SSH
   - The `gcloud` command (a command-line tool from GCP)
   - Using another ssh client

9. We are going to select SSH (the default one) and click on the SSH button. A popup should appear on the screen, and after a few seconds, we should see something similar to an ssh Terminal, which is a Terminal in our machine:

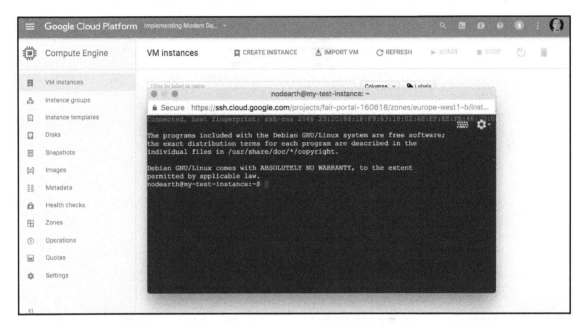

This is a very neat and useful feature that basically enables the engineer to avoid carrying a set of cryptographic keys that are always a risk as if they get leaked, your machines are exposed.

Networking

One thing I cannot stress enough about the Google Cloud Platform is how it simplifies the concepts and make them look similar to the real-world physical data center concepts. The case of the networking was not an exception: all the concepts and names can be mapped one to one to real world physical network concepts.

In Google Cloud, we can implement any required design that follows the principles of the IP networking (the same as AWS) with pretty much a few clicks. Another interesting feature that Google Cloud offers (along with other providers such as AWS) is the possibility of extending your data center into the cloud with a VPN network taking the benefits of the cloud products but achieving the level of security required by the most sensitive data that you could imagine.

Google Container Engine

The **Google Container Engine** (**GKE**) is a proposal from Google for the container orchestration making use of one of the most powerful container clusters available in the market: Kubernetes.

As we will discuss further in `Chapter 7`, *Docker Swarm and Kubernetes- Clustering Infrastructure,*Kubernetes is a feature-full cluster used for deploying and scaling container-based applications in a controlled manner, with a special emphasis on defining the common language between development and operations: a framework that blends development and operation concepts into a common ground: a YAML (or JSON) description of resources.

One of the big problems of Kubernetes is ensuring high availability. When you deploy a cluster on premises or in a cloud provider, making use of the computing power (EC2 in AWS or Compute Engine in GCP), you are responsible for upgrading the cluster version and evolving it with the new releases of Kubernetes. In this case, Google Cloud Platform, through the container engine, has solved the operational problem: GCP keeps the master and is responsible for keeping it up to date and the users upgrade the nodes when a new version of Kubernetes is released, which allows us to articulate different procedures for upgrading our cluster.

Setting up a cluster

In Chapter 7, *Docker Swarm and Kubernetes- Clustering Infrastructure,*you are going to learn how to operate Kubernetes, but it is worth teaching you how to set up a cluster in the GKEin this chapterin order to show how easy it is before diving deepinto the core concepts of Kubernetes:

1. First, go toContainer Engine withinGoogle Cloud Platform:

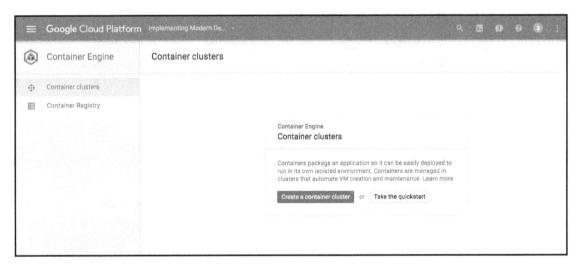

2. As you can see, there are no clusters set up, so we have two options:
    * **Create a new container cluster**
    * **Take the quickstart**

3. We are just going to click on **Create a container cluster** and follow up the onscreen instructions (a form) in order to set up our cluster:

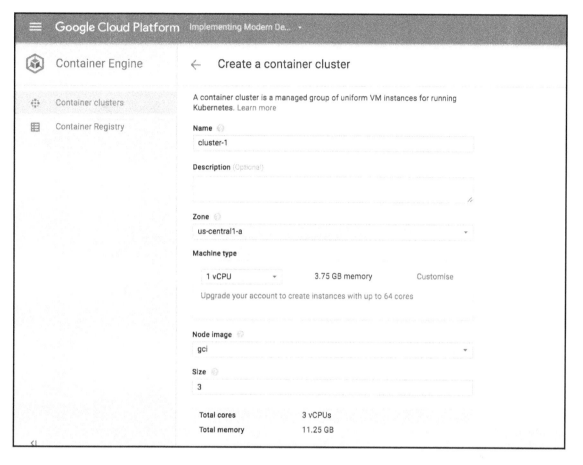

4. Ensure that **Zone** is the closest to your geographical area (even though right now it doesn't really matter) and the size is 3. This parameter, the size, is going to ask GCP to create 3 instances in the Compute Engine in order to set up the cluster plus a master that is managed by GCP itself. Regarding the image, we have two options here, `gci` or `container-vm`. In this case, again, it doesn't really matter as it is just a test cluster, but just note that if you want to use NFS or any other advanced filesystem, you will need to use `container-vm`.

5. Click on **Create**, and after few minutes, you should see two things:
   - The cluster is created in the Google Container Engine section
   - Three new VMs are provisioned in the Compute Engine section

6. This is a very smart setup because with some commands using the google cloud platform command tool (`gcloud`), we can scale up or down or cluster as well as change the size of our instances in order to satisfy our needs. If you explore the cluster (by clicking on its name), you will find a **Connect to the cluster** link,which leads to a screen with instructions to connect to the Kubernetes dashboard.

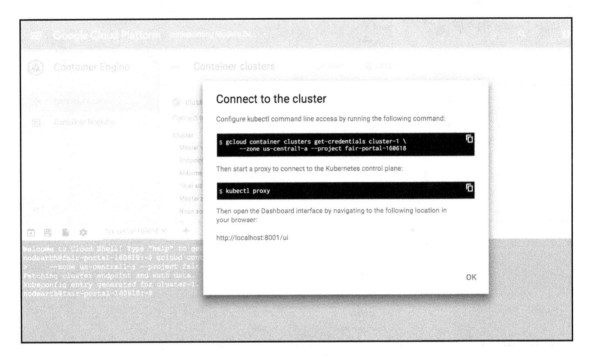

7. Sometimes, these instructions fail, and that is because `gcloud` is badly configured. If you find an error trying to configure the access to the cluster, run the following command:

```
gcloud auth login <your email>
```

8. Then, follow the instructions. Assuming that you have already configured the Google Cloud SDK, everything should work fine, and after running the `kubectl proxy`command, you should be able to access the Kubernetes dashboard at`http://localhost:8001/ui`.

9. In order to test whether everything works as expected, just run a simple image in Kubernetes (in this case, a `busybox` image):

```
kubectl run -i busybox --image=busybox
```

10. If we refresh the dashboard (`http://localhost:8001/ui`) while running the Kubernetes proxy (as specified earlier), we should see something similar to what is shown in the following figure in the **Deployments** section:

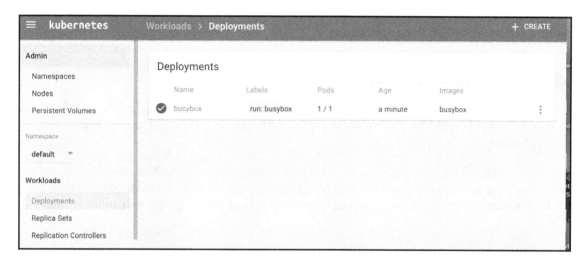

This indicates that the deployment (a Kubernetes concept that we will explore in `Chapter 7`, *Docker Swarm and Kubernetes- Clustering Infrastructure*) was successful.

Other Google Cloud Platform products

Google Cloud platform is not only Compute Engine and Container Engine, but it is also a collection of services that are very interesting for different purposes. As things are limited in scope, we won't see the majority of them and will only focus on the ones that are more relevant to the DevOps world.

Google App Engine

Up until now, we have been working with a side of DevOps called **IaaS**. Google Cloud platform also offers something called **Platform as a Service (PaaS)**. In an IaaS model, we need not worry about the underlying infrastructure: provisioning machines, installing the software, patching the software. With **Google App Engine** (or any other major PaaS), we forget about the ops of our infrastructure and focus on the development of our application, leveraging the underlying infrastructure to Google. Instead of launching a machine and installing Java to run our Spring Boot-based application, we just specify that we want to run a Java application, and GCP takes care of everything else.

This product, the Google App Engine, fits the necessity of the majority of the small to mid sized projects, but in this book, we are going to focus on the DevOps that maintaining an IaaS involves.

Google App Engine also provides us with features such as user management, which is a recurring problem in all the applications.

Machine Learning APIs

Google has always been famous for its innovation across the technology products that it has released. It has changed how people use e-mail with Gmail and how people use phones with Android.

Regarding **Machine Learning**, they are also shaking up the world with an innovative set of APIs that people can use to process images (with the vision APIs), translate documents (with the translations API), and analyze large amounts of text with the natural language API.

One of the most amazing uses that I have seen of the vision API is a company that had to do some level of photo ID verification for its customers. There was a huge problem of people uploading invalid images (random images or even images with part of the face covered or similar), so we used the vision API to recognize images that contained a face without facial hair, hat, or any other accessories aside from glasses.

The result was that the people doing the ID verification focused just on valid images instead of having to classify them as valid or invalid before proceeding to the verification.

Big data

Big data is now a big thing. Everybody is trying to take the advantage of big data to explore new areas of business or unleash their potential in traditional businesses.

Google Cloud Platform offers a set of big data APIs that enable the users to carry on pretty much any task in large sets of data. With tools such as BigQuery, a data analyst can run queries on terabytes of information in seconds without setting up a massive scale infrastructure.

In general, the big data APIs from Google are what is called no-ops toolsin the DevOps world: they don't require maintenance from users as they leverage it into Google. This means that if a big query requires a lot of processing power, Google isthe one responsible for transparently offering this power to the user.

Other cloud providers

Unfortunately, there is a limit to the number of concepts we can develop in a book, and in this case, we are going to focus on AWS and GCP, as they are the most feature-full cloud providers in the market.

I always try to adopt an open mindset regarding technology, and there are three providers that I think you should know about:

- DigitalOcean
- Heroku
- Azure

They have a lot to offer and they all are up to speed with the new trends of DevOps and security.

Heroku

Heroku's battle horse is this phrase: build apps, not infrastructure. That is a powerful message. Basically, Heroku is going full throttle with the **PaaS** concept **Platform as a Service**, allowing you to avoid maintaining the underlying infrastructure: just specify what you want to run (for example, a Node.js application) and the scale.

With this powerful philosophy, Heroku allows you to easily deploy instances of your application, databases, or communication buses, such as Kafka, with a few clicks and without all the hassle of having to provision them with a DevOps tool, such as Ansible, Chef, or similar.

Heroku is one of the cloud providers preferred by start-ups as you can save a lot of time as opposed to using AWS or Google Cloud Platform, as you just need to focus on your applications, not the infrastructure.

DigitalOcean

DigitalOcean is a provider that, even though not as well-known as AWS or GCP, offers a very interesting alternative to small to mid sized organizations to run their cloud systems. They have developed a very powerful concept: the droplet.

Basically, a droplet is a component that can run your software and be connected to different networks (private or public)through some configuration.

In order to assemble a droplet, we just need to define a few things:

- The image (the operating system or one-click images)
- The size
- The region

And once you have chosen your configuration, the droplet starts running. This is very simple and effective, which is usuallywhat companies look for.

Azure

Azure is the Microsoft push for cloud systems and one of the providers that has grown the most in the last couple of years. As expected, Azure is aparticularly good platform for running Windows-based applications, but that's not to say we can overlook its capability of running Linux applications as well.

The catalog of products is as complete as the catalog for AWS or Google Cloud Platform, and there is absolutely no reason not to choose Azure as a cloud provider for your systems.

Azure is also one of the newest providers (it became widely available in 2013) in the market, so it has the advantage of being able to solve problems that other providers have presented.

Summary

Up until now, we showcased the features of AWS and GCP and introduced some other providers that are very interesting choices when building our systems. One of the advantages of having a good number of competitors in the market is the fact that each one of them has their own strong points and we can combine them by making use of VPNs, creating a big and extended virtual data center across different providers.

Through the rest of the book, we are going to give special attention to AWS and GCP, as they have the most interesting characteristics for a DevOps book (not to overlook the rest of them, but remember, things are limited in terms of space).

We are also going to take a special interest in container clusters such as Kubernetes or Docker Swarm as they are, without any kind of doubt, the future.

3
Docker

For many years, the contact point between development and operations has been always a source of problems when deploying a new version of an application to production. Different languages generate different types of artifacts (war or JAR for Java, the source code for Node.js.), which led to heterogeneity in the procedures when rolling out new versions.

This heterogeneity led into bespoke solutions to roll out versions, which are pretty much sorceries with weird habits, such as deploying at 4 a.m. to avoid an outage in the system and creating error-prone bash scripts that are harder to maintain than the software itself. The problem, aside from the complexity, is that new hires need to ramp up into your systems, and this always introduces a level of risk that we are not aware of for the majority of the time until something goes very wrong.

Docker came to the rescue. With Docker, we can generate a deployable artifact, which is not only the software that you built but also its runtime. If you are deploying a Java application, with Docker, you will bundle the application plus the version of Java that is going to be running your application.

This sounds like a dream: a controlled environment that gets promoted as an artifact from development to QA and later production (sometimes stopping in preproduction for a sanity check) that is repeatable and the only thing that changes across environments is the configuration, usually injected via environment variables. It is not a dream; it is the reality in 2017, and in this chapter, we are going to accelerate from 0 to the speed of light on when it comes to running containers in Docker and building images.

In this chapter, we will cover the following topics:

- The Docker architecture
- The Docker client
- Building `docker images`
- Docker registries
- Volumes
- Docker networking
- Docker Compose

We will also stop at `docker-compose`, a tool used to run several containers in combination, so we can compose our system in the development machine, simulating our production configuration or, at the very least, approaching the interconnection of components, but before that, we are going to also dive deep into Docker networking: how can we choose the most appropriate networking for our system and what are the main differences between the different networks that Docker offers?

Another interesting feature of Docker is how the images get built: basically, we choose a base image (we will look at how to build one), and with a reduced set of commands, we can build a Docker file which is basically a script that instructs Docker on how to build our image with the configuration that we need.

Docker architecture

One of my preferred ways of learning is through experimentation. In order to explain the Docker architecture, we are going to show an example, but first, we need to install Docker itself. In this case, I am working with Mac, but at https://docs.docker.com/engine/installation/, you can find the distribution that suits your needs with a very clear set of instructions (usually a package that needs to be installed).

Once you have installed Docker, run the following command:

```
docker run hello-world
```

Once it finishes, the output should be very similar to the following one:

```
Unable to find image 'hello-world:latest' locally
latest: Pulling from library/hello-world
78445dd45222: Pull complete
Digest:
sha256:c5515758d4c5e1e838e9cd307f6c6a0d620b5e07e6f927b07d05f6d12a1ac8d7
```

```
Status: Downloaded newer image for hello-world:latest
Hello from Docker!
```

This message shows that your installation appears to be working correctly.

To generate this message, Docker took the following steps:

1. The Docker client contacted the Docker daemon.
2. The Docker daemon pulled the `hello-world` image from the Docker Hub.
3. The Docker daemon created a new container from that image, which runs the executable that produces the output you are currently reading.
4. The Docker daemon streamed that output to the Docker client, which sent it to your Terminal.

To try something more ambitious, you can run an Ubuntu container with the following:

```
$ docker run -it ubuntu bash
```

Share images, automate workflows, and more with a free Docker ID at `https://cloud.docker.com/`.

For more examples and ideas, visit: `https://docs.docker.com/engine/userguide/`.

As you can see, the `hello-world` image gives you some insights into what is going on when running the preceding command.

Some new concepts have been introduced here:

- **Docker Hub**: This is a central repository, which is public and private, where users can push images that they build locally. A Docker registry is used to carry the images across different stages of the deployment pipeline (or even between systems).
- **Layer**: Docker images are composed of layers. A layer is basically an ordered filesystem difference. A Docker image is a stack of these layers leading into the final image. When you change a file in an existing image, a new layer is created, but the rest of the layers of the images are reused so we can save a lot (believe me, a lot) of space.
- **Docker daemon**: Docker follows a client-server architecture. In this case, the Docker daemon is the server part that can be operated via a **Representational State Transfer** (**REST**) API.
- **Docker client**: Docker client is a **Command-Line Interface** (**CLI**) used to operate a Docker daemon. It might be a local daemon or a remote one.

The last three concepts are the key for drafting the architecture of Docker. Take a look at the following figure:

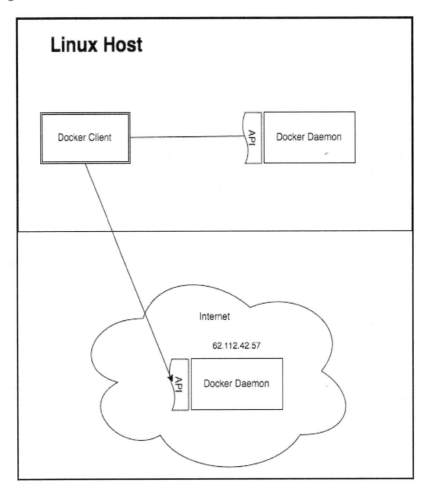

The client/server architecture predominates the software. You might think that this is an overkill for a system such as Docker, but it actually gives you a lot of flexibility. For example, in the previous diagram, we can see how the Docker CLI (the client) is able to manage a local instance of the Docker daemon but is also able to talk to a remote daemon by setting an environment variable called DOCKER_HOST, in this case, to the value of 62.112.42.57.

One of the key points of Docker is that it completely leverages the virtualization to the Linux kernel, making it impossible to run (as of today) Docker on Windows or even Mac as it uses the capabilities of the Linux kernel. The solution to this is to create a virtual machine with Linux that runs the Docker daemon, and the CLI will talk to the virtual machine to run Docker commands.

In Mac, for example, the old versions of Docker use a distribution called `Boot2Docker` that runs the Docker daemon, whereas the newer versions of Docker use something called **HyperKit**, which is a lightweight virtualization solution for Mac.

Docker for Windows uses a different type of virtualization that is equivalent to the one in Mac so all the assumptions made for Mac are valid for Windows.

Docker internals

Up until now, we have seen how Docker works regarding the overall architecture, but what happens at the operating system level in the Docker daemon?

Roughly explained, Docker provides you with only a runtime for your applications: you can limit the number of cores and the amount of memory to be used by the container, but at the end of the day, the kernel running your container is going to be the same as the kernel running your host machine.

The proof of that is in the way Docker organizes images: it calculates filesystem differences and packs them in layers that can be reused. Let's pull a fairly big image (not the hello-world from the preceding example):

```
docker pull ubuntu
```

This will produce the following output:

```
Using default tag: latest
latest: Pulling from library/ubuntu
d54efb8db41d: Pull complete
f8b845f45a87: Pull complete
e8db7bf7c39f: Pull complete
9654c40e9079: Pull complete
6d9ef359eaaa: Pull complete
Digest:
sha256:dd7808d8792c9841d0b460122f1acf0a2dd1f56404f8d1e56298048885e45535
Status: Downloaded newer image for ubuntu:latest
```

As you can see, Docker has pulled five layers, which basically tells us that the Ubuntu image was built in five steps (not quite true, but it is a good approach). Now we are going to run an instance of Ubuntu. In Docker, an instance of an image is what we call a container, and the main difference between an image and a container is the top writable layer (layers in Docker are stacked in the read-only mode to compose the image, such as the diffs in several patch files). Let's demonstrate this:

```
docker run -it ubuntu /bin/bash
```

The preceding command runs /bin/bash in an instance of the Ubuntu image. The i and t flags allow you to use the container as if it were a virtual machine allocating a virtual TTY (t flag) and creating the interactive session (i flag). Now, you can see how your prompt has changed to something like the following:

```
root@329b2f9332d5:/#
```

It does not necessarily have to be the same, but it should be similar. Note that your prompt is now a root prompt, but don't get too excited; it is just inside the container.

Create a file to alter the filesystem:

```
touch test.txt
```

Now you can disconnect from the container with the exit command.

As you can see, the prompt is back to your system prompt, and if you run docker ps, you can see that there are no running containers, but if you run docker ps -a (show all the containers, not just the running ones), you should see something similar to this:

CONTAINER ID	IMAGE	COMMAND	CREATED	STATUS	PORTS	NAMES
329b2f9332d5	ubuntu	"/bin/bash"	About a minute ago	Exited (0) 4 seconds ago		gracious_spence

This is a container that has been created from an image but is not running anymore. As we said earlier, the only difference between this container and the image is the top writable layer. In order to prove this, we are going to create a new image out of the container that we ran a few minutes ago:

```
docker commit 329b2f9332d5 my-ubuntu
```

In this case, I am using the reference 329b. because it is the one shown in the preceding image (the output of docker ps -a), but you need to change the hash to the one shown in your output. In fairness, you don't need to type it all; just few characters will do the job. If everything went well, the command should output a SHA256 checksum and return the control to you. Now run docker images (to list the images in your Docker) and the output should be similar to the following:

CONTAINER ID	IMAGE	COMMAND	CREATED	STATUS	PORTS	NAMES
329b2f9332d5	ubuntu	"/bin/bash"	About a minute ago	Exited (0) 4 seconds ago		gracious_spence

As you can see, there is a new image called `my-ubuntu` that we just created.

Now we want to check the difference between the `ubuntu` image and the `my-ubuntu` image. In order to do that, we need to inspect the layers for each image and see the difference. The command we are going to use to accomplish this task is `docker history`, with the name of the image as the third parameter.

First, for the `ubuntu` image:

IMAGE	CREATED	CREATED BY	SIZE
0ef2e08ed3fa	2 weeks ago	/bin/sh -c #(nop) CMD ["/bin/bash"]	0 B
<missing>	2 weeks ago	/bin/sh -c mkdir -p /run/systemd && echo '...	7 B
<missing>	2 weeks ago	/bin/sh -c sed -i 's/^#\s*\(deb.*universe\...	1.9 kB
<missing>	2 weeks ago	/bin/sh -c rm -rf /var/lib/apt/lists/*	0 B
<missing>	2 weeks ago	/bin/sh -c set -xe && echo '#!/bin/sh' >...	745 B
<missing>	2 weeks ago	/bin/sh -c #(nop) ADD file:efb254bc677d66d...	130 MB

Then for `my-ubuntu`: image (just created from `ubuntu`):

IMAGE	CREATED	CREATED BY	SIZE
2309b9c4202b	3 days ago	/bin/bash	5 B
0ef2e08ed3fa	2 weeks ago	/bin/sh -c #(nop) CMD ["/bin/bash"]	0 B
<missing>	2 weeks ago	/bin/sh -c mkdir -p /run/systemd && echo '...	7 B
<missing>	2 weeks ago	/bin/sh -c sed -i 's/^#\s*\(deb.*universe\...	1.9 kB
<missing>	2 weeks ago	/bin/sh -c rm -rf /var/lib/apt/lists/*	0 B
<missing>	2 weeks ago	/bin/sh -c set -xe && echo '#!/bin/sh' >...	745 B
<missing>	2 weeks ago	/bin/sh -c #(nop) ADD file:efb254bc677d66d...	130 MB

Quite illuminating. The image `my-ubuntu` ;is the same image as `ubuntu` except for the top writable layer that we just created by logging in to the machine and creating a file. This is very smart because even though both of the two images use around 130 MB of space, the only extra space used for the second image is the top layer that, in this case, uses only 5 bytes, leading to a usage of 130 MB and 5 bytes for the two images. This also has a side-effect in line with what we talked earlier: a container is the exact same thing as an image but with a different top writable layer, so running an instance of the container uses only 5 bytes of space. As you can see, the engineers that created Docker thought about everything!

The way in which how Docker stores the images in the hard drive is the responsibility of the storage driver: Docker can make use of different drivers and store the images in different ways (and places, such as S3 in AWS), but the most common use case, the default driver, stores the images on the hard drive, creating one file per layer with the checksum of the layer as the name of the file.

Docker client

We have made use of the Docker client already in the previous section, but we need to go a bit deeper into the options that the Docker CLI can offer. My favorite way of learning is through experimentation, and what we are going to be doing through this section is building concepts from top to bottom (more decomposing, than building), so I advise you to read the full section in the order without skipping parts, as the latter examples will be based on the previous ones.

If you have dug into Docker a bit before, you can see that the commands are **quite** verbose and not as intuitive as you might think. The most common use case is the following combination:

```
docker run -i -t <docker-image>
```

This command basically does one simple thing: it runs a container in the interactive mode and allocates `pseudo-tty`. This allows us to interact with the container executing the commands (not on every image, but it is true for all the base images of Linux distributions). Let's see what that means:

```
docker run -i -t ubuntu
```

This should return a prompt similar to the following one:

```
root@248ff3bcedc3:/#
```

What just happened? The prompt changed to root with a strange number in the host section. We are in the container. Basically, now we can run commands that are going to be run within the container. To exit the container, just type exit and the control should be returned in the terminal to your host machine, leaving the container running in the background.

The majority of the time, the preceding command suits our needs, but sometimes, we want to run the container in the background: imagine that you spin up a Jenkins server and you don't want to have your Terminal attached to it. In order to do that, we just need to add the -d option (daemon) and drop -i and -t:

```
docker run -d jenkins
```

Once the image is pulled and it starts running, the control is returned to your Terminal. The last line in the output, and it should be a long string of characters similar to the following one:

```
9f6a33eb6bda4c4e050f3a5dd113b717f07cc97e2fdc5e2c73a2d16613bd540b
```

This is the hash of the running container. If you execute docker ps, the following output (similar) will be produced:

> Note that the value under CONTAINER ID in the screenshot matches the first few digits of the hash from the preceding command.

Now in theory, we have a running instance of Jenkins that, as you can see in the preceding image, is listening on port 8080 and port 50000. Let's try to browse http://localhost:8080 with an internet browser. Nothing. Basically, our browser cannot open that URL.

This is because we haven't told to Docker to bind the container ports to the local ports of the host machine. In order to do that, we need to first stop the container and then start it again with a special parameter.

Time to learn how to stop containers. We have two options here:

- **Stop the container**: With the stop option, we send SIGTERM to the main process within the container and wait for it to finish (for a grace period). Then, we send SIGKILL.
- **Kill the container**: With the kill option, we send SIGKILL to the main process in the container, which forces an immediate exit without being able to save the state.

In this case, which one you choose is irrelevant, but please be careful. When you are running in a production environment, make sure it's fine to kill a container before doing that, as with the stop option, we are giving the running software the option to save the current transactions and exit gracefully. In this case, I am going to kill the container:

```
docker kill 9f6a
```

Docker is smart. I did not need to specify the full container identifier, as with only a few characters, Docker is able to identify the container (or the image in other commands) and kill it.

If you remember from previous examples, when we kill a container, we have a layer left that leads into a dead container that we can explore, adding the -a option to the docker ps command. For this example, we are going to remove this layer as well with the following command:

```
docker rm 9f6a
```

That's it. The container never existed in our host.

Now, going back to the Jenkins example, we want to run Jenkins in a way that we can access the running instance from our browser. Let's modify the preceding command and explain why:

```
docker run -p 8080:8080 -p 50000 -d jenkins
```

After a few seconds, if we go to http://localhost:8080 in a browser, we should see the initial configuration for Jenkins, which asks for the initial password to be able to proceed.

Let's explain the previous command first. We can see a new option: -p. As you can guess, -p comes from the port. In fairness, you could change -p for --port, and everything will work as expected. With the -p option, we map ports from the host, your machine, to the container. In this case, we are mapping port 8080 from the host to port 8080 and port 50000 of the host to port 50000 of the container, but how can we map a different port in the host? Well, it is fairly simple:

```
docker run -p 8081:8080 -p 50001:50000 -d jenkins
```

After running the preceding command, we have two instances of Jenkins running:

- The first one is exposed in port 8080 of your machine
- The second one is exposed in port 80801 of your machine

Note that even though we don't use port `50000`, I have changed it to `50001` as your machine's port `50000` is already busy with the first instance of Jenkins that we ran earlier on.

As you can see, Jenkins is asking for a password, and the initial web page in `http://localhost:8080` states that this password is in the logs or in the filesystem. Focusing on the logs, with Docker, we can fetch the logs for any container registered by the daemon at any time. Let's try this:

```
docker logs 11872
```

In my case, the running instance of Jenkins on port `80801` has an ID that starts with `11872`. Executing the previous command should retrieve the starting log of Jenkins that we can use for troubleshooting or, in this case, to recover the password to initialize Jenkins.

Another interesting and common option in Docker is passing environment variables to an application running inside the container. If you think about it, there are only three ways in which we can configure an application within a Docker container:

- Environment variables
- A volume with data
- Fetching the configuration from the network

Let's take a look at the official MySQL image from the Docker Hub:

- `https://hub.docker.com/_/mysql/`

MySQL is a popular database server that has also been `dockerized`. If you read a bit through the documentation, one of the config options is the root password for the MySQL database. In fairness, the quick start example points to the right direction:

```
docker run --name some-mysql -e MYSQL_ROOT_PASSWORD=my-secret-pw -d mysql
```

The new option here is `-e`. This option allows you to pass an environment variable to the container with the value that you want to specify after =. After running the preceding command, we are going to run another command:

```
docker inspect caa40cc7d45f
```

In this case, `caa40cc7d45f` is the ID that results from running MySQL on my machine (yours should be different). There should be a huge JSON output in the terminal, but one section in particular, Config, has a subsection called `Env` , which should look very similar to the following one:

```
...
"Env": [
    "MYSQL_ROOT_PASSWORD=my-secret-pw",
    "no_proxy=*.local, 169.254/16",
    "PATH=/usr/local/sbin:/usr/local/bin:/usr/sbin:/usr/bin:/sbin:/bin",
    "GOSU_VERSION=1.7",
    "MYSQL_MAJOR=5.7",
    "MYSQL_VERSION=5.7.17-1debian8"
  ],
...
```

There it is. The preceding environment variable that we passed, `MYSQL_ROOT_PASSWORD`, is now accessible from within the container as the environment variable.

In the `docker inspect` command, there is a lot of very valuable information. Just have a read through, as you might be surprised with how familiar you are with the majority of the info: it is mainly Linux terminology.

So far, we have visited the most common commands as of January 2017. As you know, the software evolves very quickly, and by the time you are reading this book, new versions (such as secrets) have already been added to Docker. The best way to check what is going on is through the documentation on `http://www.docker.com`, which, in my opinion, is quite comprehensive. There is also a reference of the commands of your current Docker installation available under the `docker help` command.

Building Docker images

In the previous sections, we built an image using the commit command of Docker. Although it works, I can see a big problem with it: it is not repeatable. There is no easy way of rebuilding the image once and over again when the software installed in the image is patched due to new vulnerabilities or versions.

In order to solve this problem, Docker provides a better way of building images: Dockerfiles.

A Dockerfile is a file that contains a set of ordered commands required to leave the image, ready to be used. Things such as installing software or upgrading the version of the kernel as well as adding users are common activities that can be carried in a Dockerfile. Let's look at an example:

```
FROM node:latest

RUN mkdir -p /app/
WORKDIR /app/

COPY package.json /app/
RUN npm install

COPY . /app

EXPOSE 8080
CMD [ "npm", "start" ]
```

If you have been in the IT field for a few years, you really don't need an explanation on what it is going on, but let's make sure that we are all on the same page:

- We are creating our image based on the latest Node.js image.
- A new folder is created in /app. Our application will be installed there.
- The working directory is set to this new folder.
- Copy package.json and install the Node.js dependencies. Remember that we have already set up the working directory to /app, so the RUN command will be run in the /app folder.
- Copy the rest of the source code.
- Expose port 8080 to the outer world.
- Run npm start.

It is very simple once you have done it few times. One thing to keep in mind that might drive beginners crazy is this: CMD versus RUN.

In the preceding Dockerfile, sometimes, we use RUN, and sometimes, we use CMD, but both of them seem to do the same thing: run a command. There is one difference:

- RUN: This will run the command when building the image
- CMD: This will run the command when the container based on the generated image starts

Also, RUN (generally) creates a new layer, whereas CMD uses the writable layer of the container.

Now, it's time to test the Dockerfile from earlier. Before building the image, we need to build a small Node.js application that is going to be used as the software running in the image. Create a new folder with three files:

- package.json
- index.js
- Dockerfile (the one from before)

The content of package.json will be as follows:

```
{
  "name": "test",
  "version": "1.0.0",
  "description": "Test",
  "main": "index.js",
  "scripts": {
  "start": "node index.js"
  },
  "author": "Test",
  "license": "MIT"
}
```

The content of index.js will be as follows:

```
console.log('Hello world!')
```

And now, with the preceding files and the Dockerfile described before in the same folder, run the following command:

```
docker build . -t my-node-app
```

After a few seconds, your image would be ready for use. Let's check it. If you list your images with the docker images command, you should see an image called my-node-app. Now create a container based on the image:

```
docker run my-node-app
```

You should see something similar to the following:

```
npm info it worked if it ends with ok
npm info using npm@4.1.2
npm info using node@v7.7.4
npm info lifecycle test@1.0.0~prestart: test@1.0.0
```

```
npm info lifecycle test@1.0.0~start: test@1.0.0
> test@1.0.0 start /app
> node index.js
hello world!
npm info lifecycle test@1.0.0~poststart: test@1.0.0
npm info ok
```

As you can see in the highlighted section, the output of running our application is here.

Dockerfile reference

As you can see in the previous section, Dockerfiles are very simple, and if you have any queries, the official documentation for the Dockerfile language is very comprehensive.

In general, the language used for creating Dockerfiles is very similar to the batch processing language of windows (.bat files) from a few years ago.

Let's look at the most used commands:

FROM	This instruction is used to specify the base image. Every single Docker image is created starting from a base image (you can create base images from a running Linux distribution).
COPY	As you can guess, COPY allows you to copy files and folders inside the image. For example, we could copy our application, a war file, or any other artifact that will be packed with the image once it is distributed.
ADD	This does the exactly the same thing as COPY but with three differences: • The origin of the files could be a URL that gets downloaded before copying • The origin of the files could be a packed file (such as a TAR file) that will be unpacked in the image filesystem
RUN	This runs a command in the image. For example, it can be used to install software in the image. It always creates a new layer in the Docker image, so be careful and keep the RUN commands to a minimum.
CMD	This is the default command to be run when the image gets instantiated as a container. As you can see in the preceding example, we are using CMD to execute npm start, which runs node index.js (refer to package.json). It does not create a new layer as it uses the top writable layer to store the changes.

ENTRYPOINT	`ENTRYPOINT` is similar to `CMD`, but it overrides the default command on a docker image that is `/bin/sh -c`. In order to override an specified entry point, you need to pass the `--entrypoint` flag when running an instance of the image. `ENTRYPOINT` is ideal for configuring containers as command-line tools, as you can pack a fairly complex command with a fairly complex setup in a single container.
MAINTAINER	With `MAINTAINER`, you can specify who is the maintainer of the image (also specify the email).
EXPOSE	This exposes the port specified in the first parameter so that the container can listen to it. It actually does not expose the port in the `docker` client host, forcing the user to pass the `-p` flag in order to access the given port.

With these commands, you can build pretty much anything that you want, and particularly with RUN, this allows the user to run any command within the container that enables us to run scripts (`python`, `bash`, and `ruby`.) or even install software using package managers.

Aside from the preceding instructions, the Dockerfile language also comes with support for adding environment variables, volumes, and a few other features that make it quite powerful.

Docker registries

In the previous section, we created a new image with our application installed and ready to be used (in this case, a very simple `Hello world` Node.js application).

Now, we need to distribute the image so it can be installed in all the stages of our deployment pipeline or even used by other developers. Docker is interesting for running applications but it is also a very interesting choice to create command-line tools that other developers can benefit from.

In order to distribute images, we have to rely on exporting/importing the image or using a registry. A registry is basically a software that allows us to store and distribute Docker images. There are two types of registries:

- Public registries
- Private registries

Let's take a look at the different registry types.

Public registries

The most known of the public registries is Docker Hub. It is the official and default registry that every Docker installation knows of. Also, it offers private repositories, but the most interesting feature is the fact that all the official images are available on Docker Hub.

Let's see how can we use it. First, you need to create an account. Once you are registered, create a new repository:

This repository hosts an image called `modern-devops`, and we are going to push one image into it. Once it is created, you can see that Docker Hub suggests that you pull the image with the following command:

```
docker pull dagonzadub/modern-devops
```

In your case, `dagonzadub` will need to be replaced with your username. Obviously, we are not going to pull an image that is not there yet, so let's push an image. In the previous section, we created an image called `my-node-app`. We are going to use this image to test Docker Hub. Docker relies on a tag system to know where to push the image or where to pull from. As we are working with the `default` registry, we don't need to specify the URL, but we need to specify the user and the repository name. If you haven't deleted the image created in the previous section, run the following command:

```
docker tag my-node-app dagonzadub/modern-devops
```

And then, run this command:

```
docker push dagonzadub/modern-devops
```

After a few seconds (depending on your upload speed, even minutes), your image is available on Docker Hub. As we marked it as `public`, everybody can pull and use your image.

Private registries

But what happens if we want to store our images in our private registry within our infrastructure?

Well, we have some options. If we are using cloud providers, such as Google Cloud Platform or Amazon Web Services, they provide a Docker registry that is only accessible from within your account, and you can specify the region in which your images live (remember, the type of data that we are handling might be under strict compliance rules about where we should store the data).

In AWS, the container registry is called **EC2 Container Registry (ECR)**, and in GCP, it is called a container registry. If your infrastructure is in one of these private clouds, I encourage you to use it as you can leverage the access to the access controls provided by the platforms.

Sometimes, we might find ourselves in a situation where we cannot use a cloud provider as our system has to be built on premises. This is when we need to use a private on-premises Docker registry.

Nowadays, there are quite a few options, but it is highly likely that the market widens in the coming months or years as the companies are using Docker more and more.

From all the range of registries, there are three that I find particularly interesting:

Quay: This is a complete registry in the current market (at the time of writing this). It has some interesting features, but the one that is probably the most interesting is the ability to scan the images searching for security vulnerabilities in the installed software. It can also build images based on changes in your git repository, so if your Dockerfile is altered in GitHub, Quay will automatically trigger a build and deploy the new version of the image. Quay is not free, so a license has to be paid in order to use it.

Registry: This is the plain name for a plain concept. It is the official implementation of the registry API and comes packed in a container. It has no interface or access controls by default, but it does the job. It also provides storage management drivers, so we can deploy our images to S3 or Google Cloud Storage buckets as well as many other options. Registry is free and can be pulled from Docker Hub.

Docker Trusted Registry: This is part of the enterprise version of Docker. Like pretty much any other commercial registry, it provides static container analysis as well as storage management drivers. **Docker Trusted Registry** (**DTR**) is not free, so a license has to be paid for in order to use it.

Docker volumes

So far, we have seen how to create images, how to store the images in a registry, and how Docker images work in general (layers and containers versus images).
An important part of any application is the storage. In general, Docker applications should be stateless, but with the new orchestration software, such as Kubernetes, Docker Swarm, and similar, every day, more and more engineers are moving toward containerized databases.
Docker solves this problem in a very elegant way: you can mount a folder from the local machine into the container as if it were a normal folder.
This is a very powerful abstraction as it leverages the ability to push data out of the container to be saved into a **Network Attached Storage** (**NAS**) or any other storage technology (it is possible to use a bucket in the Google Cloud Storage or S3 as the volume mounted in a container).

Let's start with the basics. Just run a MySQL database:

```
docker run --name my-mysql -e MYSQL_ROOT_PASSWORD=my-secret-pw -d
mysql:latest
```

This works. It actually does what is expected: it launches a container with a mysql instance in it. The problem is that all the data is going to be written to /var/lib/mysql and this folder is mapped to the top writable layer of the container (remember, in the previous section, we explained the difference between a container and an image). The only way to save data is actually committing the changes and create a new image that is not manageable and, of course, this not the way you want to do it. Think about it: if you remove a file in Docker, you are doing it in the top layer, which is the only one writable, so in reality, you are not removing the file; you are just hiding it. The file is in one of the layers using the space but it is not visible. Docker records differences and a layer itself is a set of differences from the previous stacked layers (think about how Git works; it is the same principle). Instead of committing the changes into a new image, we are going to mount a folder from our docker host into the container. Let's alter the previous command a bit:

```
docker run --name my-mysql-2 -v /home/david/docker/data:/var/lib/mysql -e
MYSQL_ROOT_PASSWORD=my-secret-pw -d mysql:latest
```

Now we have a new flag, -v, followed by the data:/var/lib/mysql value. The meaning of the command is very simple: mount the /home/david/data folder into the /var/lib/mysql path of my container.

As you can guess, the data folder, in my case, /home/david/data, should be present in your current directory, so if it wasn't present, create it or modify the path to suit your setup and launch the container. This use case can only be achieved through the -v flag: mount a selected folder from the host into the container.
Now, execute ls inside the data folder (in the Docker host):

```
ls /home/david/data
```

You can see how mysql has actually written data files corresponding to the databases created in bootstrap.
Docker volumes are not limited to one per container, so you can replicate the -v flag as many times as you need in order to match your requirements.

Another way of mounting a shared folder between the container and the host is just specifying the path inside the container:

```
docker run --name my-mysql-3 -v /var/lib/myysql -e MYSQL_ROOT_PASSWORD=my-
secret-pw -d mysql:latest
```

This command will mount a folder from our Docker host into the container, but the folder in the docker host will be managed by the storage driver and docker itself:

```
docker inspect my-mysql-3
```

The output is familiar. We have seen it before in the previous sections, but now we are looking for different information. We are actually looking for a section called `Mounts`, which looks like this (at least similar to it):

```
"Mounts": [
 {
 "Type": "volume",
 "Name":
"572c2303b8417557072d5dc351f25d152e6947c1129f596f08e7e8d15ea2b220",
 "Source":
"/var/lib/docker/volumes/572c2303b8417557072d5dc351f25d152e6947c1129f596f08
e7e8d15ea2b220/_data",
 "Destination": "/var/lib/mysql",
 "Driver": "local",
 "Mode": "",
 "RW": true,
 "Propagation": ""
 }
 ]
```

This is also possible through the VOLUME instruction in a Dockerfile.

The preceding JSON is telling us which local folder is going to be mounted in the container (the Source value of the JSON) and provides an interesting insight: the volume has been named by docker (the Name value of the JSON).

This means that Docker tracks the volumes that are (or have been) mounted in any container and can be listed through an API call:

```
docker volume ls
```

This should produce output similar to the following:

```
DRIVER VOLUME NAME
 local 13b66aa9f9c20c5a82c38563a585c041ea4a832e0b98195c610b4209ebeed444
 local 572c2303b8417557072d5dc351f25d152e6947c1129f596f08e7e8d15ea2b220
 local 695d7cbc47881078f435e466b1dd060be703eda394ccb95bfa7a18f64dc13d41
 local b0f4553586b17b4bd2f888a17ba2334ea0e6cf0776415e20598594feb3e05952
```

As you can guess, we can also create volumes through an api call:

```
docker volume create modern-devops
```

This volume is created in the same way as the previous example: it is up to Docker to decide which folder on the local machine is going to be mounted in the specified path in the container, but in this case, first, we are creating the volume and then mounting it to a container. You can even inspect the volume:

```
docker volume inspect modern-devops
```

And this should return you something similar to the following:

```
[
{
"Driver": "local",
"Labels": {},
"Mountpoint": "/var/lib/docker/volumes/modern-devops/_data",
"Name": "modern-devops",
"Options": {},
"Scope": "local"
}
]
```

Now we can use this named resource and mount it into our containers, just referencing the name:

```
docker run --name my-mysql-4 -v modern-devops:/var/lib/myysql -e
MYSQL_ROOT_PASSWORD=my-secret-pw -d mysql:latest
```

The last (but not least) interesting use case in volumes helps us share the configuration across different containers. Just imagine that you have a fairly complex setup that leads to a gigantic Docker command with several -v. Docker provides us with a much simpler way of sharing volume configuration across containers:

```
docker run --name my-mysql-5 --volumes-from my-mysql-4 -e
MYSQL_ROOT_PASSWORD=my-secret-pw -d mysql:latest
```

This is very simple and intuitive: my-mysql-5 will spawn with the volume configuration of my-mysql-4.

Docker networking

Networking is an important part of Docker. By default, Docker comes with three networks that we can inspect by executing the following command:

```
docker network ls
```

This should produce output similar to the following:

```
NETWORK ID        NAME           DRIVER         SCOPE
96e541123c53      bridge         bridge         local
931d65d41ab0      host           host           local
49d59417736c      none           null           local
```

Let's explain the different networks:

- `bridge`: This is the default network. It is an entirely different stack from the host machine with a different IP range in the `bridge` mode (the host machine acts as a `router` for the containers in this network). The containers created without specifying the network are attached to the default bridge network.
- `host`: In this network, containers share the network stack with the Docker host. If you inspect the configuration in the container, you will find that it is the exactly the same as in the Docker host.
- `none`: This is easy to guess; the container gets attached to no network: just the loopback interface in the container.

Now it is time to look at some examples. We are going to use `busybox`, which is the `swiss` army knife of the Docker images. It has several Unix tools that we could benefit from, but in this case, the characteristic that is going to benefit us is the fact that it is a functional Linux on a reduced space.

Let's run the following command:

```
docker run -it busybox /bin/sh
```

If you have followed the previous sections, by now, you can understand the outcome: we gain root access to a running container.

The next step is to execute `ifconfig` inside the container. It should give us two interfaces:

- eth0 - 172.17.0.2
- lo - 127.0.0.1

The IP might change, but you should see these two interfaces. Comparing the IP with the IP in your Docker host, we can validate the fact that the container is running in the bridge network as the IP and network are completely different; in my case, the IP on my Docker host is `10.0.0.12`.

Now, let's spawn another container with `busybox` in a different terminal:

```
docker run -it busybox /bin/sh
```

By now, we should have two `busybox` instances running, and they should have consecutive IPs, in my case, `172.17.0.2` and `172.17.0.3`. If you go back to the terminal of the first instance of `busybox`, you can ping the second container by IP. This is because they both belong (or are connected to) the same network, which is the default bridge one.
In order to run the containers in the host network, we just need to pass `--network=host` flag to the `docker run` command and that's it; our container is sharing the network stack with the Docker host, but be careful, if you are on Mac or Windows. The Docker host is a virtual machine so don't attempt to access it through localhost; you will need to find the IP of the virtual machine running `docker`.

User-defined networks

It is also possible to create custom and isolated networks in Docker. This is interesting from the security point of view, as it enables us to segregate different containers on the network level so we can enforce a higher level of access control.

In order to create a network, we just need to execute the following command:

```
docker network create my-network
```

And that's it. Well, that is a simplistic approach, but it works as expected. As you know, networking is a complicated subject, so Docker provides options to customize ranges, masks, and other parameters. The user-defined networks are of the type bridge.
Once the network is created, you can run new containers in that network, as follows (on a new terminal):

```
docker run -it --network=my-network busybox /bin/sh
```

As expected, these containers will be isolated from the other networks. In this case, the two containers are launched in the `bridge` network. In my case, the third container (the one just launched) has the IP `172.19.0.2`, whereas the two launched in the bridge network are `172.17.0.2` and `172.17.0.3`. Issuing a ping command between containers in different networks results in 100% packet loss.

Docker Compose

The majority of the time, Docker is synonymous to microservices. Running a big monolithic application in Docker does not make too much sense as the whole Docker Engine is thought to be running big applications split into different and smaller services. There is no technical limitation to running a monolithic app on Docker, but when the orchestration software comes into place (in the following chapters), it really defeats the purpose of containerization.

When dealing with microservices, it is very common to have several services running at the same time when developing, as the new services will lean on the existing ones to execute operations.

In order to achieve this setup, Docker facilitates a tool called `docker-compose` that, by creating a YAML file with the definition of our containers, can spawn a full ecosystem of containers.

Docker compose used to be very popular in the beginning of Docker. Nowadays, it is still widely used, but its space has been slowly reduced to development stages as the container orchestration tools in Kubernetes have taken over the production space.

Let's look at how Docker Compose works:

```
version: '2'
services:
my_app:
build: .
depends_on:
- db
db:
image: postgres
```

The preceding YAML file is a `docker-compose` definition. As you can guess, there are two components:

- A web application (the current folder)
- A database (postgres)

Save the file to a folder with the name `docker-compose.yaml`.

This is a typical case of an application connecting to a database. In order to simplify this, our application is just going to be a dummy application (no database connection) with the following code:

```
let dns = require('dns')

dns.lookup('db', (err, result) => {
console.log('The IP of the db is: ', result)
})
```

```
{
 "name": "modern-devops",
 "version": "1.0.0",
 "description": "Test",
 "main": "index.js",
 "scripts": {
 "start": "node index.js"
 },
 "author": "",
 "license": "ISC"
 }
package.json
```

And our Dockerfile is very simple:

```
FROM node:onbuild
```

This Dockerfile will install the required dependencies and run `npm start` in the root of our app folder.

As you can see, the application is very simple, and it only tries to resolve the name `db` instead of connecting to the database (in fairness, we didn't even specify the ports for connecting to it). We are going to demonstrate how `docker-compose` wires up the containers. By now, there should be four files in the work folder:

- `index.js`
- `package.json`
- Dockerfile
- `docker-compose.yaml`

Going back to our `docker-compose` file, we can see that in the `my_app` definition, we ask to build the current folder (build the image described by the Dockerfile), and we specify that the container itself is dependent on another container called `db`. This makes Docker take action and connect the two containers, being able to reach `db` from `my-app` by name. In order to achieve this, there is an entry created in `/etc/hosts` with the IP of `db`, so we `my-app` will be able to resolve it. Docker compose is very easy to understand: it is nearly self-explanatory, and the fact that it makes use of YAML makes everything so much more readable. Now we need to run it:

```
docker-compose up
```

Once it finishes, there should be a quite a long output, but there are some lines that indicate our success:

```
my_app_1  | > my_app@1.0.0 start /usr/src/app
my_app_1  | > node index.js
my_app_1  |
my_app_1  | The IP of the db is 172.20.0.2
my_app_1  | npm info lifecycle my_app@1.0.0~poststart:my_app@1.0.0
web_1 | npm info ok
```

The highlighted section tells us that `my_app` is able to reach db by IP as they are on the same bridge network. Let's see what happened here:

- Docker built the image for the current folder (as specified in `my_app`) from the Dockerfile
- Docker pulled the `postgres` image from the Docker Hub
- Docker started the images in order: first `db` and second `my_app`, as specified in the dependencies

In this book, we are going to give a special emphasis to orchestration technologies, and then we will come back to Docker Compose in `Chapter 5`, *Infrastructure as Code,* where we will take a deep dive into Docker Swarm, which is where compose becomes really helpful.

Summary

In this chapter, we walked through Docker from the internals to the command-line interface to operate a Docker host. Now, we have enough knowledge to understand the consequences and benefits of running Docker in production. We have not looked into how to develop Docker plugins as well as different storage drivers, as unfortunately, we have a limited amount of space in this book to introduce the most interesting concepts, but we have dived deep enough into Docker to be able to learn more from the resources (official documentation, videos, and so on) available to us on the Internet.

In the next chapter, we will have a look on how to automate tasks around our software: running tests, building images and many other tasks that shouldn't be done manually. This automation is called **continuous integration** because allows our team to integrate new features on a seamless way.

4
Continuous Integration

When building software, quality assessment is something that usually is pushed toward the end of the life cycle, just before the release. When the team is working in a 6-months release cycle, the drawbacks are not as obvious as when the release cycle is just a few days old (or even hours!), but from my experience, I can tell you that getting early feedback in your software is crucial in order to raise the quality to a good level we are comfortable to live with.

There is a misconception in the software that puts the average software projectin danger: the software has to be perfect.This is totally incorrect. Think about some of these real-world systems: the engine of your car, a nuclear plant, the water purification system in major cities, and so on; human lives depend upon all of them and they fail. A fair amount of money is spent on these systems without being able to ensure the total safety, so what makes you think that the software that your company writes will be perfect?

Instead of investing resources in making your software perfect, the experience has taught me (through the hard path) that it is a lot better to invest the resources in building the software in a way that makes it easy for the engineers to fix the problems as quickly as possible, being able to shorten the release cycles with enough level of confidence. In this chapter, we are going to examine the key components of the continuous integration:

- Software development life cycle
- Traditional CI servers:
    - Bamboo
    - Jenkins
- Modern CI servers:
    - Drone

This has the objective of building an effective continuous integration pipeline to ensure reliability and enables us to deliver faster.

Software development life cycle

The software development life cycle is the diagram of our day to day activity as software engineers wait, this book is about DevOps; what are we doing talking about software engineering? Well, in theory, DevOpsis the role of the IT activity that covers the full life cycle of a software component, from the inception to the release and further maintenance. Nowadays, many companies are hiring DevOps engineers on the basis of hiring system administrators on steroids that even though it works, it completely misses the biggest advantage of the DevOps role: having someone on the team with exposure to all the aspects of the software so that problems can be solved quickly without involving people from different teams in the majority of the cases.

Before proceeding further, let's take a look at how the software development life cycle works:

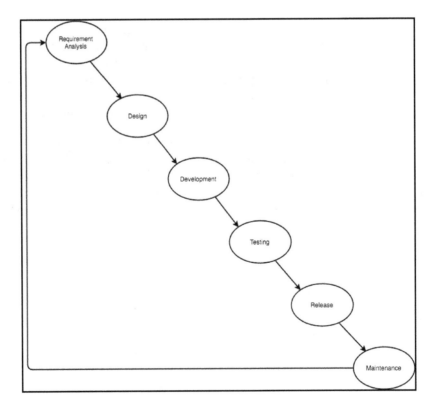

This is the most classical and studied software development life cycle in IT literacy, something that everyone has gone through in college and everyone has as a mental model of even if we have not seen it before. Nowadays, with the agile methodologies, people tend to think that the model is obsolete. I think it is still a very valid model, but what it has changed is the scale and the involvement of the different stakeholders through the previous diagram. Let's take a brief look at the objectives of every step in a top-to-bottom approach:

- **Requirement analysis**: This is where we are going to encounter the majority of the problems. We need to find a common language between people outside of IT (accountants, marketers, farmers, and so on) and people in IT, which often leads to different problems around terminology and even business flows being captured incorrectly.

- **Design**: In this phase, we are going to design our flows in a language that the IT crowd can understand straight away, so they will be able to code efficiently. Often, this phase overlaps with the requirement analysis (if the stakeholder is into IT) and that is desirable as diagrams are the perfect middle language that we are looking for.

- **Development**: As the name suggests, this is where the software is built. This is what developers do well: build technical artifacts that work and work well-- according to a potentially flawed specification. This is where we need to be clever: no matter what we do, our software is going to be imperfect, and we need to plan accordingly. When we are working in agile environments, deliver early and deliver often is the mantra followed to minimize the impact of a wrong specification so that the stakeholders can test the product before the problem is too big to be tackled. I also believe that involving the stakeholders early enough is a good strategy, but it is not a silver bullet, so no matter what we do, our software has to be modular so we can plug and play modules in order to accommodate new requirements. In order to ensure the functionality of our modules on their own, we write unit tests that can be run quickly in order to ensure that the code is doing what it is supposed to do.

- **Testing**: This is where continuous integration lives. Our continuous integration server will run the testing for us when appropriated and inform us about the potential problems in our applicationas quickly as possible. Depending on the complexity of our software, our testing can be very extensive in this phase, but in general, the continuous integration server focuses on running integration and acceptance (that said, the integration server usually runs all the tests as the unit tests should be inexpensive to run).

- **Release**: In this phase, we deliver the software to what we call production; people start using the software, and no matter how much effort we put in the previous phases, there will be bugs and that is the reason why we planned our software to be able to fix the problems quickly. In the release phase, we can create something that we will see later on in this book, called **Continuous Delivery (CD)** pipelines, which enables the developers to execute the build-test-deploy cycle very quickly (even a few times a day).
- **Maintenance**: There are two types of maintenance: evolutive and corrective. Evolutive maintenance is where we evolve our software by adding new functionalities or improving business flows to suit the business needs. Corrective maintenance is the one where we fix bugs and misconceptions. We want to minimize the latter but we cannot totally avoid it.

Testing types

In the previous section, we talked about different types of tests:

- **Unit tests**: What we call white box tests are what mock the dependencies and test the business flow of a particular piece of code.
- **Integration tests**: These are designed to test the integration between different components of an application and they do not test the business logic extensively. Sometimes, when the software is not very complex, the integration tests are used as unit tests (especiallyin dynamic languages), but this is not the most common use case.
- **Acceptance tests**: Designed to test business assumptions, these are usually built on the principle of what we know as user stories describing situations with the style of beinggiven an assumption.

Every test has a different objective, and they work well together, but keep the following diagram in your mind:

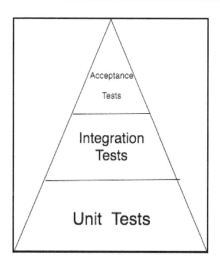

This is what I call the pyramid of testing, and there are years of experience (not only mine) behind it: your software should have a whole bunch of unit testing, fewer integration tests, and some acceptance tests. This ensures that the majority of your business logic is covered by the unit tests and the integration and acceptance tests are used for more specific functions. Also, the integration and acceptance tests are usually more expensive, so minimizing their its usage is usually something that's recommended (but not at the cost of dropping the test coverage).

When working with a CI server, usually, the developer runs the **unit tests** on his computer as they are quick and should spot a big amount of the potential problems, leaving the integration and acceptance tests to the CI server, which will run while the developer is working on other tasks.

Traditional CI servers

In this section, we are going to walk through the most traditional CI servers:

- Bamboo
- Jenkins

They have been around for quite a while and even though they are heavily used in the enterprise world, they are losing some grasp against the new and more modern CI servers such as Drone or Travis (although Travis has been around for a while, it has been reinvented to work on the cloud).

Bamboo

Bamboo is a proprietary CI server that is developed by Atlassian. Atlassian is a software company that specializes in tools for developers. Products such as JIRA and Bitbucket are created by Atlassian and they are well known in the IT world. Bamboo is their proposal for CI activities, and it is quite popular as it integrates fairly well with their other products.

Let's install it. In order to do that, please visit Bamboo's home page at `https://confluence.atlassian.com/bamboo/` and follow the instructions in the quick start guide. As you can see, the installation is quite simple, and after generating the evaluation license and some steps (express installation), you should have bamboo running on your local computer:

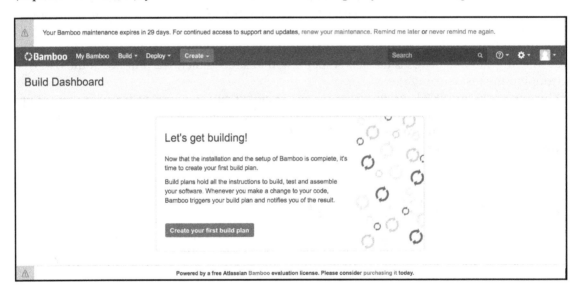

If you click on the button labeled **Create your first build plan**, you can see how easy it is to set up jobs in Bamboo. In this case, we can use one of the open source projects that I created in the past called **Visigoth**, a load balancer with circuit breaking capabilities used for interconnecting microservices. The GitHub repository is located at `https://github.com/dgonzalez/visigoth`.

Fork it into your GitHub repository if you want to modify it. Visigoth is a single component that does not interact with others, so only unit tests were created for it. Enter the clone URL of the repository into the appropriate field, in this case, Git repository, and submit the form.

> If you have the **Time-based One-Time Password** (**TOTP**) protection in your GitHub account, you might need to choose Git repository with no authentication instead of GitHub repository in the source part of the form to create a test plan.

Once you finish creating the plan, it will ask you to add tasks to your test plan, which, at the moment, is only checking out the source code from Git. In this case, Visigoth is a Node.js application, and as such, the tests are run by executing thenpm testcommand. In order to run the command, we need to add two tasks of the type command. The first task will be used to install the dependencies of the application and the second one to run the tests. Let's add the first one:

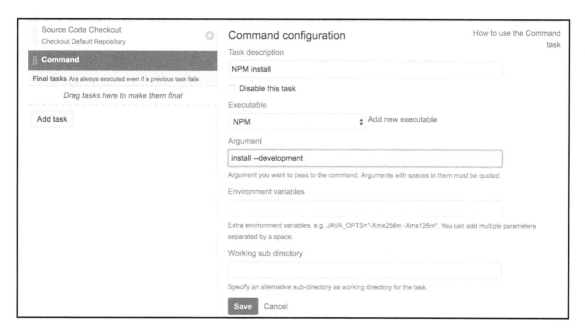

As you can see, I have added one executable by clicking on **Add new executable**by specifying the path where NPM is, which can be found by executing which npm in the terminal of the machine where you installed Bamboo.

You will need to install Node.js on the same machine where you installed Bamboo in order to run the tests. The current LTS version will work fine with it, but Visigoth was tested with Node 6.x.

Now we are going to add the second command, which will execute `npm test` in order to run the tests. This command will only be executed if the two previous steps (checking out the code [**Checkout Default Repository**) and installing the dependencies (**NPM install**)] are successful:

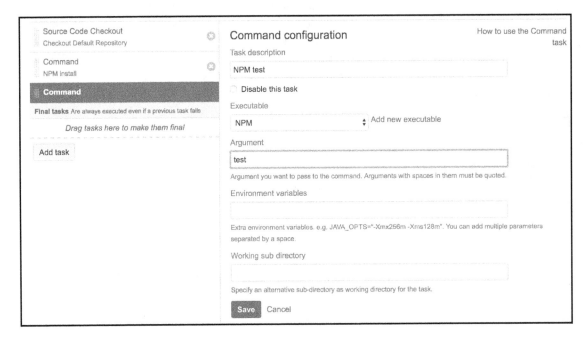

Once you save the task, we have completed all the actions that we need to execute in order to run the tests in Visigoth. Now, the only thing left is to run the job:

If everything is correct, you should get a green badge and a message of success. As you can see, my build failed in previous runs as I was adjusting the CI server to run Visigoth.

You can check the logs of the job to see how many tests were successful and other useful information. If you explore this even further, you can see how Bamboo also offers different types of tasks, such as mocha test runners, which allows Bamboo to understand the result of the tests. At the moment, with the current configuration, if any of the tests fails, Bamboo won't be able to understand which one failed. I'd suggest you to play around with different configurations and even different applications to get yourself familiar with it. As you can see by yourself, the interface is very friendly, and usually, it is quite simple to achieve your desired setup by creating new tasks.

By default, Bamboo creates something called **trigger**. A trigger is an action that leads to a test plan being executed. In this case, if we change the GitHub repository from where the job was created, the test plan will be triggered to verify the changes, ensuring the continuous integration of new code.

Another interesting type of trigger is the time-based one. This type of trigger allows us to run the build overnight, so if our tests take several minutes or even hours to run, we can do it when no one is using the server. This type of trigger has saved me from bugs derived from the daylight time savings hour adjustment, causing some tests to fail due to code fragments not handling the change across different time zones well.

In general, Bamboo can deal with every situation, and it has adapted to the modern times: we can even build Docker images and push them to remote registries once the tests have passed in order to be deployed later on. Bamboo is also able to take actions in the post-build phase, for example, alerting us if the build failed overnight with an email or other communication channels.

Jenkins

I have worked with Jenkins for quite a while now, and I have to say that I feel really comfortable working with it as I know it is free, open source, and also highly customizable. It has a powerful and well-documented API that enables users to automate pretty much anything related to continuous integration. In Chapter 8, *Release Management – Continuous Delivery*, we are going to set up a continuous delivery pipeline with Jenkins in order to be able to release new versions of an application in a transparent manner once the test results are satisfactory, enabling our team to focus on development and automating all the deployment-related activities.

Jenkins is also modular, which enables developers to write plugins to extend functionalities, for example, sending messages to a Slack channel if the build fails or running Node.js scripts as a part of a job.

On the scalability side, Jenkins, like Bamboo, can be scaled to hundreds of nodes through a master/slave configuration so that we can add more power to our CI server in order to execute some tasks in parallel.

On its own, Jenkins will be enough to provide contents for a couple of books, but we are going to visit what we need to set up automated jobs for testing our applications. It is also possible to write plugins for Jenkins, so virtually, there is no limit to what it can do.

Let's focus on the operational side of Jenkins for now. In order to run Jenkins, we have two options:

- Running it as a Docker container
- Installing it as a program in your CI server

For now, we are going to install Jenkins, using its Docker image as it is the simplest way of running it and it fits our purpose. Let's start. The first thing is running a simple instance of Jenkins from the command line:

```
docker run -p 8080:8080 -p 50000:50000 jenkins
```

This will run Jenkins, but be aware that all the information about configuration and builds executed will be stored within the container, so if you lose the container, all the data is lost as well. If you want to use a volume to store the data, the command that you need to execute is as follows:

```
docker run --name myjenkins -p 8080:8080 -p 50000:50000 -v
/var/jenkins_home jenkins
```

This will create a volume that you can reuse later on when upgrading to new versions of Jenkins or even restarting the same container. After running the command, the logs will show something similar to what is shown in the following figure:

This is the initial password for Jenkins and it is necessary in order to set up the instance. After a few seconds, the logs of the container will stop, which means your Jenkins server is ready to be used. Just open the browser and go to `http://localhost:8080/`, and you will see something similar to this:

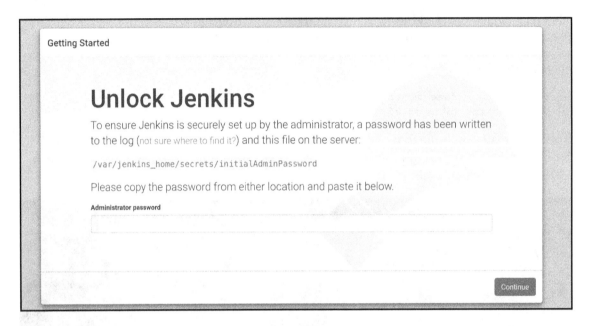

This is where you can enter**Administrator password**, which we saved earlier, and click on the **Continue**button. The next screen will ask you whether it should install the suggested plugins or whether you want to select which plugins to install. Choose the suggested plugins. After a few minutes, it will let you create a user and that's it. Jenkins is up and running in a container:

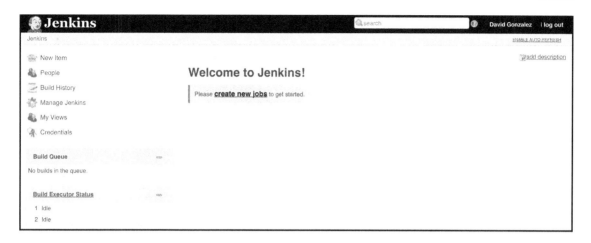

Now we are going to create a new job. We are going to use the same repository as we used with Bamboo so we can compare the two integration servers. Let's click on **Create a new project**. You should be presented with the following form:

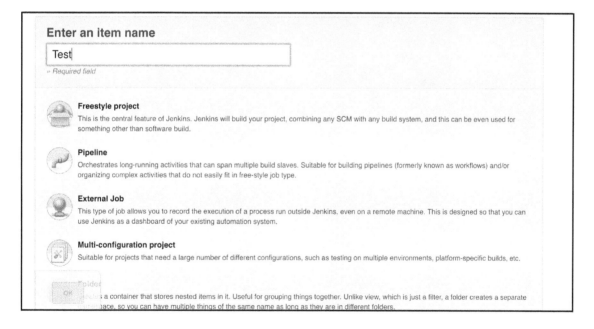

Just enter a name for the project and choose the first option: **Freestyle project**. Jenkins has different types of projects. Freestyle project is a type of project where we can define the steps, as we did in Bamboo. Another interesting option is the type **Pipeline** where we can, through a **DSL** (known as **Domain Specific Language**), define a set of steps and stages, creating a pipeline that can be saved as code.

The following screen is where we configure the project. We are going to use Git with the repository hosted at `https://github.com/dgonzalez/visigoth.git`.
You can use your fork if you previously forked it while working with Bamboo. Your configuration should be similar to the what is shown in the following screenshot:

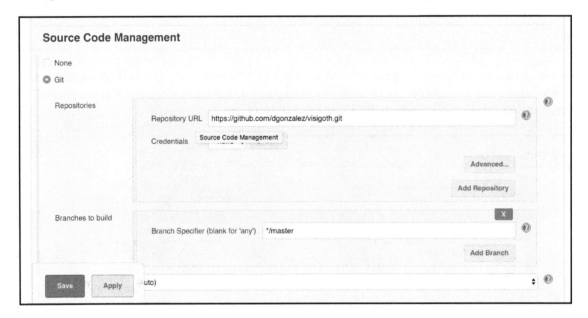

Now we need to install the dependencies of Visigoth with the `npm install --development` command and execute the tests with the `npm test` command, but we are running Jenkins from a container and this container does not have Node.js installed. We are going to use our Docker knowledge to install it. Inspecting the Dockerfile of the Jenkins image in the Docker Hub, we can verify that it is based on Debian Jessie (it is based on OpenJDK but that is based on Debian Jessie) so we can install the required software in it. The first thing that needs to be done in order to install software is gain root access to the container. As you learned in `Chapter 2`, *Cloud Data Centres - The New Reality*, we can execute commands on the running container. Let's run the following command:

```
docker exec -u 0 -it eaaef41f221b /bin/bash
```

This command executes `/bin/bash` in the container with the ID `eaaef41f221b` (it will change in your system as it is unique per container) but with the user that matches the user ID `0`, in this case, root. We need to do this because the Jenkins image defines and uses a new user called `jenkins` with a known UID and GID so if the `-u 0` flag is not passed, the `/bin/bash` command will be executed by the user `jenkins`.

Once we are root in the container, proceed to install Node.js:

```
curl -sL https://deb.nodesource.com/setup_7.x | bash -
```

And once the execution of the previous command is finished, run the following one:

```
apt-get install -y nodejs build-essentials
```

And that's it. From now on, our Jenkins container has an installation of Node.js available to run Node.js scripts. That said, we should avoid installing software in production containers. Our containers should be **immutable artifacts** that do not change through their life cycle, so what we should do is commit the changes in this image and tag it as a new version in order to release it into our production container. As we don't have a production container, we are making the changes as we go.

 Our containers in production should be immutable artifacts: if we need to change their status, we create a new version of the image and redeploy it instead of modifying the running container.

Once Node.js is installed, we can just exit the root shell within the container and go back to Jenkins to complete our tasks. As we did with Bamboo, here are our tasks in order to run our tests:

In the very bottom of the job configuration, there is a section called **post-build** actions. This section allows you to execute actions once the job is finished. These actions include sending e-mails, adding commit messages to the Git repository, among others. As we previously mentioned, Jenkins is extensible and new actions can be added by installing new plugins.

Jenkins can also parametrize builds with input from the user.

Once you have added these two steps to the build, just click on **Save**and we are all set: you now havea fully functional Jenkins job. If we run it, it should successfully run the tests on Visigoth.

Secrets Management

One of the possibilities of the CI server is the ability to talk to third-party services that usually rely on some sort of credentials (such as access tokens or similar) to authenticate the user. Exposing these secrets would be discouraged as they could potentially cause major harm to our company.

Jenkins handles this in a very simple way: it provides a way to store credentials in a safe way that can be injected into the build as environment variables so that we can work with them.

Let's look at some examples. First, we need to create the secrets in Jenkins. In order to do that, we have to go to **Manage Jenkins** from the home page.

Once we are there, you should see a screen very similar to this one:

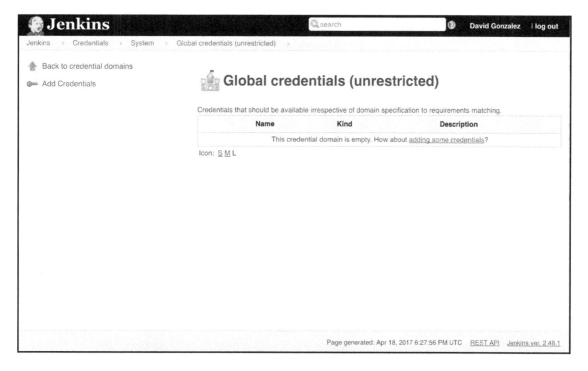

We are using the **Global credentials** store as we just want to showcase how it works, but Jenkins allows you to box credentials so you can restrict access across different usages. In Jenkins, credentials, aside from being injected into the build context, can be connected to plugins and extensions so that they can authenticate against third-party systems.

Now, we click on **Add Credentials** on the left-hand side:

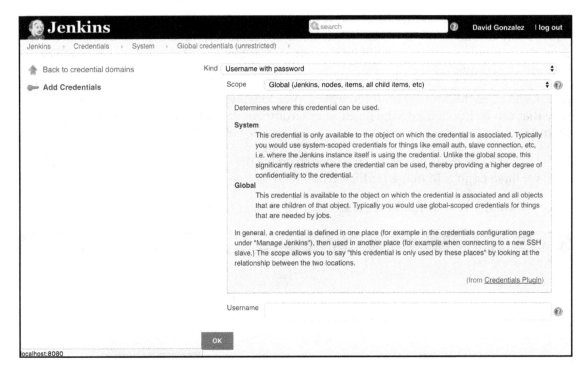

There are some fields that we need to fill before proceeding, but they are very basic:

- **Kind**: This is the type of secret that we want to create. If you open the drop-down, there are several types, from files to certificates, walking through usernames and passwords.

- **Scope**: This is the scope of our secret. The documentation is not 100% clear (at least not in the first read) but it allows us to hide the secret from certain stances. There are two options: **Global** and **System**. With **Global**, the credentials can be exposed to any object within Jenkins and its child, whereas with **System**, the credentials can be exposed only to Jenkins and its nodes.

The rest of the fields are dependant on the type of secret. For now on, we are going to create a `Username with password`secret. Just select it in the dropdown and fill in the rest of the details. Once it is created, it should show in the list of credentials.

The next step is to create a job that is bound to those credentials so we can use them. Just create a new freestyle project, as we saw in the beginning of this section, but we are going to stop on the screen where we can configure the job, precisely in the **Build Environment**section:

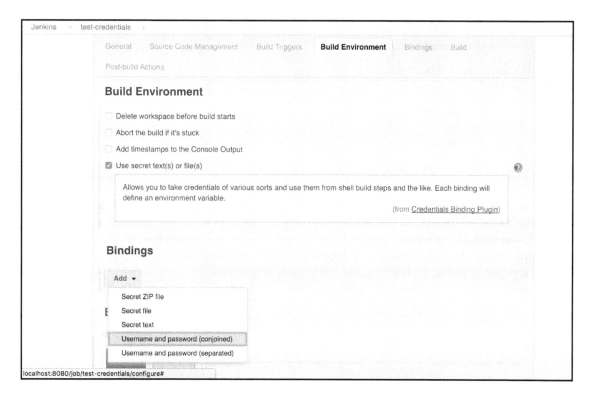

Now select **Username and password (conjoined)**. Conjoined username and password means that we get the full secret (the username and the password) in a single variable, whereas with separated, we get the secret split in two variables: one for the username and another one for the password.

Once we select it, the form to create the binding is fairly simple:

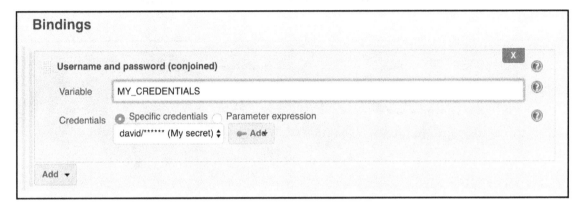

We get to choose the **Variable** where we want to store the secret and we also get to choose which secret. There is a radio button that lets you choose between **Parameter expression** or **Specific credentials** as we can parametrize the job to get input from the user on the triggering screen. In order to showcase how well thought Jenkins is, we are going to add a **Build** step that uses the secret by just echoing it into the logs:

Click on the **Save** button to save the job and run it. Once the job execution finishes, go to the result and click on**Console Output**. If you were expecting to see the secret in here, Jenkins has a surprise for you:

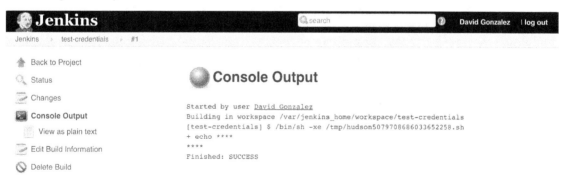

The secret has been masked in order to prevent exposure to unauthorized users. This is not bullet proof, as someone could easily dump the secret from a test within an application checked out by Jenkins, but it adds some level of security in there, leaving the rest to the code reviews and processes.

Modern CI servers

One thing that is clear in IT is that the market moves very fast, and every few years, a new trend breaks what was considered the perfect solution for a problem. CI software is not an exception to this. In the last few years (taking into account that this book was written in 2017), Infrastructure as Code has drawn a lot of attention to the DevOps world, but in CI, its equivalent is Pipelines as Code.

Jenkins and Bamboo have added support for declarative pipelines recently, but they are not built around them.

Drone CI

Drone is probably the newest CI server in the market. I decided to introduce it in this chapter as it was a big revelation to me when I found out about it working in nearForm Ltd. By that time, I was well used to Jenkins and it suited every single use case that I could come across in my professional life, from CI to continuous delivery and sometimes even as a bastion host using a feature called callback URL, where a job could be triggered by sending an HTTP request to a specific URL.

Drone is built around the concept of containers. Everything in Drone is a container, from the server to where the test runs, but the most interesting part is that even the plugins are containers. This makes it easy to write new plugins for executing custom actions, as the only requirement is that the containers return0 as the exit code if it was successful and a nonzero exit code if it was not successful.

For Jenkins or Bamboo, writing a plugin requires a few hours of testing and reading documentation. For Drone, we just need to know how to build a Docker image and what task we want to accomplish.

Be aware that Drone is still in the version 0.5 and moves very quickly, so by the time you read this book, Drone might have changed significantly, but I wanted to include it as I think it is a very promising software.

Installing Drone

In order to install Drone, we are going to use `docker-compose`, and it is going to be configured to work with GitHub.

Drone, like Docker, follows a client-server architecture, so we can find two differentiated components, the server and the CLI. The first part we are going to proceed with is with the server. Take a look at the following `docker-compose` file:

```
version: '2'

services:
drone-server:
image: drone/drone:0.5
ports:
- 80:8000
volumes:
- ./drone:/var/lib/drone/
restart: always
environment:
- DRONE_OPEN=true
- DRONE_GITHUB=true
- DRONE_GITHUB_CLIENT=${DRONE_GITHUB_CLIENT}
- DRONE_GITHUB_SECRET=${DRONE_GITHUB_SECRET}
- DRONE_SECRET=${DRONE_SECRET}

drone-agent:
image: drone/drone:0.5
command: agent
restart: always
depends_on: [ drone-server ]
volumes:
- /var/run/docker.sock:/var/run/docker.sock
environment:
- DRONE_SERVER=ws://drone-server:8000/ws/broker
- DRONE_SECRET=${DRONE_SECRET}
```

There are two containers running in the preceding Docker Compose file: a server and an agent. Up until version 0.4, Drone master could execute builds, but after that, an agent is needed to run builds. There are some secrets that we need to configure before proceeding that are being passed into compose via environment variables (with the ${VAR_NAME} notation):

- DRONE_GITHUB_CLIENT: As we specified earlier, we are going to use GitHub as the origin of our source code to be tested. This is provided on GitHub when registering a new OAuth application needed for Drone. You can create OAuth applications in the settings section of GitHub. Be careful; one of the parameters that you need in order to create a GitHub OAuth application is the callback URL. In this case, we are going to use http://localhost/authorize as we are working on our local machine.
- DRONE_GITHUB_SECRET: In the same way as DRONE_GITHUB_CLIENT, this is provided when a new OAuth application is created on GitHub.
- DRONE_SECRET: This is an arbitrary string shared with the agent and the master. Just create a simple string, but when running a drone in production, make sure that the string is long enough so it cannot be guessed.

In order to get Drone working with the GitHub integration, we need to receive callbacks from GitHub. Once we have all the values, we just need to run the following command:

```
DRONE_GITHUB_CLIENT=your-client DRONE_GITHUB_SECRET=your-secret
DRONE_SECRET=my-secret docker-compose up
```

In one line, we are setting the three variables that we need, apart from running docker-compose up. If everything went as expected, when you browse http://localhost, you should see a window similar to the following one:

If you click on **login**, Drone should redirect you to GitHub for authorization and then GitHub will redirect you to the callback URL specified when creating the OAuth application, which is your local Drone installation, `http://localhost/authorize`. Sometimes, it might require some tweaking, but in general, it is very easy to make it work. As you can see, Drone leverages the authentication to GitHub so a GitHub account is required to log in.

Now we are going to proceed with the CLI. It is as easy as visiting`http://readme.drone.io/0.5/install/cli/` and choosing the right version for your platform, in my case, macOS. Just place the binary in the path and you are ready to go. In order to configure the location of the Drone server, you need to specify two environment variables:

- `DRONE_SERVER`: This is the URL to your Drone server, in this case, `http://localhost`

- `DRONE_TOKEN`: Once you are logged into Drone, navigate to **Account**and click on **Show token**. This is the value that you need

Once you have set up the two variables, execute the following command:

```
drone info
```

This should show your GitHub username and the e-mail that you used to register.

Running builds

Drone has a different philosophy when it comes to running builds: it reacts to changes in the code on the remote repository by triggering the pipeline. Let's create a super simple repository with a very simple Node.js application. I have created it on my GitHub account in order to make everything easier:`https://github.com/dgonzalez/node-example-drone/`. Just fork it into your own account, and you are good to go.

The first thing that we need to do is activate the project in your local Drone installation. Just go to **Account**, and in the list of repositories, activate `node-example-drone`. Now it should show in the home screen in a manner similar to the following screenshot:

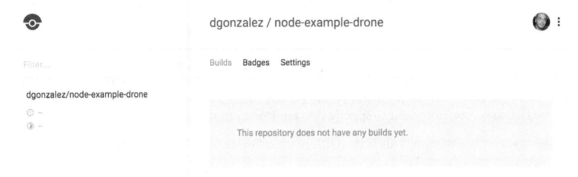

Now we are facing a small problem: Drone was created to trigger builds using a webhook delivered from GitHub into our Drone server. As we are working in a private network, we need to somehowexpose our server to the Internet. In this case, we are going to use a service called **Ngrok** (`http://www.ngrock.com`) in order to expose Drone to the internet, which is not necessary when working in a production environment as it should be accessible over the internet (or at least through a proxy). Just follow the instructions, and once you run it in the Terminal, it should look very similar to what is shown in the following screenshot:

```
ngrok by @inconshreveable                                                      (Ctrl+C to quit)

Session Status        online
Account               David Gonzalez (Plan: Free)
Version               2.2.4
Region                United States (us)
Web Interface         http://127.0.0.1:4040
Forwarding            http://852cc48a.ngrok.io -> localhost:80
Forwarding            https://852cc48a.ngrok.io -> localhost:80

Connections           ttl     opn     rt1     rt5     p50     p90
                      4       0       0.01    0.01    121.98  122.97

HTTP Requests
-------------

POST /hook                200 OK
GET  /static/favicon.ico  200 OK
GET  /ws/feed             101 Switching Protocols
GET  /static/drone.svg    200 OK
GET  /api/user/feed       401 Unauthorized
GET  /static/app.js       200 OK
GET  /static/app.css      200 OK
GET  /                    200 OK
```

This specifies which host is being forwarded to your local address, in my case,`http://852cc48a.ngrok.io`. Just open it in your browser and check whether Drone is accessible from there.

One thing left to do is edit the webhook that Drone installed in our GitHub repository when we activated it. You will find it in the repository settings on GitHub. Just edit the webhook to change the URL from `http://localhost` to your Ngrok URL, in my case, `http://852cc48a.ngrok.io`.

Executing pipelines

Now the setup is complete, before doing anything else, take a look at the `.drone.yaml` fileof the forked repository:

```
debug: true
pipeline:
  build:
    image: node
    commands:
      - npm install --development
      - npm test
```

This is our pipeline, and as you can guess, it gets committed alongside our code into our repository. Drone is going to execute the instructions in this pipeline when GitHub delivers the webhook into our Drone installation. As Drone works with containers, the first thing that Drone is going to do is create an image based on the node (as we specified) and run the following operations:

- It installs the dependencies
- It runs the tests

If the exit code of the container that executes these commands is 0, our build is successful and you can test it by pushing some changes to your GitHub repository and watching how Drone reacts to them.

There is also another way to re-trigger builds (not for the first time) via the CLI interface. Open the Terminal, and after configuring the environment variables previously stated (if you haven't done it yet), run the following command:

```
drone build list dgonzalez/node-example-drone
```

This will return a list of all the previously executed builds. Just change dgonzalez to your username, as you can see in the web interface. In order to rerun a previous build, we can run the following command:

```
drone build run dgonzalez/node-example-drone 1
```

This command fires off a build in Drone that was already built. This is particularly useful when you suspect that the build failed due to external factors.

 Sometimes, the webhook fails (particularly with the setup that we have with Ngrok), but GitHub allows you to debug that in the webhooks section of your repository.

This is the simplest case of a pipeline. As mentioned earlier, Drone is based on plugins, and those plugins are also Docker images. The list is quite comprehensive and can be found at https://github.com/drone-plugins.

Let's assume that we want to push our image to the **Google Container Registry** in Google Cloud. We are going to use the plugin called drone-gcr from https://github.com/drone-plugins/drone-gcr. Here is our pipeline:

```
debug: true
pipeline:
  build:
    image: node
    commands:
      - npm install --development
      - npm test
  publish:
    gcr:
      repo: myrepo/node-example-drone
      token: >
          {
             ...
          }
```

What we have here is a two-stage pipeline: it first executes the tests, and once they are successful, it deploys the image to Google Cloud Registry. We have different phases in the pipeline that we can use:

- **Build**: For building the tests and the related commands
- **Publish**: Used to publish the artifact in a remote repository

- **Deploy**: Very useful for continuous integration as it allows us to deploy our software in a continuous delivery manner
- **Notify**: Used to send notifications via email, slack, or any other channel

For example, if we wanted to send a Slack notification, we would just need to add the following linesto our pipeline:

```
notify:
  image: plugins/slack
  channel: developers
  username: drone
```

 Remember, YAML is sensitive to tabs and spaces so notify needs to be at the same level as publish or build.

Other features

At the time of writing this, Drone is being actively developed, with new features being added and along with some major reworks. It also offers other features, such as secret management and support services.

With secret management, we can inject secrets that get encrypted and stored in a database and only injected into builds that have been cryptographically signed by our drone CLI with a valid token from our Drone server.

Drone also offers support services, which are services that run alongside your tests. This is very helpful when our integration tests depend on a database or when we need to spin third-party software such as Hashicorp Vault or a service discovery infrastructure such as Consul or Eureka.

It is expected that in future, Drone will have more features, but at the moment, it is going through major changes as it is being actively developed (unlike more mature servers, such as Jenkins, that have been around for a while).

Summary

In this chapter, we walked through three different CI tools:

- Bamboo, a commercial tool
- Jenkins, an industry standard open source tool
- Drone, a cutting-edge technology CI server

We discussed the key features of Jenkins that we are going to use going forward in this book, but we also showcased how Drone has leveraged the concept of containers into a very powerful CI system that, even though not mature yet, I expect to become the norm in the coming years.

The important concepts that we need to be aware of were explained, but to summarize, we use our integration server to run our tests for us so we can offload developers from doing that but also run the tests overnight in order to ensure that the daily build is stable.

In the next chapter, we will visit what the community has called **Infrastructure as Code:** basically, a way of dealing with our infrastructure as if code was, managing resources on a very elegant way.

5
Infrastructure as Code

In the previous chapters, we demonstrated how the new cloud data centers can help us create online resources (virtual machines, Docker repositories, cryptographic keys) in a very easy way, shortening the hardware provisioning cycle from weeks (buying, shipping, and installing new computers) to seconds. We have also seen that there are different providers in the market that can offer us very similar features with different strong points that we can take advantage of when building our systems.

You learned how to create resources through the web interface that they offer, but how scalable is that? Creating resources manually prevents us from keeping an automated inventory of resources that can be used for security purposes as well as manage our infrastructure as if it were software components.

In this chapter, you are going to learn how to build resources in the cloud first, through the SDK provided by the cloud data center vendor and then by a software component called **Terraform**, which is an industry standard for managing online resources. We are going to focus on **Google Cloud Platform** for several reasons:

The command-line interface, in my opinion, is easier to use.

The Google Cloud Platform trial covers a good bunch of resources that you can use to experiment with throughout this book as you can create pretty much any resource in the full set of products.

At the time of writing this (April 2017), Google Cloud Platform is the best value for money when it comes to cloud data centers.

That said, AWS, Azure or any other provider also offer a very interesting range of trial accounts, but unfortunately, we cannot cover everything in a single book.

Google Cloud Platform SDK - gcloud

Google offers us a very comprehensive SDK that can be used for operating Google Cloud Platform as well as installing software components related to cloud operations.
The first thing we need to do is install `gcloud`.
There are installers for Windows but, in general, for Unix-based systems (Linux and Mac mainly), we have an interactive installer that can be executed from the command line and the unattended mode (for automatic provisioning).
The different options can be found at `https://cloud.google.com/sdk/downloads`.
In order to install it (in my case, on Mac), the first thing we need to do is run the following command:

```
curl https://sdk.cloud.google.com | bash
```

This will initiate the interactive installed in the online mode: we will be asked a number of questions during the installation process.

The first one is the installation directory. By default, this is the home of the user, but you can change it to the folder of your choice. Once you have selected the folder, it will start downloading and installing the required base components.

The question is whether you want to help improve the Google Cloud SDK through the collection of anonymized data. Just answer as per your preferences.

Now, Google Cloud SDK will start installing the core components.

```
Your current Cloud SDK version is: 152.0.0
Installing components from version: 152.0.0

┌─────────────────────────────────────────────────────────────┐
│              These components will be installed.              │
├───────────────────────────────────────┬───────────┬─────────┤
│                  Name                  │  Version  │  Size   │
├───────────────────────────────────────┼───────────┼─────────┤
│ BigQuery Command Line Tool             │    2.0.24 │ < 1 MiB │
│ BigQuery Command Line Tool (Platform Specific) │ 2.0.24 │ < 1 MiB │
│ Cloud SDK Core Libraries (Platform Specific)   │ 2017.03.24 │ < 1 MiB │
│ Cloud Storage Command Line Tool        │      4.25 │ 2.9 MiB │
│ Cloud Storage Command Line Tool (Platform Specific) │ 4.23 │ < 1 MiB │
│ Default set of gcloud commands         │           │         │
│ gcloud-deps (Mac OS X, x86_64)         │ 2017.03.31 │ 2.1 MiB │
└───────────────────────────────────────┴───────────┴─────────┘

For the latest full release notes, please visit:
  https://cloud.google.com/sdk/release_notes
```

As you can see in the preceding figure, Google SDK installs few packages that will be used to operate the basic services on Google Cloud Platform. Once it is finished (no need to do anything), it will ask you whether you want to modify the PATH variable of your system or not. Just reply Y and press *Enter* so that the gcloud command is available from the console. It will ask you in which file you want to modify the PATH variable. Usually, the default option that the installer provides you with is good enough. Before changing the file, the Google Cloud SDK installer will create a backup of the file with the same name with the .backup extension so you can revert the changes.

And we are done. It will ask you to start a new shell for the changes to take effect. Close your Terminal and open it again to check whether the gcloud command is available. Now that we have installed Google Cloud SDK, it is time to configure the authentication. Execute the following command:

```
gcloud init
```

It will ask you to log in, so reply yes, which will open a browser window asking you to enter your Google credentials. Enter the ones associated with your trial account (if you didn't sign for the trial, do it before configuring your credentials). If you had a project already created in the Google Cloud Platform, it will ask you in the console to choose which one to use. In my case, I had one configured from Chapter 2, *Cloud Data Centers – The New Reality*, so I selected the one called implementing-modern-devops in my case.

The next topic is configuring the Google Compute Engine. Reply yes and select your availability zone. In my case, anywhere in Europe will work for me.

After this step, we are done. The prompt will tell us that we have a configuration called 'default' created. This means that the Google Cloud SDK can work with multiple credentials but, in this case, we are going to work with just one set of credentials and a single project.

Creating resources with Google Cloud SDK

Once we are set up, it is time to start creating resources. As you can guess, the commands for creating resources can be quite complicated or extremely simple depending on your requirements. Luckily, Google engineers have thought about it when creating the interface for Google Cloud Platform.

The first thing you need to do is log in to your Google Cloud Platform account. Once you are there, go to **Compute Engine** and fill the form to create a new resource. Enter the name of the instance, choose your closest region (Europe in my case), machine type (the default one will do), API access (we don't need that but the default is OK) and **Allow HTTP traffic** and **Allow HTTPS traffic**. Before clicking on create, take a look at the following screenshot:

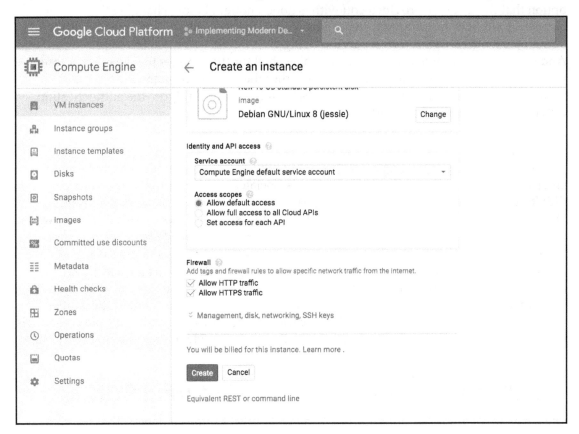

If you take a look at the very bottom, below the **Create** button, there are two links:

- **REST** equivalent
- **Command line**

For now, we are going to focus on the **command line** link. Click on it and you should get a window with a few commands. Let's explain them:

```
gcloud compute --project "implementing-modern-devops" instances create
"test-instance" \
              --zone "europe-west1-c" --machine-type "n1-standard-1" --
subnet "default" \
              --maintenance-policy "MIGRATE" \
              --service-account "1085359944086-
compute@developer.gserviceaccount.com"
              --scopes \
                  "https://www.googleapis.com/auth/devstorage.read_only",
\
                  "https://www.googleapis.com/auth/logging.write", \
                  "https://www.googleapis.com/auth/monitoring.write", \
                  "https://www.googleapis.com/auth/servicecontrol", \
"https://www.googleapis.com/auth/service.management.readonly", \
                  "https://www.googleapis.com/auth/trace.append" \
              --tags "http-server","https-server" --image "debian-8-
jessie-v20170327" \
              --image-project "debian-cloud" --boot-disk-size "10" --boot-
disk-type "pd-standard" \
              --boot-disk-device-name "test-instance"
```

The first command creates the VM. As you can see, no one can expect to learn to create this command easily, but luckily, Google Cloud Platform provides it to you for every single resource that will be created for you so you can use the UI to generate the commands. That said, the preceding command sets every single potential setting that **Google Cloud** provides, so in other words, we will be able to run the preceding command with the same results no matter what settings we change in our cloud account.

There is a shorter version:

```
gcloud compute --project "implementing-modern-devops" instances create
"test-instance"
```

This command does exactly the same as the very long command from earlier but assuming that the settings are the default (remember, you have already chosen some parameters, such as the default zone).

The other two commands are simpler:

```
gcloud compute --project "implementing-modern-devops" firewall-rules create
"default-allow-http" --allow tcp:80 --network "default" --source-ranges
"0.0.0.0/0" --target-tags "http-server"
```

Take a look at this too:

```
gcloud compute --project "implementing-modern-devops" firewall-rules create
"default-allow-https" --allow tcp:443 --network "default" --source-ranges
"0.0.0.0/0" --target-tags "https-server"
```

As you can guess, these commands allow the HTTP and the HTTPS traffic into our host as described in the UI form.

These are the basics of infrastructure as code. We could potentially write those commands on a bash script and off we go; our infrastructure is created automatically for us. In the same way, if we don't want to depend on Google Cloud SDK, we could choose the REST option that will show us the list of HTTP requests that we need to issue to Google Cloud in order to create the same resources. If you are familiar with languages such as Python, JavaScript (Node.js), and others, you know how easy is to issue HTTP requests in order to create the resources so you could manage your infrastructure as if it were code following the same life cycle.

This is a massive step forward in managing resources on the cloud, but it is still incomplete. Imagine this situation: you work in a company with a fairly complex setup, say, a few machines across different time zones and a fairly entangled network setup. How can you know at first glance which machines are running and what are the firewall rules are?

The answer is simple: it is not possible with what we know today. In the next section, you are going to learn how to use something called **Terraform** from HashiCorp in order to manage not only the creation, but also the complete life cycle of online resources on different cloud providers.

Terraform

Terraform is a product developed by **HashiCorp**. HashiCorp is a company with a strong focus on DevOps tools such as Consul, a highly available distributed key value storage, or Vagrant, a tool to reproduce development environments using the same provisioners as production.

Terraform, as the name hints, allows you to create infrastructure in cloud data centers in a declarative way, keeping track of what was created where, allowing you to apply changes to the infrastructure from the code perspective: your infrastructure is described as the code and, as such, it can follow its life cycle.

The first thing we need to do is download and install Terraform. Just open the `https://www.terraform.io/downloads.html` URL in a browser and select your platform, in my case, Mac. Terraform is a single binary compressed in a ZIP file (as far as I am aware, it is the same for every platform) that I unzip and place somewhere in my path, in my case, in `/usr/local/bin/terraform`.

 Be careful as some OSX setups do not include `/usr/local/bin/` in the PATH environment variable, so you might need to do it before being able to execute Terraform from any path.

Once it is installed and the `PATH` variable includes `/usr/local/bin/` as one of the values separated by semi colons, we can check whether everything works as expected:

```
terraform version
```

This should return the following output:

```
Terraform v0.9.4
```

This confirms that everything is correct. Also, be aware that DevOps tools move very quickly nowadays as they are required to do more things day by day. We are going to use the latest available version, 0.9.4, but by the time you are reading this book, a newer version might be available with new features and even some breaking changes. Luckily, Terraform comes with a very powerful documentation embedded in it. Let's look at all the available commands. Just execute this:

```
terraform
```

This should output something similar to the following:

```
Usage: terraform [--version] [--help] <command> [args]

The available commands for execution are listed below.
The most common, useful commands are shown first, followed by
less common or more advanced commands. If you're just getting
started with Terraform, stick with the common commands. For the
other commands, please read the help and docs before usage.

Common commands:
    apply              Builds or changes infrastructure
    console            Interactive console for Terraform interpolations
    destroy            Destroy Terraform-managed infrastructure
    env                Environment management
    fmt                Rewrites config files to canonical format
    get                Download and install modules for the configuration
    graph              Create a visual graph of Terraform resources
    import             Import existing infrastructure into Terraform
    init               Initialize a new or existing Terraform configuration
    output             Read an output from a state file
    plan               Generate and show an execution plan
    push               Upload this Terraform module to Atlas to run
    refresh            Update local state file against real resources
    show               Inspect Terraform state or plan
    taint              Manually mark a resource for recreation
    untaint            Manually unmark a resource as tainted
    validate           Validates the Terraform files
    version            Prints the Terraform version

All other commands:
    debug              Debug output management (experimental)
    force-unlock       Manually unlock the terraform state
    state              Advanced state management
```

Now, in order to display the help dialog on any of the commands, we just need to execute the command with the flag -h. For example, let's display the help for `apply`:

```
terraform apply -h
```

It will output the list of all the options available for the command in the prompt.

Creating resources

Now that we have all the requirements installed, we are going to create our first resource in order to help us to understand how Terraform works and how powerful it is. Create a folder called `implementing-modern-devops` somewhere in your computer and add a file called `resources.tf` with the following content:

```
provider "google" {
 credentials = "${file("xxx.json")}"
 project = "implementing-modern-devops"
 region = "europe-west1-b"
}

resource "google_compute_instance" "my-first-instance" {
 }
```

As you can see, the preceding snipped is very similar to JSON but it is actually called HCL: HashiCorp Configuration Language. Let's explain what the code is doing.

The first section is where we configure our credentials. As you can see, Terraform is expecting a file called xxx.json, which we don't have at the moment. If we check the official documentation of Terraform for Google Cloud Platform, it specifies that we need to create a **Service account** from the API Manager section of the Google Cloud Platform, as shown in the following screenshot:

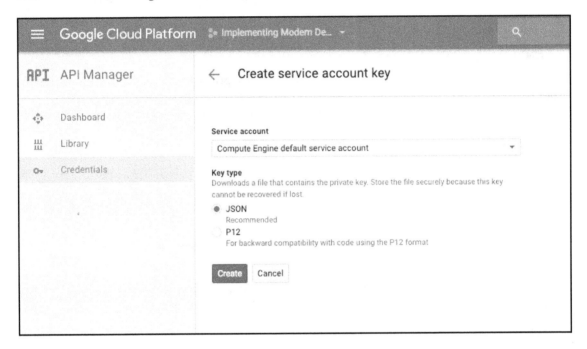

Once we create it by choosing JSON as a format, a file will automatically be saved on our computer, containing the credentials that we need in order to operate Google Cloud Platform.

 Be careful. If you leak these credentials, someone could create or destroy resources on your behalf, which may lead to significant charges or data loss.

Copy the file to the previously created folder (implementing-modern-devops) and rename it to xxx.json so it matches our configuration.

The second section is the description of our virtual machine, the instance to be created in Google Cloud. In this case, we are creating a resource called `my-first-instance` of the type `google_compute_instance`. We did not specify any configuration on purpose as I want to show you how to troubleshoot problems with Terraform, which, due to the high-quality error logs produced, is rather simple.

Let's see what happens. From the root of our project, the `implementing-modern-devops` folder, we run the following command:

```
terraform plan
```

This command will describe the steps required to create our infrastructure in Google Cloud. In this case, it is rather simple as we have only one machine, but it is going to be helpful to learn about Terraform.

Let's look at what happened and and how it has been explained in the output:

```
Errors:

  * google_compute_instance.my-first-instance: "disk": required field is not
set
  * google_compute_instance.my-first-instance: "name": required field is not
set
  * google_compute_instance.my-first-instance: "machine_type": required
field is not set
  * google_compute_instance.my-first-instance: "zone": required field is not
set
```

The preceding command failed. Basically, our compute instance requires four fields that we did not specify: `machine_type`, `name`, `zone`, and `disk`. In this case, we can specify them, but if you need to check extra parameters, all the documentation for the resource `google_compute_instance` can be found at https://www.terraform.io/docs/providers/google/r/compute_instance.html.

Visit it and read around to get familiar with it.

We are also going to specify the network interface (basically the network we want to connect to our machine) as it will fail later on in the `apply` command if we don't do it now.

Now, we are going to fix the problems that we found on the first run. Replace the `google_compute_instance` block with the following one:

```
resource "google_compute_instance" "my-first-instance" {
  name = "my-first-instance"
  machine_type = "n1-standard-1"
  zone = "europe-west1-b"
```

```
disk {
image = "ubuntu-os-cloud/ubuntu-1704-zesty-v20170413"
}

network_interface {
  network = "default"
  access_config {
  // Ephemeral IP
  }
}
}
```

Go back to the Terminal and execute `terraform plan`' again. The output will be similar to this:

```
+ google_compute_instance.my-first-instance
can_ip_forward: "false"
disk.#: "1"
disk.0.auto_delete: "true"
disk.0.image: "ubuntu-os-cloud/ubuntu-1704-zesty-v20170413"
machine_type: "n1-standard-1"
metadata_fingerprint: "<computed>"
name: "my-first-instance"
network_interface.#: "1"
network_interface.0.access_config.#: "1"
network_interface.0.access_config.0.assigned_nat_ip: "<computed>"
network_interface.0.address: "<computed>"
network_interface.0.name: "<computed>"
network_interface.0.network: "default"
self_link: "<computed>"
tags_fingerprint: "<computed>"
zone: "europe-west1-b"


Plan: 1 to add, 0 to change, 0 to destroy.
```

For space reasons, I have omitted an explanatory text that comes before the resource explanation but basically tells us that we can save this plan in a file in order to pass it as a parameter to the apply the command that we are going to run next.

This enables us to ensure that what is executed is what we have seen in the plan just in case someone else has modified the online infrastructure before calculating what needs to change, Terraform syncs the configuration in the resources files with the existing infrastructure in Google Cloud. So, it might be the case that we can execute `terraform plan` and someone changes our cloud infrastructure (with another Terraform script or manually) and then our `terraform apply` command differs from the plan calculated.

Now once we have verified that our Terraform plan is to create a VM, execute the following command:

```
terraform apply
```

After a few seconds, the script should finish presenting the output of what was created, changed, or destroyed:

```
google_compute_instance.my-first-instance: Creating...
 can_ip_forward: "" => "false"
... (lines omitted: they should match the ones in the plan) ...
 zone: "" => "europe-west1-b"
google_compute_instance.my-first-instance: Still creating... (10s elapsed)
google_compute_instance.my-first-instance: Still creating... (20s elapsed)
google_compute_instance.my-first-instance: Still creating... (30s elapsed)
google_compute_instance.my-first-instance: Creation complete

Apply complete! Resources: 1 added, 0 changed, 0 destroyed.

The state of your infrastructure has been saved to the path
below. This state is required to modify and destroy your
infrastructure, so keep it safe. To inspect the complete state
use the `terraform show` command.

State path: terraform.tfstate
```

If everything went as per plan, we should have a file called `terraform.tfstate` in our folder which is the state of our virtual infrastructure created in the cloud. We also have the same file with the extension `backup`, which is the status of our infrastructure before running our last `apply` command.

This file is important. Terraform is able to refresh it with changes made on the cloud, but it is not able to rebuild it. Some people keep this file alongside the Terraform scripts and some other people prefer to use a backend to store this file and manage the Terraform state.

Remote state management

A backend is a system that is going to store our status in a shared environment where everyone using the same configuration can quickly access it. Let's look at how is this done using **Google Cloud Storage**. Just execute the following command:

```
terraform remote config –backend=gcs –backend-config="bucket=my-terraform"
–backend-config="path=terraform/infrastructure"
```

Here are a few considerations: we need to create a bucket called `my-terraform` in the Google Cloud Storage interface and we need to configure Application default credentials for Google Cloud. The easiest way to do this is by setting an environment variable called `GOOGLE_APPLICATION_CREDENTIALS` to the path where the `xxx.json` file that we have used to authenticate against GCP when running our infrastructure is. If you are in the same folder, just run the following command:

```
export GOOGLE_APPLICATION_CREDENTIALS=./xxx.json
```

Once this is done and the Terraform command succeeds, if we check our bucket in Google Cloud Storage, we have a new item with the content of `terraform.tfstate` that we had in our local file system.

Now we can test that it works by altering our infrastructure and seeing how this is reflected in our bucket on Google Cloud Storage. You can do this easily by running `terraform destroy` and checking what happens to our remote state in Google Cloud.

 Be careful with the state files. They have very valuable information about your company's infrastructure and can be used as an attack vector.

This feature is used to share configuration across a team of engineers, and it is fully managed by Terraform: you don't need to pull or push state files as Terraform will do it for you.

Modifying your infrastructure

Up until now, we have only created resources and stored the state of or cloud data center in an online bucket. Now you are going to learn how to modify the existing infrastructure from a project such as the one we built earlier on.

As you can see, we started from a very simple example: create a single virtual machine with an ephemeral IP address (the default one assigned by Google, not fixed).

Now, we are going to create a static IP and assign it to our machine so it always uses the same IP. The way of doing this through Terraform is creating a resource of the type `google_compute_address`, as follows:

```
resource "google_compute_address" "my-first-ip" {
 name = "static-ip-address"
}
```

Now, we can execute `terraform plan` to see what will change if we apply the infrastructure change. As you can see in your new execution plan, Terraform identifies that we need to create a new resource of type `google_compute_address`, but... how do we attach this IP to our VM? Let's revisit the configuration of our VM:

```
resource "google_compute_instance" "my-first-instance" {
 name = "my-first-instance"
 machine_type = "n1-standard-1"
 zone = "europe-west1-b"
 disk {
 image = "ubuntu-os-cloud/ubuntu-1704-zesty-v20170413"
 }

 network_interface {
 network = "default"
 access_config {
 nat_ip = "${google_compute_address.my-first-ip.address}"
 }
 }
}
```

In the highlighted line of the code, you can see how simple it is to associate our VM with the new address that we are going to create: our created resource, the address, will have computed attributes (attributes calculated at runtime) that can be used in other resources. In Terraform, the syntax for interpolating values is `${}` with the value of the attribute to interpolate between the brackets, in this case, the IP address of the resource called `my-first-ip`.

If you head to the Google Cloud Console and open the external IP's section, you can see something similar to what is shown in the following screenshot:

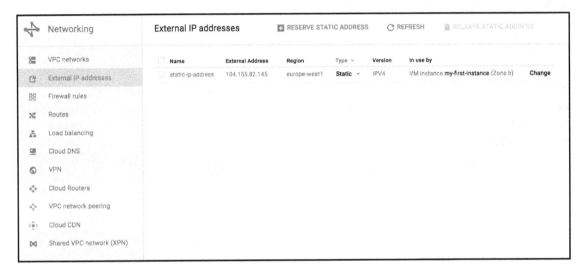

The IP was associated with our VM, as expected.

Terraform variables

One thing we did not mention earlier is the fact that Terraform can work with variables. Take a look at the following definition:

```
provider "google" {
 credentials = "${file("xxx.json")}"
 project = "implementing-modern-devops"
 region = "europe-west1"
}
```

This is the configuration of our provider. There are few strings that, quite likely, are going to be used in other places, such as the region or the name of the project. Terraform has the concept of variable, which is a value that is susceptible to change so we can extract it into a separated file. Up until now, we have created a file called `resources.tf`. Let's create a file called `vars.tf` with the following content:

```
variable "project_name" {
 type = "string"
 default = "implementing-modern-devops"
}
```

```
variable "default_region" {
  type = "string"
  default = "europe-west1"
}
```

Now, we are going to use these variables in our files. By default, Terraform will look into all the files with the extension `.tf` in our current folder, build the knowledge base of all the facts that have been described, and start creating our infrastructure as appropriated (internally building a graph of dependencies that can be checked with the `terraform graph` command). This means that we don't need to do anything special for Terraform to pick up our variables file:

```
provider "google" {
  credentials = "${file("xxx.json")}"
  project = "${var.project_name}"
  region = "${var.default_region}"
}
```

We can use variables pretty much anywhere to facilitate our infrastructure creation. As you can see, the syntax is the same as the syntax used for interpolation; in fact, it is an interpolation.

In the variables file, we have specified the default values for the variables, but it is possible that we want to change them depending on the environment or even for tweaking the configuration. Terraform also allows you to override variables in three ways:

- On the command line
- With a file called `terraform.tfvars`
- With environment variables

The first way is as easy as passing extra flags to the `terraform` commands. For example, if we want to change `project_name` when applying the changes to our infrastructure, we just need to pass an extra flag with the value of the variable:

```
terraform apply -var 'project_name=my-new-name'
```

And that's it. You can experiment by changing the project name or the zone and see how `terraform plan` creates new resources (as they don't exist in a different project).

The second method is using a file with the variable definitions. In order to test it, create a file called `terraform.tfvars` in the root of your project with the following content:

```
project_name = "my-new-project-name"
```

Now, if you run `terraform plan`, you will see how Terraform plans to create new resources as they don't exist in a project called `my-new-project-name`. The filename does not need to be `terrafrom.tfvars`, but if you create it with a different name, Terraform won't pick it up by default and you will need to pass the flag -var-file in order to load it.

 Don't forget to remove the `terraform.tfvars` file before continuing.

The third way of overriding variables is via environment variables. This is particularly interesting as it easily allows you to manage the configuration of different environments by external factors. The convention is to define an environment variable with the same name as the variable in Terraform but prefixing it with `TF_VAR_`. For example, for the variable `project_name`, we would execute the following command:

```
export TF_VAR_project_name=my-new-project-name
```

Terraform outputs

Up until now, we have worked with Terraform to create our infrastructure but we have little to no insight on what is going on in our cloud, in this case, on Google Cloud Platform. The engineers from HashiCorp have also thought about this, and they have created an element called output that allows us to print values of the resources created by our scripts.

So far, we have two files:

- `resources.tf`
- `variables.tf`

Before proceeding, make sure that your online infrastructure is created by running `terraform apply` as we did earlier.

Now, we are going to create another file called `outputs.tf`. This is not coincidental. In Terraform, this is the recommended layout for your projects as it facilitates the code readability as well as segregates responsibilities.

Add the following content to the `outputs.tf` file:

```
output "instance_ip" {
 value = "${google_compute_instance.my-first-
instance.network_interface.0.access_config.0.nat_ip}"
}
```

We will come back to this command later, but now, we need to rerun the apply command in order to let Terraform create the output for us. Something has changed:

```
google_compute_address.my-first-ip: Refreshing state... (ID: static-ip-
address)
google_compute_instance.my-first-instance: Refreshing state... (ID: my-
first-instance)

Apply complete! Resources: 0 added, 0 changed, 0 destroyed.

Outputs:

instance_ip = 23.251.138.171
```

 Terraform apply needs to be run for your outputs for it to become available even if you did not change the infrastructure.

Now we can see a new section called outputs, which contain the values that we have defined in the outputs file. If you want to see it again at any time, just run the following command:

`terraform output instance_ip`

Alternatively, simply run this command:

`terraform output`

The first one will show only the IP of the instance (this is particularly handy for using it as input for other commands). The second one shows all the outputs defined in your Terraform scripts.

Now, let's explain how the outputs work. In this case, we have used the following string to identify what we want to output:

**`google_compute_instance.my-first-
instance.network_interface.0.access_config.0.nat_ip`**

The first two keys (separated by dots) are clear: the type and the name of our resource. Then, the IP belongs to `network_interface` in the `acccess_config` section and the value is stored in `nat_ip`, but what are those 0ses in there?

Easy; we can define more than one network interface by repeating the `network_interface` block as many times as you need: the first one in the code will be 0, the second one will be 1, and so on...

This attribute path can be tricky to calculate sometimes, although the majority of the time is quite obvious from the configuration file. If you experience problems finding what you want to output, here is a shortcut: When you run `terraform apply`, in the output, you will see something similar to this:

```
google_compute_instance.my-first-instance: Creating...
  can_ip_forward:                                         "" => "false"
  disk.#:                                                 "" => "1"
  disk.0.auto_delete:                                     "" => "true"
  disk.0.image:                                           "" => "ubuntu-os-cloud/ubuntu-1704-zesty-v20170413"
  machine_type:                                           "" => "n1-standard-1"
  metadata_fingerprint:                                   "" => "<computed>"
  name:                                                   "" => "my-first-instance"
  network_interface.#:                                    "" => "1"
  network_interface.0.access_config.#:                    "" => "1"
  network_interface.0.access_config.0.assigned_nat_ip:    "" => "<computed>"
  network_interface.0.access_config.0.nat_ip:             "" => "23.251.138.171"
  network_interface.0.address:                            "" => "<computed>"
  network_interface.0.name:                               "" => "<computed>"
  network_interface.0.network:                            "" => "default"
  self_link:                                              "" => "<computed>"
  tags_fingerprint:                                       "" => "<computed>"
  zone:                                                   "" => "europe-west1-b"
```

This is the list of all the attributes that you can show in your outputs; the key is the column on the left-hand side. For example, if we want to show the zone where our VM is created, it is as simple as this:

```
output "instance_zone" {
  value = "The zone is ${google_compute_instance.my-first-instance.zone}"
}
```

As you can see, the interpolation also works here, letting you mix strings with values of the Terraform resources.

Summary

Terraform is the basic tool that every DevOps engineer needs to master in order to work efficiently with cloud providers such as Google Cloud Platform or AWS as it allows you to manage the infrastructure as if code was, with a lifecycle the ability to deploy infrastructure.

In this chapter, we saw the most important aspects of Terraform regarding the creation of virtual infrastructure. You learned enough to be able to, with the help of the online documentation, create resources and connect them in order to create much bigger projects.

Even though the examples that we followed through this chapter were pretty basic, in the next chapter, we will create a more complex infrastructure and install the required software to run it in an automated fashion.

We will also use more advanced Terraform capabilities such as modules to create highly reusable components that can be shared with different teams or even as open source components.

6
Server Provisioning

In the previous chapter, you learned how to create the infrastructure that is going to hold our applications. As we saw, the infrastructure automation is something that's new, and we used Terraform for it. The problem with Terraform is that it can only be used to build the infrastructure, but in order to provision the software, we need something different.

Through this chapter, we are going to dive deep into Ansible as, together with Puppet and Chef, it is the most predominant server provisioning tool in the market right now.

Here are the main topics that will be covered in this chapter:

- Server provisioning software
    - Chef
    - Puppet
    - Ansible
- Ansible
    - Ansible configuration
    - Ansible variables
        - Variables
        - Remote facts
        - Templates
    - Flow control
    - Ansible roles
- Ansible tower

As you can see, it is quite an extensive chapter with many examples that will enable you to learn the most important features of Ansible.

One thing that you need to be aware while reading through this chapter is the fact that it is impossible to showcase all the features from Ansible in a single chapter. In fairness, it would take us over a book to master all the features up to a proficient level. As you can guess by now, when I need to deal with Ansible, the first thing I do is open the official documentation and have it side by side with the code so that I can always refer to it for examples and features that I have either never dealt with or it has been a long time since I did not work with it.

We will also explore a section Ansible Tower, which is a software used to run Ansible playbooks on a bastion host mode from within your infrastructure instead of running it from a workstation.

Server provision software

As mentioned earlier, there are few options for software provisioning. Through this chapter, you will learn how to use Chef and Ansible, focusing on the latter as it is widely used across many companies and is easier to master than Chef.

There are also other options in the market that are valid and good solutions, but we are going to take a special interest in Ansible, which, to me, seems the easiest to learn and extend out of all of them.

Chef

Chef is a very interesting software that follows the bastion host principle to run configurations on our servers. A bastion host is a server placed in our private network that is able to reach our servers directly or via proxy in order to execute the actions needed to set them up with the desired state. This is an option not to be overlooked, as one of the biggest challenges that server provisioning presents is the management of secrets and authorization that, for example, Ansible needs to improve via third-party software such as Ansible Tower from Red Hat.

Chef uses recipes to configure parts of the server. A recipe is basically a set of declarative instructions that define what needs to happen in order to get the server to the desired status. For example, take a look at this:

```
execute "update-upgrade" do
    command "apt-get update && apt-get upgrade -y"
```

```
   action :run
end

package "apache2" do
   action :install
end
```

The preceding code will upgrade our system and then install the Apache2 web server.

This recipe, once finished, gets uploaded into the Chef server from a workstation, and here is the key: in Chef, there are three actors:

- Server
- Workstation
- Nodes

The server is where the recipes and configuration live. It needs to be installed prior to doing any work, and the instructions can be found at `https://docs.chef.io/install_server.html`.

There are three modalities of the Chef server:

- **Enterprise:** This can be installed inside your infrastructure and it is licensed, so you need to pay depending on the numbers of nodes that it is managing.
- **Open source:** This can also be installed in your infrastructure but **it does not have any support**. It is free and has to be configured and maintained by your company. It is also a cut-down version of the Enterprise Chef.
- **Hosted:** The Chef server is hosted on third-party hardware and you don't need to worry about maintaining and upgrading it. It might not be an option depending on the setup of your company.

The nodes are the target hosts. Every node is registered in the Chef server and has a run list: a list of recipes that are going to be run on a host when the `chef-client` command is executed.

The workstation is the computer used to configure and upload the Chef server. This computer uses a software called knife that can do everything on the Chef server:

- Configuring roles
- Looking for VMs depending on the roles and other parameters
- Configuring run lists
- Managing secrets

Knife uses cryptographic keys to communicate with the Chef server so all the communication happens in a trusted way.

Now, if we want to picture everything, it looks like that is shown in the following diagram:

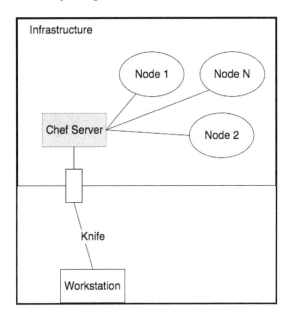

As you can see, even though the setup is quite complex (you need to set up a couple of software components) there are obvious benefits: our Chef server is behind the firewall in the demilitarized zone of our infrastructure, but it is managed via a CLI tool so all our secrets and configuration are safe inside our infrastructure.

Chef has a steep learning curve that, once we have gone through the initial learning phase, gets very familiar and easy to add new features and extend the DSL with the power of Ruby and a very well-thought-out interface.

Puppet

Puppet has been around for a while and is widely used in the DevOps world. Puppet comes in two flavors:

- Open source
- Enterprise

The open source version comes as is, offering a good set of features that allow you to fully automate the configuration management of your infrastructure.

The enterprise edition, aside from support, comes with an extended set of features that make the life of the engineers in your company a lot easier.

In the same way as Chef, Puppet follows the bastion host architecture: the server is installed within your infrastructure in the demilitarized zone and the nodes (your servers), via the puppet agent, will execute the specified tasks to reach the desired status.

The main difference between Chef and Puppet is the fact that puppet is declarative whereas Chef is more imperative:

- In Puppet, you specify which state you want your servers on and Puppet takes care of keeping them there
- In Chef, you declare a number of steps that will get your server to the desired state

That said, Chef also allows you to declare guards, which are conditions for steps to be executed.

Through my experience, I've found that people coming from an DevOps background feel more comfortable with Puppet as it is similar to what they have done through the years, whereas writing Chef recipes is similar to software development.

Ansible

Ansible is what we are going to be using to develop the contents of the rest of the book. In my opinion, it is the easiest to learn and extend. It is also easy to understand and offers a fairly comprehensive open source version that works with all the features from Ansible. You can also buy a license of Ansible Tower (or similar) to run Ansible Playbooks in a bastion host configuration as Chef or Puppet.

Ansible is basically a **domain-specific language** (**DSL**) for executing operations on remote hosts that are defined in an inventory.

Ansible works by running playbooks in the desired servers via SSH, so unlike Chef or Puppet, we don't need to install anything in the remote hosts; we should just be able to SSH into them. A playbook is basically a **Yet Another Markup Language (YAML)** with a set of instructions to get the server into the desired state in the same way as if we were executing a Bash script. A Playbook looks like this:

```
---
- hosts: webservers
  vars:
    http_port: 80
    max_clients: 200
  remote_user: root
  tasks:
  - name: ensure apache is at the latest version
    yum: name=httpd state=latest
  - name: write the apache config file
    template: src=/srv/httpd.j2 dest=/etc/httpd.conf
    notify:
    - restart apache
  - name: ensure apache is running (and enable it at boot)
    service: name=httpd state=started enabled=yes
  handlers:
    - name: restart apache
      service: name=httpd state=restarted
```

Reading through the file will make you understand how easy and straightforward it is to understand what the Playbook doing.

As you can see, in the second line, we are specifying that we want to run this Playbook in the hosts called `webservers`. This can be defined in the other part of Ansible: the inventory. The Ansible inventory is basically a file with the list of hosts in your infrastructure, as follows:

```
[webservers]
host1
host2

[dbservers]
192.168.0.[1:3]
```

This file is very straightforward but can get really complicated as well:

- The names between brackets are groups

- The groups contain hosts that can be defined with generators or they can just be listed
- Groups can have configuration specific to them or even override variables

In the preceding example, we have two groups: `webservers` and `dbservers`.

Web servers are only two hosts:

- `Host1`
- `Host2`

Dbservers use a generator and we have three hosts:

- `192.168.0.1`
- `192.168.0.2`
- `192.168.0.3`

As mentioned earlier, we can also define variables in the inventory. These variables can be scoped on the group and the host. Let's take a look at the following inventory:

```
[dbservers]
192.168.0.[1:3]

[webservers]
host1 role=master
host2

[dbservers:vars]
timezone=utc
```

As you can see, we have two variables:

- `timezone`: This is applied to all the hosts of the group `dbservers`.
- `role`: This is applied to the host `host1` of the group `webservers`.

This variable can be used in `playbooks` in order to have a specific configuration for specific hosts, as we will see later on in this chapter.

Groups can also be combined into bigger groups:

```
[dbservers]
192.168.0.[1:3]

[webservers]
host1
host2

[mongoservers]
10.0.0.1
10.0.0.2

[dataservers:child]
mongoservers
dbservers
```

In the preceding inventory, we can find the following:

- dbservers
- mongoservers
- webservers
- dataservers
- all
- ungrouped

Even though we did not specify it, Ansible always has two default groups called all and ungrouped that are self-descriptive: all is all the hosts in the inventory and ungrouped is all the hosts that are not specified in any group.

As stated earlier, Ansible does not follow the bastion host architecture as Chef or Puppet, but it follows the client/server architecture: our host needs to be able to reach the destination hosts (the ones on the inventory) in order to work.

This can be inconvenient depending on your infrastructure architecture, but it can be worked around using Ansible Tower or Rundeck to execute Ansible playbooks from inside your demilitarized zone.

In this chapter, we are going to use Ansible to build real production-ready examples in combination with Terraform so that we get a grasp of the real usage of the tools.

Ansible

In this section, we are going to take our first steps toward a more comprehensive example in Ansible. For now, we are going to install and configure NGINX, a very popular web server so we can showcase the main concepts of Ansible.

First, we are going to create a VM in Google Cloud Platform with an associated static IP so we can target it from our inventory. We are going to use Terraform in order to do it. First, we'll look at our resources file:

```
provider "google" {
  credentials = "${file("account.json")}"
  project = "${var.project_name}"
  region = "${var.default_region}"
}

resource "google_compute_instance"
"nginx" {
  name = "nginx"
  machine_type = "n1-standard-1"
  zone = "europe-west1-b"
  disk {
   image = "ubuntu-os-cloud/ubuntu-1704-zesty-v20170413"
  }
  network_interface {
    network = "default"
    access_config {
      nat_ip = "${google_compute_address.nginx-ip.address}"
    }
  }
}

resource "google_compute_address" "nginx-ip" {
  name = "nginx-ip"
}
```

And now, we'll look at our vars file:

```
variable "project_name" {
  type = "string"
  default = "implementing-modern-devops"
}

variable "default_region" {
  type = "string"
  default = "europe-west1"
}
```

In this case, we are reusing the project from the previous chapter as it is convenient to shut down everything once we are done. Now we run our plan so we can see what resources are going to be created:

```
+ google_compute_address.nginx-ip
  address: "<computed>"
  name: "nginx-ip"
  self_link: "<computed>"

+ google_compute_instance.nginx
  can_ip_forward: "false"
  disk.#: "1"
  disk.0.auto_delete: "true"
  disk.0.image: "ubuntu-os-cloud/ubuntu-1704-zesty-v20170413"
  machine_type: "n1-standard-1"
  metadata_fingerprint: "<computed>"
  name: "nginx"
  network_interface.#: "1"
  network_interface.0.access_config.#: "1"
  network_interface.0.access_config.0.assigned_nat_ip: "<computed>"
  network_interface.0.access_config.0.nat_ip: "<computed>"
  network_interface.0.address: "<computed>"
  network_interface.0.name: "<computed>"
  network_interface.0.network: "default"
  self_link: "<computed>"
  tags_fingerprint: "<computed>"
  zone: "europe-west1-b"


Plan: 2 to add, 0 to change, 0 to destroy.
```

So far, everything looks right. We are creating two resources:

- The static IP

- The VM

Now, we can apply our infrastructure:

```
google_compute_address.nginx-ip: Creating...
  address: "" => "<computed>"
  name: "" => "nginx-ip"
  self_link: "" => "<computed>"
google_compute_address.nginx-ip: Still creating... (10s elapsed)
google_compute_address.nginx-ip: Creation complete
google_compute_instance.nginx: Creating...
  can_ip_forward: "" => "false"
```

```
disk.#: "" => "1"
disk.0.auto_delete: "" => "true"
disk.0.image: "" => "ubuntu-os-cloud/ubuntu-1704-zesty-v20170413"
machine_type: "" => "n1-standard-1"
metadata_fingerprint: "" => "<computed>"
name: "" => "nginx"
network_interface.#: "" => "1"
network_interface.0.access_config.#: "" => "1"
network_interface.0.access_config.0.assigned_nat_ip: "" => "<computed>"
network_interface.0.access_config.0.nat_ip: "" => "35.187.81.127"
network_interface.0.address: "" => "<computed>"
network_interface.0.name: "" => "<computed>"
network_interface.0.network: "" => "default"
self_link: "" => "<computed>"
tags_fingerprint: "" => "<computed>"
zone: "" => "europe-west1-b"
google_compute_instance.nginx: Still creating... (10s elapsed)
google_compute_instance.nginx: Still creating... (20s elapsed)
google_compute_instance.nginx: Creation complete

Apply complete! Resources: 2 added, 0 changed, 0 destroyed.
```

And everything works as expected. If we check Google Cloud Platform, we can see that our VM has been created and has associated a public IP:

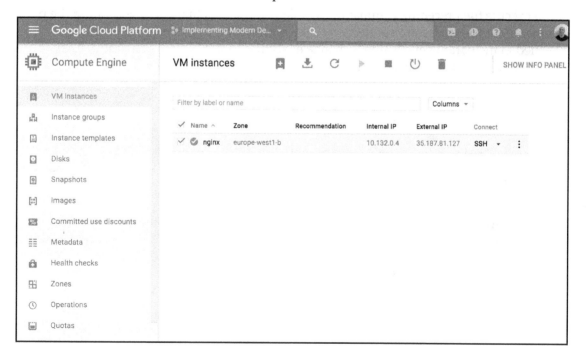

In this case, the associated public IP is 35.187.81.127. It is important to verify that we can reach the server via SSH. In order to do it, just click on the **SSH** button on the right-hand side of your instance row and it should open a Cloud Console window with terminal access.

 If SSH access fails, you need to add an ingress allow rule in the firewall to the port 22. For this example, just allow the traffic from any IP into any port, but don't do this in your real infrastructure as it is a security threat.

Once everything is up and running, it is time to start with Ansible. First, we are going to create our inventory file:

```
[nginx-servers]
35.187.81.127
```

This is very simple: a group with our public IP address that is connected to our VM. Save the file with the name inventory in a new folder named, for example, ansible-nginx. Once the inventory is created, we need to verify that all the hosts can be reached. Ansible provides you the tool to do that:

```
ansible -i inventory all -m ping
```

If you execute the preceding command, Ansible will ping (actually, it does not use the ping command but tries to issue a connection to the server) all the hosts in your inventory specified in the parameter -i. If you change everything for the name of a group, Ansible will try to reach only the hosts in that group.

Let's take a look at the output of the command:

```
35.187.81.127 | UNREACHABLE! => {
  "changed": false,
  "msg": "Failed to connect to the host via ssh: Permission denied
(publickey).\r\n",
  "unreachable": true
}
```

We are experiencing problems in connecting to our remote host and the cause is that we don't have any key that the host can validate to verify our identity. This is expected as we did not configure it, but now, we are going to solve it by creating a key pair and installing it on the remote host using the Google Cloud SDK:

```
gcloud compute ssh nginx
```

This command will do three things:

- Generate a new key pair
- Install the key pair in our remote VM
- Open a shell in our VM in GCP

The new key generated can be found under `~/.ssh/` with the name `google_compute_engine` and `google_compute_engine.pub` (private and public key).

Once the command finishes, our shell should look like this:

```
Welcome to Ubuntu 17.04 (GNU/Linux 4.10.0-19-generic x86_64)

 * Documentation:  https://help.ubuntu.com
 * Management:     https://landscape.canonical.com
 * Support:        https://ubuntu.com/advantage

 * Ubuntu 12.04 LTS ('precise') end-of-life was April 28, 2017
   ongoing security updates for 12.04 are available with Ubuntu Advantage
   - https://ubu.one/U1204esm
 * Aaron Honeycutt from the Kubuntu Council on art and design in Kubuntu
   - https://ubu.one/kubuart
 * The Ubuntu Desktop team wants your feedback on the move to Gnome
   - https://ubu.one/2GNome

  Get cloud support with Ubuntu Advantage Cloud Guest:
    http://www.ubuntu.com/business/services/cloud

0 packages can be updated.
0 updates are security updates.


Last login: Fri May 26 01:25:24 2017 from 79.97.8.5
davidgonzalez@nginx:~$
```

Now we have a terminal connected to our VM and we can execute commands. `gcloud` configures a user by default; in my case, `davidgonzalez` that can use `sudo` without password. In this case, we are going to execute the playbook as the root, so we need to be able to login as root into the VM. Copy the file `~/.ssh/authorized_keys` into `/root/.ssh/authorized_keys` and we should be able to do it. So, we have copied the public key that we generated earlier to the set of authorized keys of the root user.

In general, root access should be avoided as much as possible, but in this case, we will be executing the playbook as the root for convenience.

In order for Ansible to be able to use the key, we need to add it to the daemon on our server:

```
ssh-add ~/.ssh/google_compute_engine
```

This command should output the success, stating that the identity was added.

Now we can run our pin command again:

```
ansible -i inventory all -m ping
```

The output should be very different:

```
35.187.81.127 | SUCCESS => {
  "changed": false,
  "ping": "pong"
}
```

This means that now, Ansible is able to reach our server; therefore, it will be able to execute the playbook against it.

Now it is time to start writing our first `ansible` playbook. Inside the same folder, `ansible-nginx`, create a file called `tasks.yml` with the following content:

```
---
- hosts: all
  user: root
  tasks:
  - name: Update sources
    apt:
      update_cache: yes
  - name: Upgrade all packages
    apt:
      upgrade: dist
```

This is simple to understand:

- Our playbook is going to affect all the hosts
- The user running the playbook is going to be root

- And then we are going to execute two tasks:
  - Update the `apt cache`
  - Upgrade all the packages

Once we have the two files (inventory and playbook), we can run the following command:

```
ansible-playbook -i inventory tasks.yml
```

We should produce output similar to the following one:

```
PLAY [all] ******************************************************

TASK [setup] ****************************************************
ok: [35.187.81.127]

TASK [Update sources] *******************************************
changed: [35.187.81.127]

TASK [Upgrade all packages] *************************************
changed: [35.187.81.127]

PLAY RECAP ******************************************************
35.187.81.127 : ok=3 changed=2 unreachable=0 failed=0
```

We are going to run few playbooks along the chapter, so I would recommend that you keep the same VM alive and run all of them against it in order to save time and resources. The trial account from Google Cloud Platform will give you enough room to run them across several days or weeks.

Let's explain the output:

- First, it specifies against which group we are going to execute the playbook. In this case, we specified that the group is `all`.
- Then, we can see three tasks being executed. As you can see, the description matches the description specified in `tasks.yml`. This is very helpful in order to understand the output of your playbooks, especially when they fail.

- And then we get a recap:
    - Three tasks were executed
    - Two of them produced changes on the server
    - Zero failed

Simple and effective. This is the closest to executing a script in the server that we can get: a set of instructions, a target host, and its output.

In Ansible, instead of plain bash instructions, the actions are encapsulated into modules. A module is a component of the DSL, which allows you to do something special. In the playbook from earlier, apt is a module included in the core of Ansible. Documentation for it can be found at `http://docs.ansible.com/ansible/apt_module.html`.

Let's take another look to one of our usages of the `apt` module:

```
- name: Update sources
  apt:
    update_cache: yes
```

This, as you can guess, would be the equivalent to the following:

```
apt-cache update
```

So, in this case, Ansible provide us with a different module called command, which allows us to execute commands in the hosts of our inventory. Take a look at the following `yaml`:

```
- name: Update sources
  command: apt-cache update
```

This is equivalent to the `yaml` from earlier, and both do the same: update `apt-cache`.

In general, if there is a module for a given task, it is recommended that you use it as it will handle (or at least you can expect it to) the errors and the outputs better than executing the equivalent command.

Now, once our playbook has succeeded, we can expect our system to be up to date. You can check it by running the playbook again:

```
PLAY [all] ****************************************************

TASK [setup] **************************************************
ok: [35.187.81.127]

TASK [Update sources] *****************************************
changed: [35.187.81.127]

TASK [Upgrade all packages] ***********************************
ok: [35.187.81.127]

PLAY RECAP ****************************************************
35.187.81.127 : ok=3 changed=1 unreachable=0 failed=0
```

Now you can see that only one task has produced changes in the server (updating the apt sources).

Ansible configuration

One of the features of Ansible is the ability to override the defaults per project. In order to do it that, we just need to create a file called `ansible.cfg` in the root of our project and Ansible will read it and apply the configuration.

There is a big number of parameters that can be configured, and all of them can be found in the official documentation at `http://docs.ansible.com/ansible/intro_configuration.html`.

As you can see, the documentation for Ansible is quite good, and the majority of the time, it will provide an answer to your problems.

Let's see how the configuration can help us. If you remember from the previous example, we have specified the flag `-i` in order to tell Ansible where our inventory file lives. Ansible has a default for this value, which is `/etc/ansible/hosts`. In our little project, our inventory is in the same folder as our code, and in order to specify it to Ansible, we need to create a configuration file with the following content:

```
[defaults]
inventory = ./inventory
```

Now, we run our `playbook` again with the following command:

```
ansible-playbook tasks.yml
```

We did not specify the host list, but Ansible, after reading `ansible.cfg` knows that the inventory file can be located at `./inventory`.

Ansible has a hierarchy of precedence to find the configuration:

- The `ANSIBLE_CONFIG` environment variable
- `ansible.cfg`
- `.ansible.cfg`
- `/etc/ansible/ansible.cfg`

So, if we define an environment variable called `ANSIBLE_CONFIG` pointing to a file, the Ansible configuration will be read from that location and the rest of the options will be ignored. This is particularly helpful in segregating environments: our CI server can define its own configuration in the environment file, whereas developers can have the `ansible.cfg` file checked in into the source control so that is shared across everyone.

There are a few sections that can be specified in `ansible.cfg`. Sections control several aspects of of Ansible, such as connections. Under certain circumstances, we might need to add special parameters for `ssh` to work, and it is as easy as adding the following lines to your `ansible.cfg` file:

```
[ssh_connection]
ssh_args=<your args here>
```

Ansible variables, remote facts and templates

Variables and templates are an important part of Ansible. They allow us to override values in our configuration (servers and playbooks) so that we can write generic playbooks that can be reused across different configurations with minor tweaks. With templates, we can render configuration files from our host so we could potentially use Ansible to manage the configuration of remote servers with little to no effort. It also can be used to generate and install SSL certificates for different hosts transparently to the user.

Both of them (variables and templates) use a template engine called Jinja2, which allows logic and interpolation to be embedded in our configurations.

In general, there are several ways of defining variables, but we are only going to visit the most common ones (under my criteria), as otherwise, it would take us the size of several chapters to document them properly. If you want to explore further different ways of defining variables, the official documentation provides a fairly comprehensive guide at `http://docs.ansible.com/ansible/playbooks_variables.html`.

Ansible variables

Variables are the most simple of the potential customizations. With variables, we can define values that are going to be replaced in our playbooks. Let's take a look at the following playbook:

```
---
- hosts: all
  user: root
  tasks:
  - debug:
    msg: "Hello {{ myName }}! I am {{ inventory_hostname }}"
```

Replace the content of `tasks.yml` with the snippet from earlier. There are two new symbols in our task. Also, our task is new: debug is used to output values from our variables into the terminal while executing the playbook. Let's take a look at the execution (we will use the same configuration as the example from earlier):

```
ansible-playbook -i inventory tasks.yml
```

It fails:

```
PLAY [all] ***********************************************************************

TASK [Gathering Facts] ***********************************************************
ok: [35.187.81.127]

TASK [debug] *********************************************************************
fatal: [35.187.81.127]: FAILED! => {"failed": true, "msg": "the field 'args'
has an invalid value, which appears to include a variable that is undefined.
The error was: 'myName' is undefined\n\nThe error appears to have been in
'/code/ansible-variables/tasks.yml': line 5, column 5, but may\nbe elsewhere
in the file depending on the exact syntax problem.\n\nThe offending line
appears to be:\n\n tasks:\n - debug:\n ^ here\n"} to retry,
use: --limit @/Users/dgonzalez/code/ansible-variables/tasks.retry

PLAY RECAP ***********************************************************************
35.187.81.127 : ok=1 changed=0 unreachable=0 failed=1
```

The reason for the failure can be seen in in the message: we have a variable defined called `name` that does not have a value associated. Ansible will fail if there is a value that cannot be interpolated, aborting the execution of the task.

There is another interesting piece of information here: Ansible gives you a parameter to retry the playbook only on the hosts that were not successful. If we wanted to retry the playbook only on the failed hosts, we could run the following command:

```
ansible-playbook -i inventory tasks.yml --limit
@/Users/dgonzalez/code/ansible-variables/tasks.retry
```

The new parameter, `tasks.retry` is a file with a list of hosts that are okay to rerun the playlist as they failed before.

Going back to our missing variables, we need to define the variable called `myName`. There are a few ways of doing that; the first is via the command line:

```
ansible-playbook -i inventory tasks.yml -e myName=David
```

And you can see that the output of the playbook is looking better now:

```
PLAY [all] **********************************************

TASK [Gathering Facts] ******************************
ok: [35.187.81.127]

TASK [debug] ****************************************
ok: [35.187.81.127] => {
 "changed": false,
 "msg": "Hello David! I am 35.187.81.127"
}

PLAY RECAP *******************************************
35.187.81.127 : ok=2 changed=0 unreachable=0 failed=0
```

As you can see, the variables got interpolated and we can see the message `Hello David! I am 35.187.81.127`.

The second way of defining variables is via inventory, as we have seen earlier:

```
[nginx-servers]
35.187.81.127 myName=DavidInventory
```

If we modify our inventory to match the preceding snippet, the value of our variable will be `DavidInventory` and we don't need to pass a value in the command line:

```
ansible-playbook -i inventory tasks.yml
```

This will produce the message `Hello DavidInventory! I am 35.187.81.127`.

The third way to define variables in Ansible is by defining them in the playbook itself. Take a look at the following playbook:

```
---
- hosts: all
 vars:
 myName: David
 user: root
 tasks:
 - debug:
 msg: "Hello {{ myName }}! I am {{ inventory_hostname }}"
```

As simple as it sounds, once you define the variable in the `vars` section of your playbook, it becomes available; therefore, there is no need to specify the value anywhere else.

The fourth way to define variables is via files. Ansible is designed to be a self-documented component that can be easily understood by someone with not much experience in it. One of the ways in which Ansible facilitates the task of understanding playbooks is the possibility of writing every single configuration piece in a file. Variables are not the exemption, so Ansible will let you define variables in files or playbooks.

Let's start with the files. Create a file called `vars.yml` in the same folder in which you are working (where your playbook and inventory are) with the following content:

```
myName: DavidFromFile
yourName: ReaderFromFile
```

Now we can run the following command in order to use the variables file:

```
ansible-playbook -i inventory playbook.yml -e @vars.yml
```

And if you check the output, it would be the same as the one from earlier.

In this case, we have defined a new variable that we are not using (`yourName`), but that is fine. I just wanted to show you that Ansible won't complain if there are free variables, but it will raise an error if there are unbound interpolations.

In this case, we have included `vars.yml` in our playbook via the command line, referencing your local file with @ in the beginning, but there is another possibility for using variable files in Ansible: including them from within the playbook. Let's take a look at how it is done:

```
---
- hosts: all
  user: root
  tasks:
  - name: Include vars
    include_vars:
    file: vars.yml
  - debug:
    msg: "Hello {{ myName }}! I am {{ inventory_hostname }}"
```

In this case, we have used the `include_vars` module in our playbook. Now execute the playbook with the following command:

```
ansible-playbook -i inventory tasks.yml
```

You will get the following output:

```
PLAY [all] ********************************************

TASK [setup] ******************************************
ok: [35.187.81.127]

TASK [Include vars] ***********************************
ok: [35.187.81.127]

TASK [debug] ******************************************
ok: [35.187.81.127] => {
  "msg": "Hello DavidFromFile! I am 35.187.81.127"
}

PLAY RECAP ********************************************
35.187.81.127 : ok=3 changed=0 unreachable=0 failed=0
```

As you can see, there is an extra task that takes a file and injects the variables in the context.

This module is quite flexible and there are several options to include variable files in our playbook. We have used the most straightforward one, but you can check out other options in the official documentation at `http://docs.ansible.com/ansible/include_vars_module.html`.

There is another possibility for including a variable file into our playbook, and it is using the `vars_files` directive in our playbook:

```
---
- hosts: all
 user: root
 vars_files:
 - vars.yml
 tasks:
 - debug:
 msg: "Hello {{ myName }}! I am {{ inventory_hostname }}"
```

This will take the `vars.yml` file and inject all the defined variables into the context, making them available for use.

As you can see, Ansible is quite flexible around the definition of variables.

There is another interesting way of setting up variables in Ansible that helps us further customize our playbooks: `set_fact`. Setting facts allows us to set variables dynamically in our playbooks. `Set_fact` can be used in combination with another interesting instruction called register. Let's look at an example:

```
---
- hosts: all
  user: root
  tasks:
  - name: list configuration folder
  command: ls /app/config/
  register: contents
  - set_fact:
  is_config_empty: contents.stdout == ""
  - name: check if folder is empty
  debug: msg="config folder is empty"
  when: is_config_empty
  - name: installing configuration
  command: <your command here>
  when: is_config_empty
```

What we are doing here is basically setting a variable to true if the configuration folder of our app is empty (hypothetic configuration folder) so that we can regenerate it only when it is not present. This is done by making use of the instruction when that allows us to execute instructions conditionally. We will come back to it during this chapter.

We have visited the most common ways of defining variables, but there is one question pending: what is the precedence of the different methods for creating variables?

This is something that I have to query myself whenever I am working in a playbook, and the truth is that at the end of the day, you will use only a couple of methods to create variables so that it is not as important as it should be. In my case, I tend to create a file with variables (when not working with roles), and if I want to override a value, I do that on the command line (or environment variable), which is the highest priority in the chain. The complete list of variable precedence can be found at `http://docs.ansible.com/ansible/playbooks_variables.html#variable-precedence-where-should-i-put-a-variable`.

Ansible remote facts

Remote facts in Ansible are a way to specify configuration on remote hosts either by an explicit configuration file or by a script that returns data about the server. In general, this feature is very useful for operations such as maintenance, setting up flags that specifically mark the host as out of the pool so that our playbooks have no effect in the hosts.

Take a look at the following command (assuming the inventory from the previous example is present in the folder and the VM is running on Google Cloud Platform):

```
ansible all -m setup -i inventory --user=root
```

This will output an enormous amount of data (JSON-formatted data). This data is all the known facts about the remote host, such as the CPU type, machine ID, network interfaces, kernel version, and so on. They can be used within our playbooks, but they can also be extended to add more data that is controlled by the remote host without any local configuration.

In order to set up custom remote facts, we have several options, but at the end of the day, the custom facts are defined in JSON files by default under `/etc/ansible/facts.d/`. It is also possible to create an executable (a script) under the same folder so that Ansible will execute it and take the output as facts and add them to the facts scope. Take a look at the following file:

```
{
 "my_name": "David Gonzalez"
 }
```

Put into the remote box (the one used in all the examples from earlier) and create a file in `/etc/ansible/facts.d/example.facts` with the content from earlier.

Once this is done, run the following command:

```
ansible all -m setup -i inventory --user=root | grep -B 3 -A 3 my_name
```

It almost looks magical, but the output of your command should now include the facts that you created earlier:

```
 },
 "ansible_local": {
 "example": {
 "my_name": "David Gonzalez"
 }
 },
 "ansible_lsb": {
```

Now they can be used in your playbook in the `ansible_local` variable, for example, to access `my_name`:

```
---
- hosts: all
  user: root
  tasks:
  - name: Gather my_name fact.
    debug: msg="{{ ansible_local.example.my_name }}"
```

As mentioned earlier, Ansible can also gather facts from a script placed in the facts path. This script should have the x flag present, which indicates that it can be executed and have the extension `fact`. Let's look at a very interesting trick that I find quite useful. When I try to diagnose a failure in our systems, the first thing I tend to check is the CPU usage. The majority of the time, our systems are highly observable (monitored) so it is easy to check the CPU load, but sometimes, monitoring might not be in place.

First, go to the server that we have been using in the preceding examples and create a file in `/etc/ansible/facts.d/cpuload.fact` with the following content:

```
#!/bin/bash
CPU_LOAD=`grep 'cpu ' /proc/stat | awk '{usage=($2+$4)*100/($2+$4+$5)} END
{print usage "%"}'`
echo { \"cpu_load\": \"$CPU_LOAD\"}
```

This is a simple script that will output JSON with information about the CPU load in your system. Once the file is created, give it execution permissions:

```
chmod u+x /etc/ansible/facts.d/cpuload.fact
```

And we are done. Before disconnecting the SSH session, make sure that the script works as expected by executing it:

```
/etc/ansible/facts.d/cpuload.fact
```

This should output something like the following:

```
{ "cpu_load": "0.0509883%"}
```

Now it is time to test our scripted facts. What we are going to do is create a playbook that gets the CPU load and outputs it to the terminal with a debug message. This is the content:

```
- hosts: all
  user: root
  tasks:
  - name: Get CPU load
    debug: msg="The CPU load for {{ ansible_hostname }} is {{
ansible_local.cpuload.cpu_load }}"
```

Run the preceding playbook:

```
ansible-playbook -i inventory tasks.yml
```

You should get an output very similar to the following one:

```
PLAY [all] ************************************************************

TASK [Gathering Facts] ***********************************************
ok: [35.187.81.127]

TASK [Update sources] ************************************************
ok: [35.187.81.127] => {
  "changed": false,
  "msg": "The CPU load for nginx is 0.0511738%"
}

PLAY RECAP ***********************************************************
35.187.81.127 : ok=2 changed=0 unreachable=0 failed=0
```

Now we have a rudimentary tool to check the CPU load on our servers with a simple command, leveraging the host groups to Ansible.

One thing we have not explained is the first task that Ansible outputs in every playbook: gathering facts.

This task gets all those facts that we have been talking about in this section and creates the context for the playbook to run, so in this case, the CPU load that we get is the CPU load gathered at the execution of that task.

Ansible templates

Templates are another powerful tool from Ansible. They allow us to render configuration files, application properties, and anything that can be stored in a human readable file.

Templates rely heavily on variables and a template engine called Jinja2 , which is used by Ansible to render the templates. First, we are going to install `ngnix` on our server with a simple playbook:

```
---
- hosts: all
  user: root
  tasks:
  - name: Update sources
  apt:
  update_cache: yes
  - name: Upgrade all packages
  apt:
  upgrade: dist
  - name: Install nginx
  apt:
  name: nginx
  state: present
```

As you can see, it is very simple:

- Update the `apt cache`
- Upgrade the system
- Install `nginx`

Now, just run the preceding playbook using the VM created earlier:

```
ansible-playbook -i inventory tasks.yaml
```

And when the playbook is finished, you should have `nginx` running in your remote server. In order to verify it, just open the browser and use the IP of your VM as URL. You should see the `nginx` welcome screen.

Now, we are going to create a template with the `nginx` configuration, where we can add or remove servers with templates in a fairly easy manner. Create a folder called `nginx-servers` in your current directory (where the playbook is) and add a file called `nginx.yml` with the following content:

```
---
- hosts: all
```

```
user: root
vars_files:
- vars.yml
tasks:
- name: Update sources
apt:
update_cache: yes
- name: Upgrade all packages
apt:
upgrade: dist
- name: Install nginx
apt:
name: nginx
state: present
- template:
src: nginx-servers/nginx-one.conf.j2
dest: /etc/nginx/sites-enabled/default
owner: root
- service:
name: nginx
state: reloaded
```

Let's explain the file a bit:

- The system is upgraded using `apt`.
- Using apt as well, `nginx` is installed. Note that Ansible uses a declarative approach to install packages: you state the name of the package and the state that the package should be in after the playbook is executed.
- The playbook renders the configuration for a virtual server in `nginx` from a template called `nginx-one.conf.j2`. We will come back to this in a second.
- The playbook reloads the `nginx` service so that the new configuration takes effect.

We have a few blocks missing in the preceding playbook. The first block is the file called `nginx-one.conf.j2`. This file is a template that is used to render the `nginx` configuration for a virtual host in the server. Let's look at the content of that file:

```
server {
    listen {{ server_one_port }} default_server;
    index index.html;
}
```

Create a folder called `sites-enabled` and add the `nginx-one.conf.j2` file to it with the preceding content. This file is a standard `nginx` server block but with one particularity: we have a *server_one_port* as a placeholder for the port so that we can control the port where the `nginx` virtual host is exposed. This is very familiar to us: we are using the variables to render the templates.

The second block is the file called `vars.yml` () with the following content:

```
server_one_port: 3000
```

This is very simple: it just defines the variables required to render the template from earlier. One thing that you need to be aware when using templates is that all the variables in the context can be accessed in it, from the facts gathered from the remote server to the variables defined everywhere.

Once we have everything in place (the two files from earlier, the playbook from earlier, and the inventory from the previous example), we can run the playbook as usual and verify that everything works as expected:

```
ansible-playbook -i inventory nginx.yml
```

If everything worked as expected, you should have a fully functional `nginx` server (serving the default page) in your VM in Google Cloud Platform on the port `3000`.

 Google Cloud Platform has a deny by default policy in order to enhance security, so you might need to adjust the firewall to allow inbound traffic to certain ports.

Flow control

In Ansible, it is possible to use flow control statements such as loops or conditionals using variables as input. This can be used to repeat tasks on a certain dataset and avoid executing some tasks if a few conditions are not met: we might want to use different commands depending on the underlying system of our server.

We have already seen an example of conditionals using the `when` clause in our previous examples, but let's explain it a bit more:

```
---
- hosts: all
  user: root
  tasks:
  - command: /bin/false
```

```
register: result
ignore_errors: True

- debug: msg="fail!"
when: result|failed

- debug: msg="success!"
when: result|succeeded
```

The preceding code is very easy to read: a command is executed (ignoring the potential errors so our playbook continues), and it registers a variable called result. Then, we have two debug tasks:

- The first one will only be executed only if the /bin/false command fails
- The second one will be executed only if the /bin/false command succeeds

In this playbook, we are using two new tricks:

- ignore_errors: With this clause, if the task fails, the playbook will continue executing the following tasks. This is very helpful if we want to test for assumptions in the system, for example, if some files are present or a certain network interface is configured.
- Pipe symbol (|): This symbol is called pipe. It is a Jinja2 expression used to filter values. In this case, we are using the failed and succeeded filters to return true or false depending on the outcome of the command. There are many filters that can be used on Jinja2 to work in a similar way as Unix pipes transforming the data that goes through them.

Another type of control flow structure are loops. Let's look at how loops work:

```
---
- hosts: all
  user: root
  vars:
  names:
  - David
  - Ester
  - Elena
  tasks:
  - name: Greetings
  debug: msg="Greetings {{ item }}! live long and prosper."
  with_items: "{{ names }}"
```

Here, we are using something new that we did not see at the time of explaining variables: they can have a structure such as lists and dictionaries. In this case, we are defining a list with a few names and outputting a message for each of them. Now it is time to run the playbook. Save the preceding content in a file called `loops.yml` and execute the following command:

```
ansible-playbook -i inventory loops.yml
```

We will assume that the inventory is the same as the one used in the preceding examples. After finishing, you should see something similar to the following output in your Terminal:

```
PLAY [all] ***********************************************

TASK [Gathering Facts] **********************************
ok: [35.187.81.127]

TASK [Greetings] ****************************************
ok: [35.187.81.127] => (item=David) => {
 "item": "David",
 "msg": "Greetings David! Live long and prosper."
}
ok: [35.187.81.127] => (item=Ester) => {
 "item": "Ester",
 "msg": "Greetings Ester! Live long and prosper."
}
ok: [35.187.81.127] => (item=Elena) => {
 "item": "Elena",
 "msg": "Greetings Elena! Live long and prosper."
}
PLAY RECAP **********************************************
35.187.81.127 : ok=2 changed=0 unreachable=0 failed=0
```

It is also possible to define a list using the compact version of the declaration. Take a look at the following statement:

```
names:
- David
- Ester
- Elena
```

This can be redefined as follows:

```
names: ['David', 'Ester', 'Elena']
```

And it is totally equivalent.

It is also possible to define dictionaries in Ansible and use them as variables. They can also be used as iterable elements, which enable us to give structure to our data:

```
---
- hosts: all
  user: root
  vars:
  namesAge:
  - name: David
  age: 33
  - name: Ester
  age: 31
  - name: Elena
  age: 1
  tasks:
  - name: Presentations
  debug: msg="My name is {{ item.name }} and I am {{ item.age }} years old."
  with_items: "{{ namesAge }}"
```

If you are familiar with software development, the preceding snippet will make perfect sense to you: a list of structured data (an array of objects) that holds information to be accessed by the key.

In the rest of the book, we will be using more advanced features of flow control structures in Ansible, and we will explain them as we go, but if you want to learn more about it, the following links might be useful for you:

- Conditionals (http://docs.ansible.com/ansible/playbooks_conditionals.html)
- Loops (http://docs.ansible.com/ansible/playbooks_loops.html)
- Jinja2 Templating (http://docs.ansible.com/ansible/playbooks_templating.html)

Roles

We have been working on few Ansible playbooks, and as you can imagine, there is a lot that can be abstracted from them into generic units of work. As of now, with our current knowledge of Ansible, the best thing we can do is use a naming convention for playbooks and files so that we don't mix them, but Ansible provides a better approach to this: roles.

Think of roles as common reusable capabilities as you do with modules in software: a highly cohesive set of playbooks, variables, and resources that work together for one purpose. For example, if we are managing `nginx`, it makes sense to have all the related resources in a single module (role, in this case) in order to improve the reusability as well as clarity of the code.

One option would be including playbooks using Ansible features. Although we did not talk about it, with Ansible, it is possible to include YAML files with tasks to create dependencies, as shown in the following snippets:

```
---
- include: play-include.yml
- hosts: all
  user: root
  tasks:
  - debug: msg="I am the main playbook"
  - include: tasks-include.yml
```

Let's explain what is going on. We can see two files included:

- The first include is what Ansible calls a play include. It is a fully functional playbook as is, which gets included in another playbook.
- The second include is what Ansible calls a task include. It only includes a list of tasks.

This can be explained easily by looking at the content of the two files. First, look at the content of `play-include.yml`:

```
---
- hosts: all
  user: root
  tasks:
  - debug: msg="I am a play include"
```

Second, look at the content of `tasks-include.yml`:

```
---
- debug: msg="I am a task include"
- debug: msg="I am a task include again"
```

Now we are going to execute the playbooks from earlier and see what the output is. Save the content of the first playbook on a file called `tasks.yml` and use the same inventory as on all the examples from earlier. Now run the following command:

```
ansible-playbook -i inventory tasks.yml
```

Once the execution has finished, let's examine the output, which should be very similar to the following one:

```
PLAY [all] ************************************************

TASK [setup] ************************************************
ok: [35.187.81.127]

TASK [debug] ************************************************
ok: [35.187.81.127] => {
 "msg": "I am a play include"
}

PLAY [all] ************************************************

TASK [setup] ************************************************
ok: [35.187.81.127]

TASK [debug] ************************************************
ok: [35.187.81.127] => {
 "msg": "I am the main playbook"
}

TASK [debug] ************************************************
ok: [35.187.81.127] => {
 "msg": "I am a task include"
}

TASK [debug] ************************************************
ok: [35.187.81.127] => {
 "msg": "I am a task include again"
}

PLAY RECAP ************************************************
35.187.81.127 : ok=6 changed=0 unreachable=0 failed=0
```

Let's explain this:

1. The play include (`play-include.yml`) gets executed by outputting the debug message in there.
2. The debug task in the main playbook gets executed.
3. The task includes (`tasks-include.yml`) gets executed by executing the two debug messages included there.

It is not very complicated, but it gets easier if you play around a bit with the playbooks.

Although the preceding example can lead to a very clean and reusable set of files, there is a much better way of doing this: using roles. Roles are isolated sets of functionalities that allow an easy maintenance cycle like any other software component.

Following the preceding example, we can rewrite it using three roles:

- The play include (`play-include.yml`)
- The main tasks (`tasks.yml`)
- The tasks include (`tasks-include.yml`)

In order to start creating roles, first, create a new folder called `ansible-roles` and a folder called `roles` inside the same one. One thing that was not mentioned earlier is the fact that it is a good practice to create a set of folders to hold Ansible resources: tasks folders to hold the tasks, files folder to store all the files that need to be transferred to the remote hosts, and so on. In general, I agree with this setup, but for the examples, we just simplified it in order to make everything easier. For roles, this setup is mandatory. We need to create the folders as appropriated. In this case, as we are only going to use tasks to demonstrate how roles work; we will create the folder tasks inside of every role because otherwise, we won't execute the tasks from the role.

Inside the **roles** folder, we are going to create another folder called `play-include`, which is going to be the equivalent to `play-include.yml` from the preceding example but in the form of a role.

Now it is time to create our first role playbook: create a file called `main.yml` and place it inside the `play-include/tasks/` folder. This is the content of the `main.yml file`:

```
---
- debug: msg="I am a play include"
```

Now it is time to add a second role called `main-tasks` by creating a folder in *roles* and adding a file called `main.yml` inside of `roles/main-tasks/tasks`:

```
---
- debug: msg="I am the main playbook"
```

And our third and last role is called `tasks-include`. Just create the folder as earlier (inside the roles folder) and add a file called `main.yml` to it inside of the tasks folder:

```
---
- debug: msg="I am a task include"
- debug: msg="I am a task include again"
```

And that's it. You have created three roles that can be reused across different Ansible projects. Now it is time to use them. Create a file called `tasks.yml` in the root folder of your project (in my case, `ansible-roles`) and add the following content:

```
---
- hosts: all
  user: root
  roles:
  - main-tasks
  - play-include
  - tasks-include
```

This is how your project should look after adding all the files from earlier:

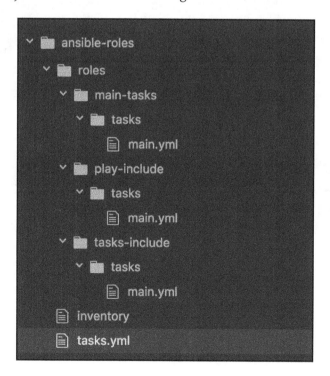

The inventory is the same one as the previous examples (remember, the recommendation was to reuse the same VM). Now it is time to run our playbook:

```
ansible-playbook -i inventory tasks.yml
```

This will produce output similar to the following one:

```
PLAY [all] *********************************************************

TASK [setup] ******************************************************
ok: [35.187.81.127]

TASK [main-tasks : debug] ****************************************
ok: [35.187.81.127] => {
 "msg": "I am the main playbook"
}

TASK [play-include : debug] **************************************
ok: [35.187.81.127] => {
 "msg": "I am a play include"
}

TASK [tasks-include : debug] *************************************
ok: [35.187.81.127] => {
 "msg": "I am a task include"
}

TASK [tasks-include : debug] *************************************
ok: [35.187.81.127] => {
 "msg": "I am a task include again"
}

PLAY RECAP ********************************************************
35.187.81.127 : ok=5 changed=0 unreachable=0 failed=0
```

If we compare the output from the previous example, we can see that it is virtually the same except for the legend of the task, which indicates the role that the task is coming from.

In roles, we can also define variables and access to the variables defined in the global scope as well as many other features. As stated earlier, Ansible is big enough to write an entire book just on it, so we are scratching the surface of the important parts (under my criteria). As usual, the documentation in Ansible is pretty good, and if you want to learn more about roles, the information can be found at `https://docs.ansible.com/ansible-container/roles/index.html`.

If I can give you some advice regarding Ansible, it would be that you should always try to use roles. It doesn't matter how big or simple your project is; you will find out very soon that the isolation and reusability that roles provide at pretty much no cost are quite beneficial.

Ansible Tower

We have seen an extensive number of features from Ansible that are very useful to any DevOps engineer wanting to automate tasks in any IT department.

There is one design challenge with Ansible, and it is the fact that the playbooks are run from your own computer against remote servers, as shown in the following figure:

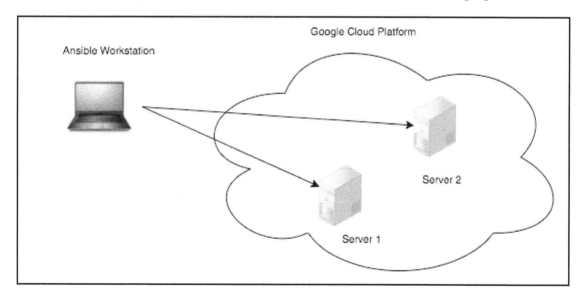

This can be a problem because as you are aware by now, Ansible uses secrets (ansible-vault secrets) and, potentially, some sensible information that can be intercepted or stolen from a workstation. This is not a problem in Chef or Puppet as they follow the bastion host approach, but it might be a problem for companies to choose Ansible.

One of the solutions for it comes from Red Hat with the name Ansible Tower. This software gets installed in your IT infrastructure (in this case, Google Cloud Platform) and offers a UI to be operated in the same way as if a CI server was, enabling the role access control to Ansible playbooks as well as a security layer that is not present in plain Ansible: the secrets are kept in a server (Ansible Tower) inside your infrastructure and they never leave it.

Ansible Tower offers all the features present in Ansible so that you don't need to rewrite any playbook,; just adjust them to the new infrastructure geometry.

Let's take a look at the following figure:

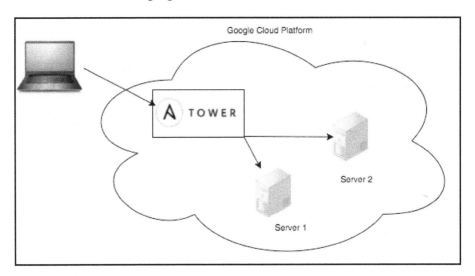

As you can see, now our Ansible host is inside of our infrastructure; therefore, it can be operated through a web interface enhancing the security of our IT operations.

Ansible Tower also offers an API that can be used to build integration points with our software or CI server.

Ansible Tower is licensed by Red Hat, so if you want to use it in your company, a license needs to be purchased. At the time of writing this, there are not that many alternatives in the market and the ones that are available are not as feature-full as Ansible Tower. Also, the UI (as shown in the next screenshot) is very sleek, which, even though not a killer, is always something to be considered.

Summary

In this chapter, you learned about the main Ansible features, but obviously, we have not covered every single possibility, as it would take us a couple of books to master them. Also, there is another catch here: DevOps tools are evolving constantly.

When you are working on the DevOps side of the IT world, you always need to be willing to learn new things on the fly.

Ansible was originally created to fully provision VMs in the cloud (and on premises), but slowly, it is gravitating toward configuration management as more modern tools, such as Kubernetes or Docker Swarm, are increasing their market share, leveraging Docker into the full software development life cycle in a continuous delivery environment.

In the next chapter, you will learn more about Kubernetes and Docker Swarm as they are the next big things in DevOps. Kubernetes, particularly, is an orchestration tool that I think will take over all the others in the next few months or years as it offers all the resources needed by any IT company leveraging the experience that Google has accumulated through years of running software in containers.

In my opinion, container engines such as Docker are about to surpass the break-even and become the norm for all the software components and architectures of the main software companies around the world.

7
Docker Swarm and Kubernetes - Clustering Infrastructure

So far, we have seen how powerful Docker is but we have not unleashed the full potential of containers. You have learned how to run containers on a single host with the local resources without the possibility of clustering our hardware resources in a way that allows us to uniformly use them as one big host. This has a lot of benefits, but the most obvious one is that we provide a middleware between developers and ops engineers that acts as a common language so that we don't need to go to the ops team and ask them for a machine of a given size. we just provide the definition of our service and the Docker clustering technology will take care of it.

In this chapter, we are going to dive deep into deploying and managing applications on Kubernetes, but we will also take a look at how Docker Swarm works.

People usually tend to see Kubernetes and Docker Swarm as competitors, but in my experience, they solve different problems:

- **Kubernetes** is focused on advanced microservices topologies that offer all the potential of years of experience running containers in Google
- **Docker Swarm** offers the most straightforward clustering capabilities for running applications in a very simple way

In short, Kubernetes is more suited for advanced applications, whereas Docker Swarm is a version of Docker on steroids.

This comes at a cost: managing a Kubernetes cluster can be very hard, whereas managing a Docker Swarm cluster is fairly straightforward.

There are other clustering technologies that are used in the current DevOps ecosystem, such as DC/OS or Nomad, but unfortunately, we need to focus on the ones that are, in my opinion, the most suited for DevOps and focus specifically on Kubernetes that, in my opinion, is eating the DevOps market.

Why clustering ?

In `Chapter 1`, *DevOps in the Real World,* you learned about organizational alignment and why is important to shift roles in a company to accommodate DevOps tools. It is not okay anymore to just be a developer or a sysadmin; now you need to be a full stack DevOps engineer in order to get success in any project. Full stack DevOps means that you need to understand the business and the technology used in the organisation. Think about it; if you became a civil engineer instead of an IT engineer, it is mandatory to know the local rules (the business) plus the commercial names of the tools used to build roads and bridges (the technology) but also be able to coordinate their building (ops). Maybe not every engineer needs to know everything but they need to be aware of in the full picture in order to ensure the success of the project.

Coming back to containers and DevOps, making concepts simple for everyone to understand is something that's mandatory nowadays. You want to ensure that all the engineers in your project are able to trace the software from conception (requirements) to deployment (ops) but also have in mind predictability so that the business people that barely speak tech are able to plan strategies around the products that you build.

One of the keys to achieving the flow described here is predictability, and the way to achieve predictability is making uniform and repeatable use of your resources. As you learned earlier, cloud data centers such as Amazon Web Services or Google Cloud Platform provide us with a virtually unlimited pool of resources that can be used to build our systems in a traditional way:

- Define the size of the VMs
- Provision VMs
- Install the software
- Maintain it

Or, if we want to draw a diagram so we can understand it better, it would be similar to the next one:

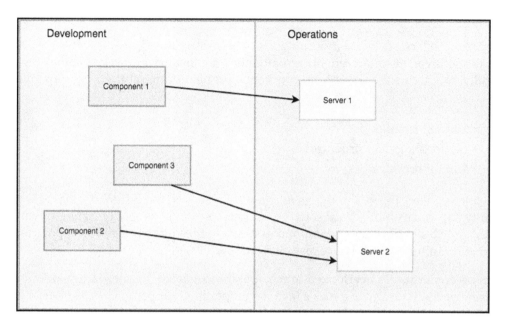

Here are a few considerations:

- Clear separation between Development and Operations (this may vary depending on the size of your company
- Software components owned by Development and deployments and configuration owned by Operations
- Some servers might be relatively underutilized (**Server 1**) and on a very low load

This has been the picture for 40 odd years of software development, and it is still the picture if we are running Docker containers, but there are few problems in it:

- If a problem arises in **Component 3** in production, who is responsible for it?
- If there is a configuration mismatch, who will fix it if developers are not supposed to see what is going on in production?

- **Server 1** is running a software component that might be called only once or twice a day (imagine an authentication server for workstations); do we need a full VM just for it?
- How do we scale our services in a transparent manner?

These questions can be answered, but usually, they get an answer too late in the game plus "the hidden requirements" are only seen once the problems arise at the worst possible time:

- Service discovery
- Load balancing
- Self-healing infrastructure
- Circuit breaking

During college years, one of the things in common across all the different subjects was reusability and extensibility. Your software should be extensible and reusable so that we can potentially build libraries of components creating the engineering sweet spot (not just software development): build once, use everywhere.

This has been completely overlooked in the operations part of the software development until recent years. If you get a job as a Java developer in a company, there is a set of accepted practices that every single Java developer in the world knows and makes use of so you can nearly hit the ground running without too many problems (in theory). Now let's raise a question: if all the Java apps follow the same practices and set of common patterns, why does every single company deploy them in a different way?

A continuous delivery pipeline has the same requirements in pretty much every company in the IT world, but I have seen at least three different ways of organizing it with a huge amount of custom magic happening that only one or two people within the company know of.

Clusters are here to save us. Let's reshuffle the image from before:

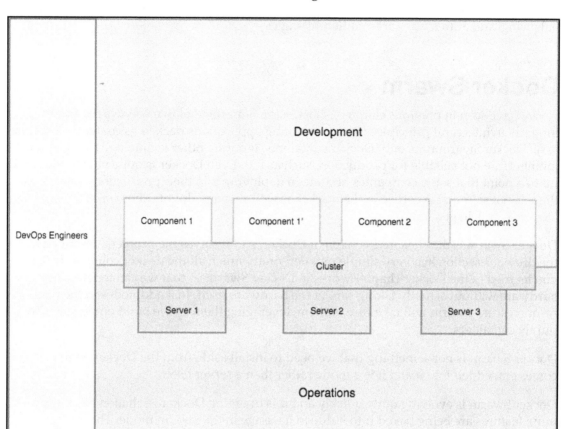

In this case, we have solved few of our problems:

- Now development and ops are connected via a middleware: the cluster.
- Components can be replicated (refer to component 1 and component 1') without provisioning extra hardware.
- DevOps engineers are the glue between the two teams (development and ops), making things happen at a fast pace.
- The stability of the full system does not depend on a single server (or component) as the cluster is built in a way that can accept some level of failure by just degrading performance or taking down the less critical services: it is okay to sacrifice e-mailing in order to keep the accounting processes of the company running.

And about the hidden requirements. Well, this is where we need to make a decision about which clustering technology we want to use as they approach the service discovery, load balancing, and auto-scaling from different angles.

Docker Swarm

As we have seen in previous chapters, Docker is a fantastic tool that follows the most modern architectural principles used for running applications packed as containers. In this case, Docker Swarm runs only Docker containers, ignoring other technologies that, at the moment, are not suitable for production, such as Rkt. Even Docker is quite new to the scene up to a point that some companies hesitate in deploying it in their production systems, as there is not so much expertise in the market as well as many doubts about security or how Docker works in general.

Docker Swarm is the clustered version of Docker, and it solves the problem described in the previous section in a very simple manner: pretty much all the docker commands that you learned in the Docker chapter works in Docker Swarm so that we can federate our hardware without actually taking care of the hardware itself. Just add nodes to the pool of resources and Swarm will take care of them, leveraging the way we build our systems to purely containers.

Docker Swarm is not something that we need to install aside from the Docker engine: it comes embedded into it and it is a mode rather than a server itself.

Docker Swarm is evolving quite quickly and it is dragging Docker itself along as more and more features are being baked into it due to its usage in the Swarm mode. The most interesting part of this is how we can leverage our Docker knowledge into it without any extra as the swarm mode of our Docker engine takes care of the resources.

This is also a problem: we are limited by the Docker API, whereas with Kubernetes (we will come back to it in a second), we are not only limited by the Docker API, but we can also extend the Kubernetes API to add new objects to fulfill our needs.

Docker Swarm can be operated through `docker-compose` (up to a certain extent), which provides a decent approach to infrastructure as code but is not very comprehensive when our application is somehow complex.

In the current IT market, Kubernetes seems to be the clear winner of the orchestration battle, and as such, we are going to focus on it, but if you want to learn more about Docker Swarm, the official documentation can be found at `https://docs.docker.com/engine/swarm/`.

Kubernetes

Kubernetes is the jewel of the crown of the containers orchestration. The product itself was vamped by Google leveraging years of knowledge on how to run containers in production. Initially, it was an internal system used to run Google services, but at some point, it became a public project. Nowadays, it is an open source project maintained by few companies (Red Hat, Google, and so on) and is used by thousands of companies.

At the time of writing this, the demand for Kubernetes engineers has skyrocketed up to a point that companies are willing to hire people without expertise in the field but with a good attitude to learn new technologies.

Kubernetes has become so popular due to, in my opinion, the following factors:

- It solves all the deployment problems
- It automates micro services' operations
- It provides a common language to connect ops and development with a clean interface
- Once it is setup, it is very easy to operate

Nowadays, one of the biggest problems in companies that want to shorten the delivery life cycle is the **red tape that has grown around the delivery process**. Quarter releases are not acceptable anymore in a market where a company of five skilled engineers can overtake a classic bank due to the fact that they can cut the red tape and streamline a delivery process that allows them to release multiple times a day.

One of my professional activities is to speak at conferences (meet-ups in Dublin, RebelCon in Cork, **Google Developer Groups** (**GDGs**) in multiple places, Google IO Extended) and I always use the same words in all the talks: release management should stop being a big bang event that stops the world for three hours in order to release a new version of your company's application and start being a painless process that can be rolled back at any time so that we remove the majority of the stress from it by providing the tools to manage a faulty release.

This (not just this, but mainly this) is Kubernetes: a set of tools and virtual objects that will provide the engineers with a framework that can be used to streamline all the operations around our apps:

- Scale up
- Scale down
- Zero downtime rollouts
- Canary deployments

- Rollbacks
- Secret management

Kubernetes is built in a technology-agnostic way. Docker is the main container engine, but all the components were designed with interchangeability in mind: once Rkt is ready, it will be easy to switch to Rkt from Docker, which gives an interesting perspective to the users as they don't get tied to a technology in particular so that avoiding vendor locking becomes easier. This applies to the software defined network and other Kubernetes components as well.

One of the pain points is the steep learning curve for setting it up as well as for using it.

Kubernetes is very complex, and being skilled in its API and operations can take any smart engineer a few weeks, if not months, but once you are proficient in it, the amount of time that you can save completely pays off all the time spent learning it.

On the same way, setting up a cluster is not easy up to a point that companies have started selling Kubernetes as a service: they care about maintaining the cluster and you care about using it.

One of the (once again, in my opinion) most advanced providers for Kubernetes is the **Google Container Engine** (GKE), and it is the one that we are going to use for the examples in this book.

When I was planning the contents of this chapter, I had to make a decision between two items:

- Setting up a cluster
- Showing how to build applications around Kubernetes

I was thinking about it for a few days but then I realized something: there is a lot of information and about half a dozen methods to set up a cluster and none of them are official. Some of them are supported by the official Kubernetes GitHub repository, but there is no (at the time of writing this) official and preferred way of setting up a Kubernetes instance either on premises or in the cloud, so the method chosen to explain how to deploy the cluster might be obsolete by the time this book hits the market. The following options are the most common ways of setting up a Kubernetes cluster currently:

- **Kops**: The name stands for Kubernetes operations and it is a command-line interface for operating clusters: creating, destroying, and scaling them with a few commands.

- **Kubeadm**: Kubeadm is alpha at the moment and breaking changes can be integrated at any time into the source code. It brings the installation of Kubernetes to the execution of a simple command in every node that we want to incorporate to the cluster in the same way as we would do if it was Docker Swarm.
- **Tectonic**: Tectonic is a product from CoreOS to install Kubernetes in a number of providers (AWS, Open Stack, Azure) pretty much painlessly. It is free for clusters up to nine nodes and I would highly recommend that, at the very least, you play around it to learn about the cluster topology itself.
- **Ansible**: Kubernetes' official repository also provides a set of playbooks to install a Kubernetes cluster on any VM provider as well as on bare metal.

All of these options are very valid to set up a cluster from scratch as they automate parts of Kubernetes architecture by hiding the details and the full picture. If you really want to learn about the internals of Kubernetes, I would recommend a guide written by Kelsey Hightower called Kubernetes the hard way, which basically shows you how to set up everything around Kubernetes, from the etcd cluster needed to share information across nodes to the certificates used to communicate with `kubectl`, the remote control for Kubernetes. This guide can be found at `https://github.com/kelseyhightower/ kubernetes-the-hard-way`.

And it is maintained and up to date with new versions of Kubernetes.

As you can guess from this explanation, in this chapter, you are going to learn about the architecture of Kubernetes, but mainly, we will focus on how to deploy and operate applications on Kubernetes so that by the end of this chapter, we have a good understanding of how we can benefit from an already running cluster.

Kubernetes logical architecture

The first problem that you will find once you start playing with Kubernetes is creating a mental map on how and where everything runs in Kubernetes as well as how everything is connected.

In this case, it took me few weeks to fully understand how it all was wiring up, but once I had the picture in my mind, I drew something similar to what is shown in the following diagram:

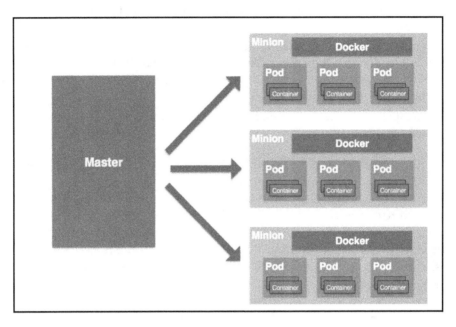

This is Kubernetes on a very high level: a master node that orchestrates the running of containers grouped in pods across different Nodes (they used to be called minions but not anymore).

This mental map helps us understand how everything is wired up and brings up a new concept: the pod. A pod is basically a set of one or more containers running in orchestration to achieve a single task. For example, think about a cache and a cache warmer: they can run in different containers but on the same pod so that the cache warmer can be packed as an individual application. We will come back to this later on.

With this picture, we are also able to identify different physical components:

- Master
- Nodes

The master is the node that runs all support services such as DNS (for service discovery) as well as the API server that allows us to operate the cluster. Ideally, your cluster should have more than one master, but in my opinion, being able to recover a master quickly is more important than having a high availability configuration. After all, if the master goes down, usually, it is possible to keep everything running until we recover the master that usually is as simple as spawning a new VM (on the cloud) with the same template as the old master was using.

 It is also possible to have a master running with the IP Tables blocking connections to key ports so that it does not join the cluster and remove the IP Tables rules once you want the master to become the lead of your cluster.

The nodes are basically workers: they follow instructions from the master in order to deploy and keep applications alive as per the specified configuration. They use a software called Kubelet, which is basically the Kubernetes agent that orchestrates the communication with the master.

Regarding the networking, there are two layers of network in here:

- Hardware network
- Software network

The hardware network is what we all know and that is used to interconnect the VMs on the cluster. It is defined in our cloud provider (AWS, Google Cloud Platform, and so on), and there is nothing special about it, just bear in mind that ideally, this network should be a high profile network (Gigabyte Ethernet) as the inter-node traffic can be quite high.

The software network (or **Software Defined Network**, **SDN**) is a network that runs on top of Kubernetes middleware and is shared between all the nodes via **etcd**, which is basically a distributed key value storage that is used by Kubernetes as a coordination point to share information about several components.

This SDN is used to interconnect the pods: the IPs are virtual IPs that do not really exist in the external network and only the nodes (and master) know about. They are used to rout the traffic across different nodes so that if an app on the node 1 needs to reach a pod living in the **Node 3**, with this network, the application will be able to reach it using the standard `http/tcp` stack. This network would look similar to what is shown in the following figure:

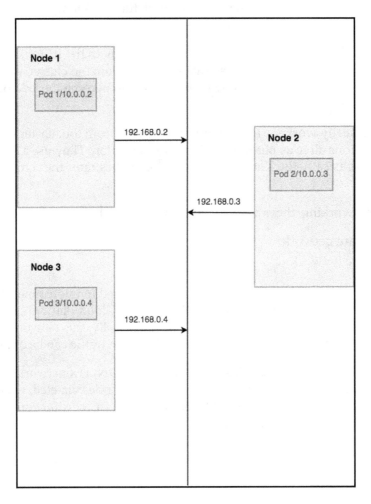

Let's explain this a bit:

- The addresses on the network 192.168.0.0/16 are the physical addresses. They are used to interconnect the VMs that compound the cluster.
- The addresses on the network 10.0.0.0/24 are the software defined network addresses. They are not reachable from outside the cluster and only the nodes are able to resolve these addresses and forward the traffic to the right target.

Networking is a fairly important topic in Kubernetes, and currently, the most common bottleneck in performance is that traffic forwarding is common across nodes (we will come back to this later on in this chapter), and this causes extra inter-node traffic that might cause a general slowdown of the applications running in Kubernetes.

In general and for now, this is all we need to know about the Kubernetes architecture. The main idea behind Kubernetes is to provide a uniform set of resources that can be used as a single computing unit with easy zero downtime operations. As of now, we really don't know how to use it, but the important thing is that we have a mental model of the big picture in a Kubernetes cluster.

Setting up a cluster in GCP

The first thing we need to start playing with in Kubernetes is a cluster. There are several options, but we are going to use GKE as we have already signed for the trial and there should be enough credit in there for going through the full book.

Another option if you did not sign for the trial on GCP is Minikube. Minikube is an out-of-the-box, easy-to-install local cluster that runs on VMs and is a very good tool for experimenting with new features without being afraid of breaking something.

The Minikube project can be found at `https://github.com/kubernetes/minikube`.

Its documentation is fairly comprehensive.

In order to create a cluster in GCP, the first thing we need to do is open the container engine in the online console in GCP that will show something similar to what is shown in the following screenshot:

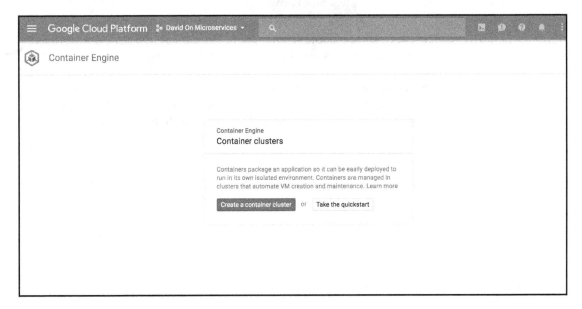

This means that you have no clusters at the moment. Click on the **Create a container cluster** button and fill in the following form:

Just a few considerations here:

- Give a comprehensive name to the cluster. In my case, I named it `testing-cluster`.
- Choose a zone that is close to you geographically, in my case, `europe-west1-c`.
- Regarding the cluster version, choose the default one. This is the version of Kubernetes that you want your cluster to run. It can be seamlessly upgraded later. Also, be aware that Kubernetes releases a new version every 2 months (apporximately), so by the time you are reading this book, it is most likely that there will be a more modern version available.
- The machine type should also be the standard one (1 vCPU 3.75 GB of RAM).

- Size is the number of machines that we want to use in our cluster. Three is a good number for testing and it can also be increased (or decreased later on).

Everything else should be default. Auto-upgrade and auto-repair are beta functionalities that I would hesitate to use in a production cluster yet. These two options allow GCP to take actions if there is a new version of Kubernetes available or one of the nodes breaks for some reason.

Once the form is completed click on **Create Cluster**, and that is everything. Now Google is provisioning a cluster for us. In order to check what is going on, open the tab of the Compute Engine in the GCP and you should see something similar to what is shown in the following screenshot:

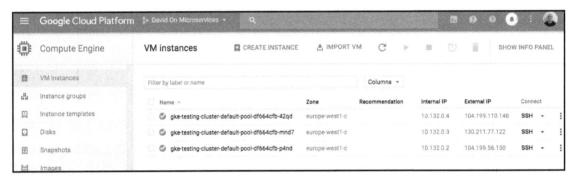

Three machines have been created in the compute engine with the prefix "gke-", which means that they belong to the GKE, **K** is for **Kubernetes**. They are regular machines, and there's nothing special about them aside from the fact that Google has provisioned all the software required to set up a Kubernetes Node, but where is the master?

Here is the interesting thing about running Kubernetes in Google Cloud Platform: they look after your master so there is no need to worry about the high availability or upgrading it as it is done automatically.

The master of our cluster is hosting one of the key components of our whole cluster: the API server. All the operations in Kubernetes are done via the API server with a component called `kubectl`. Kubectl stands for Kubernetes Control and is basically a terminal program that you can install on your local machine (or in a continuous integration server), add the configuration for a given cluster, and start issuing commands to our cluster.

First, we are going to install `kubectl`. In the previous chapters, we already installed the Google Cloud SDK (`gcloud` command), which can be used to install `kubectl` with the following command:

```
gcloud components install kubectl
```

And that's it. Now we can use `kubectl` in our system as if it was any other command, but we need to add our cluster configuration. As of now, `kubectl` is not configured to operate our cluster, so the first thing we need to do is fetch the required configuration. Google Cloud Platform makes it very easy. If you open the Google Container Engine tab, it now should look similar to the following one:

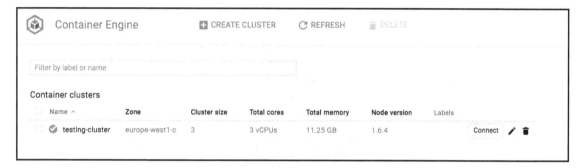

As you can see, there is a button called **Connect** on the right-hand side of the screen. By clicking on it, you will be presented with the following form:

The date in the form will be slightly different (as the name of your cluster and project will be different), but there are two commands presented in there:

- A `gcloud` command to get the configuration of our Kubernetes cluster in our local machine
- A `kubectl` command to start the proxy into the Kuberentes Dashboard UI

The first command is easy. Just execute it:

```
gcloud container clusters get-credentials testing-cluster --zone europe-west1-c --project david-on-microservices
```

And the output will be similar to the following one:

```
Fetching cluster endpoint and auth data.
kubeconfig entry generated for testing-cluster.
```

So, what happened here is that `gcloud` fetched the configuration and installed it locally for us to operate the cluster. You can try this by running the following command:

```
kubectl get nodes
```

This will output the list of nodes in your cluster. Kubectl is a very extensive command-line tool. With it, we can do pretty much anything inside the cluster, as we will learn in the rest of this chapter.

The second command in the preceding screenshot is used to start a proxy in Kubernetes:

```
kubectl proxy
```

This will output the following:

```
Starting to serve on 127.0.0.1:8001
```

Let's explain what happened here. Kubernetes makes heavy usage of client certificates. In order to communicate with the master, our machine needs to proxy the requests sending the certificate to validate them.

So, if we browse to the URL in the preceding screenshot now,
`http://localhost:8001/ui`, we get presented with the Kubernetes dashboard:

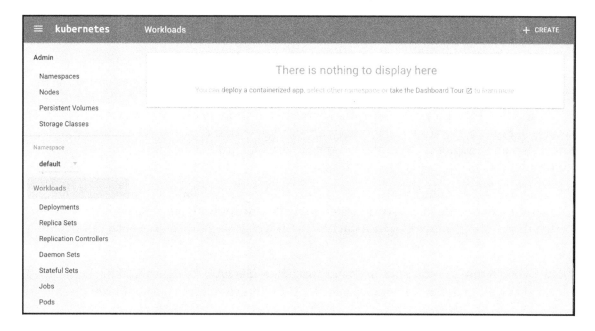

The dashboard is basically a nice way of presenting all the information of our running cluster to the end users. It is also possible to operate the cluster up to a certain extent from the dashboard, but my recommendation will be to master `kubectl` as it is way more powerful. On the dashboard, we can see a lot of information, such as the state of the nodes, the items deployed into the cluster (Pods, Replica Sets, Daemon Sets, and so on), and the namespaces as well as many other elements.

Explore around a bit and get yourself familiar with the dashboard as it is a nice tool to actually see things happening in your cluster.

Kubernetes divides the workloads into namespaces. A namespace is a virtual cluster that allows the engineers to segregate resources (up to a point) across different teams. It is also used by Kubernetes to run its own internal components. This is important because Kubernetes spreads the key components across different nodes to ensure high availability. In this case, we have three components that are running on every node:

- The Kubernetes dashboard
- Kubernetes proxy (`kube-proxy`)
- Kubernetes DNS (`kube-dns`)

The Kubernetes dashboard is what we just have seen: a user interface to represent the information within the Kubernetes cluster.

Kubernetes proxy is a proxy that the nodes use to resolve IP addresses in the SDN from Pods addresses to node addresses so that the cluster is able to redirect the traffic to the right Node.

The Kubernetes DNS is basically a load balancing and service discovery mechanism. In the next section, you will learn about the building blocks that we can use for deploying applications to Kubernetes. In particular, Services are strongly coupled with this DNS service in a way that in order to locate an application within Kubernetes, we just need to know its name and the configuration of the Service that groups the Pods compounding the given application.

The fact that we are running these components in every node enables Kubernetes to enter into an autopilot mode in case of a master going down: applications will continue working (in the majority of the cases) even without a master, so losing a master is not a catastrophic event.

Once we have configured `kubectl` in our machines, it is time to learn about the building blocks that we can use in Kubernetes in order to build extremely robust applications.

Kubernetes building blocks

In the preceding section, you learned about the cluster topology, but now we need the tools to run applications on it. We have already introduced one of the Kubernetes building blocks: the Pod. In this section, we are going to look at some of the most important API objects (building blocks) that Kubernetes provide in order to build our applications.

When I started learning Kubernetes, I was working in the second company that was deploying applications in a continuous delivery way, and I always had a question in mind: why are different companies trying to solve the same problem in different ways?

Then I realized why: The element missing was the domain-specific language for continuous delivery. The lack of a common standard and well understood way of rolling out applications was preventing them to work efficiently and deliver value early in the chain. Everybody knows what a load balancer is or a proxy or many other elements that are involved in the deployment of a new version of an app, but the way people uses the in, say, imaginative ways is where the problem lies. If you hire a new engineer, their previous knowledge of continuous delivery becomes obsolete as they need to learn your way of doing things.

Kubernetes solves this problem with a set of objects (Pods, ReplicaSets, DameonSets, and so on) that are described in YAML files (or JSON). Once we finish this section, we will already have enough knowledge to be able to, from the YAML or JSON files defining our resources, build a diagram about what the system looks like. These files, alongside the Docker images, are enough for Kubernetes to run our system, and we will look at a few examples.

Pods

Pods are the most basic element of the Kubernetes API. A Pod basically is a set of containers that work together in order to provide a service or part of it. The concept of Pod is something that can be misleading. The fact that we can run several containers working together suggests that we should be sticking the frontend and backend of our application on a single pod as they work together. Even though we can do this, it is a practice that I would strongly suggest you avoid. The reason for this is that by bundling together the frontend and the backend, we are losing a lot of flexibility that Kubernetes is providing us with, such as autoscaling, load balancing, or canary deployments.

In general, pods contain a single container and it is, by far, the most common use case, but there are few legitimate use cases for multi-container pods:

- Cache and cache warmer
- Precalculating and serving HTML pages
- File upload and file processing

As you can see, all of these are activities that are strongly coupled together, but if the feeling is that the containers within a pod are working toward different tasks (such as backend and frontend), it might be worth placing them in different Pods.

There are two options for communication between containers inside a pod:

- Filesystem
- Local network interface

As Pods are indivisible elements running on a single machine, volumes mounted in all the containers of a pod are shared: files created in a container within a pod can be accessed from other containers mounting the same volume.

The local network interface or loopback is what we commonly know as localhost. Containers inside a pod share the same network interface; therefore, they can communicate via localhost (or 127.0.0.1) on the exposed ports.

Deploying a pod

As mentioned earlier, Kubernetes relies heavily on **Yet Another Markup Language** (**YAML**) files to configure API elements. In order to deploy a pod, we need to create a yaml file, but first, just create a folder called **deployments**, where we are going to create all the descriptors that we will be created on this section. Create a file called `pod.yaml` (or `pod.yml`) with the following content:

```yaml
apiVersion: v1
kind: Pod
metadata:
  name: nginx
  labels:
    name: nginx
spec:
  containers:
  - name: nginx
    image: nginx
    ports:
     - containerPort: 80
    resources:
      requests:
        memory: "64Mi"
        cpu: "250m"
```

As you can see, the preceding `yaml` is fairly descriptive, but some points need clarification:

- `apiVersion`: This is the version of the Kubernetes API that we are going to use to define our resource (in this case, pod). Kuberentes is a living project that evolves very quickly. The version is the mechanism used to avoid deprecating resources with new releases. In general, Kuberentes works with three branches: alpha, beta, and stable. In the preceding case, we are using the stable version. More information can be found at `https://kubernetes.io/docs/concepts/overview/kubernetes-api/`.
- `metadata`: In this section, we are defining one of the most powerful discovery mechanisms that I have ever seen: the pattern matching. The section label, specifically, will be used later on to expose pods with certain labels to the outer world.

- `spec`: This is where we define our container. In this case, we are deploying an `nginx` instance so that we can easily see how everything works without focusing too much on the application itself. As expected, the image and the exposed port have been specified. We have also defined the CPU and memory limitations for this Pod, so we prevent an outbreak in resource consumption (note that the YAML file is requesting the resources; they might not be available so the pod will operate with lower profile resources).

This is the simplest configuration for an item that we can create in Kubernetes. Now it's time to deploy the resource in our cluster:

```
kubectl apply -f pod.yml
```

This will produce an output similar to the following one:

```
pod "nginx" created.
```

Disclaimer: there are several ways of creating a resource, but in this book, I will use `apply` as much as possible. Another possibility would be to use `create`:

```
kubectl create -f pod.yml
```

The advantage that `apply` has over create is that apply does a three-way diff between the previous version, the current version, and the changes that you want to apply and decides how is best to update the resource. This is letting Kubernetes do what it does best: automate container orchestration.

With create, Kubernetes does not save the state of the resource, and if we want to run apply afterward in order to gracefully change the state of a resource, a warning is produced:

```
Warning: kubectl apply should be used on resource created by either kubectl
create --save-config or kubectl apply
pod "nginx" configured
```

This means that we can push our system to an unstable state for few seconds, which might not be acceptable depending on your use case.

Once we have applied our YAML file, we can use `kubectl` to see what is going on in Kubernetes. Execute the following command:

```
kubectl get pods
```

This will output our pod:

We can do this for other elements of our cluster, such as the nodes:

```
kubectl get nodes
```

And this will output the following:

NAME	STATUS	AGE	VERSION
gke-testing-cluster-default-pool-df664cfb-42qd	Ready	5d	v1.6.4
gke-testing-cluster-default-pool-df664cfb-mnd7	Ready	5d	v1.6.4
gke-testing-cluster-default-pool-df664cfb-p4nd	Ready	5d	v1.6.4

The `kubectl get` works for all the workflows in Kubernetes and the majority of the API objects.

Another way of seeing what is going on in Kubernetes is using the dashboard. Now that we have created a pod, open the dashboard at `http://localhost:8001/ui` and navigate to the pods section on the left-hand side.

Remember that in order to access the dashboard, first, you need to execute `kubectl proxy` on a Terminal.

There; you will see the list of the current deployed pods, in this case, just **nginx**. Click on it and the screen should look very similar to what is shown here:

Here, we get a ton of information, from the memory and CPU that the pod is consuming to the node where it is running and a few other valuable items, such as the annotations applied to the pod. We can get this using the 'describe' command of kubectl, as follows:

```
kubectl describe pod nginx
```

Annotations are a new concept and are the data around our API element, in this case, our pod. If you click on L**ast applied configuration** in the Details section, you can see the data from the YAML file, as shown in the following screenshot:

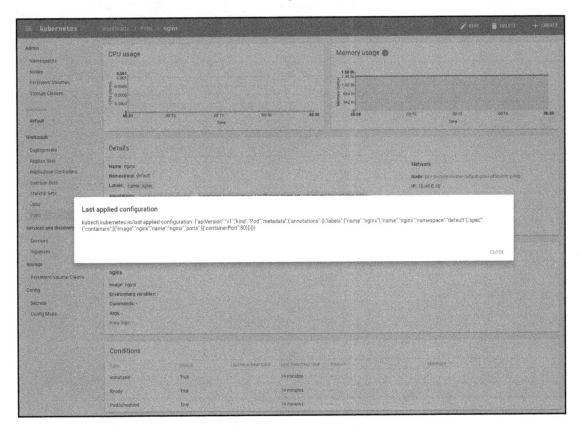

And this relates to the three-way diff that was explained earlier and is used by Kubernetes to decide the best way of upgrading a resource without getting into an inconsistent state.

As of now, our pod is running in Kubernetes but is not connected to the outer world; therefore, there is no way to open a browser and navigate to the **nginx** home page from outside the cluster. One thing that we can do is open a remote session to a bash Terminal in the container inside the pod in a manner similar to what we would do with Docker:

```
kubectl exec -it nginx bash
```

And we are in. Effectively, we have gained access to a root terminal inside our container and we can execute any command. We will use this functionality later on.

Once we have seen how pods work, you might have a few questions abound what Kubernetes is supposed to do:

- How can we scale pods?
- How can we roll out new versions of an application?
- How can we access our application?

We will answer all these questions, but first, we need to know other 'building blocks'.

Replica Sets

So far, we know how to deploy applications in pods. The sole concept of pod is very powerful, but it lacks robustness. It is actually impossible to define scaling policies or even make sure that the pods remain alive if something happens (such as a node going down). This might be okay in some situations, but here is an interesting question. If we are biting the bullet on the overhead of maintaining a Kubernetes cluster, why don't we take the benefits of it?

In order to do that, we need to work with **Replica Sets**. A Replica Set is like a traffic cop in a road full of pods: they make sure that the traffic flows and everything works without crashing and moving the pods around so that we make the best use of the road (our cluster, in this case).

Replica Sets are actually an update of a much older item: the Replication Controller. The reason for the upgrade is the labeling and selecting of resources, which we will see visit when we dive deep into the API item called Service.

Let's take a look at a Replica Set:

```
apiVersion: extensions/v1beta1
kind: ReplicaSet
metadata:
   name: nginx-rs
spec:
   replicas: 3
   template:
      metadata:
         labels:
            app: nginx
            tier: frontend
      spec:
         containers:
         - name: nginx
            image: nginx
```

```
    resources:
        requests:
            cpu: 256m
            memory: 100Mi
    ports:
    - containerPort: 80
```

Again, this a YAML file that is basically fairly easy to understand but might require some explanation:

- In this case, we have used the extensions API on the version `v1beta1`. If you remember from the pod section (previously), Kubernetes has three branches: stable, alpha, and beta. The complete reference can be found in the official documentation, and it is very likely to change often as Kubernetes is a vibrant and always evolving project.
- In the spec section is where the important things happen: we have defined a set of labels for the Replica Set, but we have also defined a pod (in this case, with a single container) and specified that we want three instances of it (replicas: three).

Simple and effective. Now we have defined a resource called Replica Set, which allows us to deploy a pod and keep it alive as per configuration.

Let's test it:

```
kubectl apply -f replicaset.yml
```

Once the command returns, we should see the following message:

```
replicaset "nginx-rs" created
```

Let's verify it using `kubectl`:

```
kubectl get replicaset nginx-rs
```

As the output of the preceding command, you should see the Replica Set explaining that there are three desired pods, three actually deployed, and three ready. Note the difference between current and ready: a pod might be deployed but still not ready to process requests.

We have specified that our `replicaset` should keep three pods alive. Let's verify this:

```
kubectl get pods
```

No surprises here: our `replicaset` has created three pods, as shown in the following screenshot:

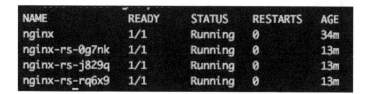

We have four pods:

- One created in the preceding section
- Three created by the Replica Set

Let's kill one of the pods and see what happens:

```
kubectl delete pod nginx-rs-0g7nk
```

And now, query how many pods are running:

NAME	READY	STATUS	RESTARTS	AGE
nginx	1/1	Running	0	36m
nginx-rs-j829q	1/1	Running	0	15m
nginx-rs-rq6x9	1/1	Running	0	15m
nginx-rs-s93s4	1/1	Running	0	35s

Bingo! Our `replicaset` has created a new pod (you can see which one in the AGE column). This is immensely powerful. We have gone from a world where a pod (an application) being killed wakes you up at 4 a.m. in the morning to take action to a world where when one of our application dies, Kubernetes revives it for us.

Let's take a look at what happened in the dashboard:

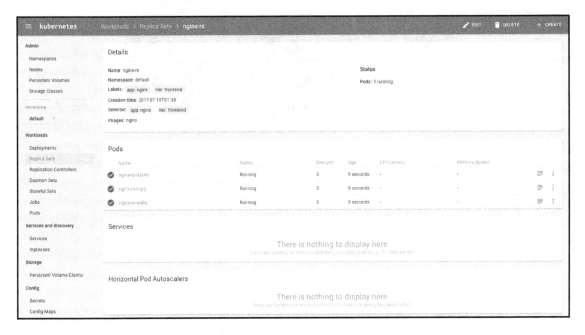

As you can expect, the Replica Set has created the pods for you. You can try to kill them from the interface as well (the period icon to the very right of every pod will allow you to do that), but the Replica Set will re-spawn them for you.

Now we are going to do something that might look like it's from out of this world: we are going to scale our application with a single command, but first, edit `replicaset.yml` and change the `replicas` field from three to five.

Save the file and execute this:

```
kubectl apply -f replicaset.yml
```

Now take a look at the dashboard again:

As you can see, Kubernetes is creating pods for us following the instructions of the Replica Set, `nginx-rs`. In the preceding sreenshot, we can see one pod whose icon is not green, and that is because its status is **Pending**, but after a few seconds, the status becomes **Ready**, just like any other pod.

This is also very powerful, but there is a catch: who scales the application if the load spike happens at 4 a.m. in the morning? Well, Kubernetes provides a solution for this: **Horizontal Pod Autoscalers**.

Let's execute the following command:

```
kubectl autoscale replicaset nginx-rs --max=10
```

With the preceding command, we have specified that Kubernetes should attach a **Horizontal Pod Autoscalers** to our Replica Set. If you browse the Replica Set in the dashboard again, the situation has changed dramatically:

Let's explain what happened here:

- We have attached an **Horizontal Pod Autoscalers** to our Replica Set: minimum 1 pod, maximum 10, and the trigger for creating or destroying pods is the CPU utilization going over 80% on a given pod.
- The Replica Set has scaled down to one pod because there is no load on the system, but it will scale back to up to 10 nodes if required and stay there for as long as the burst of requests is going on and scale back to the minimum required resources.

Now this is actually the dream of any sysadmin: no-hassle autoscaling and self-healing infrastructure. As you can see, Kubernetes starts making sense altogether, but there is one thing disturbing in the autoscaler part. It was a command that we ran in the terminal, but it is captured nowhere. So how can we keep track of our infrastructure (yes, an Horizontal Pod Autoscaler is part of the infrastructure)?

Well, there is an alternative; we can create a YAML file that describes our Horizontal Pod Autoscaler:

```
apiVersion: autoscaling/v1
kind: HorizontalPodAutoscaler
metadata:
    name: nginx-hpa
spec:
    maxReplicas: 10
    minReplicas: 1
    scaleTargetRef:
        kind: ReplicaSet
        name: nginx-rs
    targetCPUUtilizationPercentage: 80
```

First, from the dashboard, remove `HorizontalPodAutoscaler` created from the previous example. Then, write the preceding content into a file called `horizontalpodautoscaler.yml` and run the following command:

```
kubectl apply -f horizontalpodautoscaler.yml
```

This should have the same effect as the `autoscale` command but with two obvious benefits:

- We can control more parameters, such as the name of the HPA, or add metadata to it, such as labels
- We keep our infrastructure as code within reach so we know what is going on

The second point is extremely important: we are in the age of the infrastructure as code and Kubernetes leverages this powerful concept in order to provide traceability and readability. Later on, in Chapter 8, *Release Management – Continuous Delivery*, you will learn how to create a continuous delivery pipeline with Kubernetes in a very easy way that works on 90% of the software projects.

Once the preceding command returns, we can check on the dashboard and see that effectively, our Replica Set has attached an Horizontal Pod Autoscaler as per our configuration.

Deployments

Even though the Replica Set is a very powerful concept, there is one part of it that we have not talked about: what happens when we apply a new configuration to a Replica Set in order to upgrade our applications? How does it handle the fact that we want to keep our application alive 100% of the time without service interruption?

Well, the answer is simple: it doesn't. If you apply a new configuration to a Replica Set with a new version of the image, the Replica Set will destroy all the Pods and create newer ones without any guaranteed order or control. In order to ensure that our application is always up with a guaranteed minimum amount of resources (Pods), we need to use Deployments.

First, take a look at what a deployment looks like:

```
apiVersion: apps/v1beta1
kind: Deployment
metadata:
  name: nginx-deployment
spec:
  strategy:
    type: RollingUpdate
    rollingUpdate:
      maxUnavailable: 0
      maxSurge: 1
  replicas: 3
  template:
    metadata:
      labels:
        app: nginx
    spec:
      containers:
      - name: nginx
        image: nginx
        resources:
          requests:
            cpu: 256m
            memory: 100Mi
        ports:
        - containerPort: 80
```

As you can see, it is very similar to a Replica Set, but there is a new section: strategy. In strategy, we are defining how our `rollout` is going to work, and we have two options:

- RollingUpdate
- Recreate

`RollingUpdate` is the default option as it seems the most versatile in modern 24/7 applications: It coordinates two replica sets and starts shutting down pods from the old replica set at the same time that it is creating them in the new Replica Set. This is very powerful because it ensures that our application always stays up. Kubernetes decides what is best to coordinate the pods' rescheduling, but you can influence this decision with two parameters:

- `maxUnavailable`
- `maxSurge`

The first one defines how many pods we can loose from our Replica Set in order to perform a `rollout`. As an example, if our Replica Set has three replicas, a `rollout` with the `maxUnavailable` value of 1 will allow Kubernetes to transition to the new Replica Set with only two pods in the status `Ready` at some point. In this example, `maxUnavailable` is 0; therefore, Kubernetes will always keep three pods alive.

`MaxSurge` is similar to maxUnavailable, but it goes the other way around: it defines how many pods above the replicas can be scheduled by Kubernetes. In the preceding example, with three replicas with `maxSurge` set on 1, the maximum amount of pods at a given time in our `rollout` will be 4.

Playing with these two parameters as well as the replicas' number, we can achieve quite interesting effects. For example, by specifying three replicas with `maxSurge 1` and `maxUnavailable 1`, we are forcing Kubernetes to move the pods one by one in a very conservative way: we might have four pods during the `rollout`, but we will never go below three available pods.

Coming back to the strategies, Recreate basically destroys all the pods and creates them again with the new configuration without taking uptime into account. This might be indicated in some scenarios, but I would strongly suggest that you use `RollingUpdate` when possible (pretty much always) as it leads to smoother deployments.

It is also possible to attach a Horizontal Pod Autoscaler to a Deployment in the same way that we would do with a Replica Set.

Let's test our deployment. Create a file called `deployment.yml` and apply it to our cluster:

```
kubectl apply -f deployment.yml --record
```

Once the command returns, we can go to the Kubernetes dashboard (`localhost:8001/ui` with the proxy active) and check what happened in the **Deployments** section in the menu on the left-hand side:

We have a new **Deployment** called `nginx-deployment`, which has created a Replica Set that also contains the specified pods. In the preceding command, we have passed a new parameter: `--record`. This saves the command in the `rollout` history of our deployment so that we can query the `rollout` history of a given deployment to see the changes applied to it. In this case, just execute the following:

```
kubectl rollout history deployment/nginx-deployment
```

This will show you all the actions that altered the status of a deployment called `nginx-deployment`. Now, let's execute some change:

```
kubectl set image deployment/nginx-deployment nginx=nginx:1.9.1
```

We have used `kubectl` to change the version of the `nginx` container back to version 1.9.1 (`kubectl` is very versatile; the official documentation offers shortcuts for pretty much everything), and a few things happened. The first one is that a new Replica Set has been created and the pods have been moved over to it from the old replica set. We can verify this in the **Replica Sets** section of the menu on the left-hand side of the dashboard:

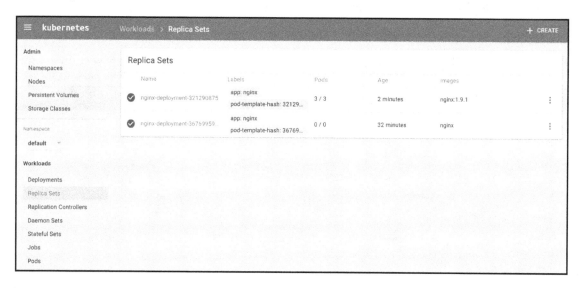

As you can see, the old replica set has 0 pods, whereas the new one that took over has three pods. This all happened without you noticing it, but it is a very clever workflow with a lot of work from the Kubernetes community and the companies behind it.

The second thing that happened was that we have a new entry in our rollout history. Let's check it out:

```
kubectl rollout history deployment/nginx-deployment
```

Which one should produce an output similar to the following one:

```
deployments "nginx-deployment"
REVISION        CHANGE-CAUSE
1               kubectl apply --filename=deployment.yml --record=true
2               kubectl set image deployment/nginx-deployment nginx=nginx:1.9.1
```

Now we have two entries that describe the changes applied to our deployment.

If you have been into IT for few years, by now, you have reached the conclusion that a rollback strategy is always necessary because bugs flowing into production are the reality no matter how good our QA is. I am a big fan of building the systems in a way that deployments are unimportant events (from a technical point of view), as shown with Kuberentes, and the engineers always have an easy way out if things start to fail in production. Deployments offer an easy rollback if something goes wrong:

```
kubectl rollout undo deployment/nginx-deployment
```

Execute the preceding and browse back to the dashboard on the **Replica Sets** section again:

That's right. In a matter of seconds, we have gone from instability (a broken build) to the safety of the old known version without interrupting the service and without involving half of the IT department: a simple command brings back the stability to the system. The rollback command has a few configurations, and we can even select the revision where we want to jump to.

This is how powerful Kubernetes is and this is how simple our life becomes by using Kubernetes as the middleware of our enterprise: a modern CD pipeline assembled in a few lines of configuration that works in the same way in all the companies in the world by facilitating command `rollouts` and rollbacks. That's it...simple and efficient.

Right now, it feels like we know enough to move our applications to Kubernetes, but there is one thing missing. So far, up until now, we have just run predefined containers that are not exposed to the outer world. In short, there is no way to reach our application from outside the cluster. You are going to learn how to do that in the next section.

Services

Up until now, we were able to deploy containers into Kubernetes and keep them alive by making use of pods, Replica Sets, and Horizontal Pods Autoscalers as well as Deployments, but so far, you have not learned how to expose applications to the outer world or make use of service discovery and balancing within Kubernetes.

Services are responsible for all of the above. A Service in Kubernetes is not an element as we are used to it. A Service is an abstract concept used to give entity to a group of pods through pattern matching and expose them to different channels via the same interface: a set of labels attached to a Pod that get matched against a selector (another set of labels and rules) in order to group them.

First, let's create a service on top of the deployment created in the previous section:

```
kind: Service
apiVersion: v1
metadata:
    name: nginx-service
spec:
    selector:
        app: nginx
    ports:
        - protocol: TCP
          port: 80
          targetPort: 80
```

Easy and straightforward, but there's one detail: the selector section has a hidden message for us. The selectors are the mechanisms that Kubernetes uses to connect components via pattern matching algorithms. Let's explain what pattern matching is. In the preceding Service, we are specifying that we want to select all the Pods that have a label with the `app` key and the `nginx` value. If you go back to the previous section, you'll understand our deployment has these labels in the pod specification. This is a match; therefore, our service will select these pods. We can check this by browsing in the dashboard in the **Services** section and clicking on `nginx-service`, but first, you need to create the `service`:

```
kubectl apply -f service.yml
```

Then, check out the dashboard:

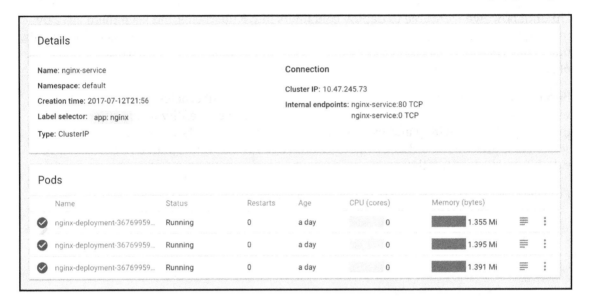

As you can see, there are three pods selected, and they all belong to the deployment `nginx` that we created in the preceding section.

 Don't remove the deployment from the previous section; otherwise, there will be no pods to select by our service.

This screen has a lot of interesting information. The first piece of information is that the service has an IP: this IP is denominated as `clusterIP`. Basically, it is an IP within the cluster that can be reached by our pods and other elements in Kubernetes. There is also a field called `Type`, which allows us to chose the service type. There are three types:

- `ClusterIP`
- `NodePort`
- `LoadBalancer`

`ClusterIP` is what we just created and explained.

`NodePort` is another type of service that is rarely used in Cloud but is very common on premises. It allocates a port on all the nodes to expose our application. This allows Kubernetes to define the ingress of the traffic into our pods. This is challenging for two reasons:

- It generates extra traffic in our internal network as the nodes need to forward the traffic across to reach the pods (imagine a cluster of 100 nodes that has an app with only three pods, it is very unlikely to hit the node that is running one of them).
- The ports are allocated randomly so you need to query the Kubernetes API to know the allocated port.

`LoadBalancer` is the jewel in the crown here. When you create a service of type `LoadBalancer`, a cloud load balancer is provisioned so that the client applications hit the load balancer that redirects the traffic into the correct nodes. As you can imagine, for a cloud environment where infrastructure is created and destroyed in matter of seconds, this is the ideal situation.

Coming back to the previous screenshot, we can see another piece of interesting information: the internal endpoints. This is the service discovery mechanism that Kubernetes is using to locate our applications. What we have done here is connect the pods of our application to a name: `nginx-service`. From now on, no matter what happens, the only thing that our apps need to know in order to reach our `nginx` pods is that there is a service called `nginx` that knows how to locate them.

In order to test this, we are going to run an instance of a container called `busybox`, which is basically the Swiss army knife of command-line tools. Run the following command:

```
kubectl run -i --tty busybox --image=busybox --restart=Never -- sh
```

The preceding command will present us with a shell inside the container called `busybox` running in a pod so we are inside the Kubernetes cluster and, more importantly, inside the network so that we can see what is going on. Be aware that the preceding command runs just a pod: no deployment or replica set is created, so once you exit the shell, the pod is finalized and resources are destroyed.

Once we get the prompt inside `busybox`, run the following command:

```
nslookup nginx-service
```

This should return something similar to the following:

```
Server: 10.47.240.10
Address 1: 10.47.240.10 kube-dns.kube-system.svc.cluster.local

Name: nginx-service
Address 1: 10.47.245.73 nginx-service.default.svc.cluster.local
```

Okay, what happened here? When we created a service, we assigned a name to it: `nginx-service`. This name has been used to register it in an internal DNS for service discovery. As mentioned earlier, the DNS service is running on Kubernetes and is reachable from all the Pods so that it is a centralised repository of common knowledge. There is another way that the Kubernetes engineers have created in order to carry on with the service discovery: the environment variables. In the same prompt, run the following command:

```
env
```

This command outputs all the environment variables, but there are few that are relevant to our recently defined service:

```
NGINX_SERVICE_PORT_80_TCP_ADDR=10.47.245.73
NGINX_SERVICE_PORT_80_TCP_PORT=80
NGINX_SERVICE_PORT_80_TCP_PROTO=tcp
NGINX_SERVICE_SERVICE_PORT=80
NGINX_SERVICE_PORT=tcp://10.47.245.73:80
NGINX_SERVICE_PORT_80_TCP=tcp://10.47.245.73:80
NGINX_SERVICE_SERVICE_HOST=10.47.245.73
```

These variables, injected by Kubernetes at creation time, define where the applications can find our service. There is one problem with this approach: the environment variables are injected at creation time, so if our service changes during the life cycle of our pods, these variables become obsolete and the pod has to be restarted in order to inject the new values.

All this magic happens through the selector mechanism on Kubernetes. In this case, we have used the equal selector: a label must match in order for a pod (or an object in general) to be selected. There are quite a few options, and at the time of writing this, this is still evolving. If you want to learn more about selectors, here is the official documentation: `https://kubernetes.io/docs/concepts/overview/working-with-objects/labels/`.

As you can see, services are used in Kubernetes to glue our applications together. Connecting applications with services allows us to build systems based on microservices by coupling REST endpoints in the API with the name of the service that we want to reach on the DNS.

Up until now, you have learned how to expose our applications to the rest of our cluster, but how do we expose our applications to the outer world? You have also learned that there is a type of service that can be used for this: `LoadBalancer`. Let's take a look at the following definition:

```
kind: Service
apiVersion: v1
metadata:
    name: nginx-service
spec:
    type: LoadBalancer
    selector:
        app: nginx
 ports:
  - protocol: TCP
        port: 80
        targetPort: 80
```

There is one change in the preceding definition: the service type is now `LoadBalancer`. The best way to explain what this causes is by going to the **Services** section of the dashboard:

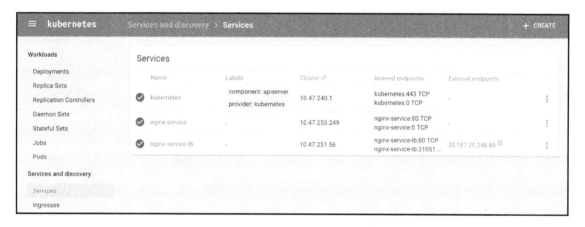

As you can see, our newly created service got assigned an external endpoint. If you browse it, bingo! The `nginx` default page is rendered.

We have created two services, `nginx-service` and `nginx-service-lb`, of the type `ClusterIP` and `LoadBalancer`, respectively, which both point to the same pods that belong to a deployment and are managed through a replica set. This can be a bit confusing, but the following diagram will explain it better:

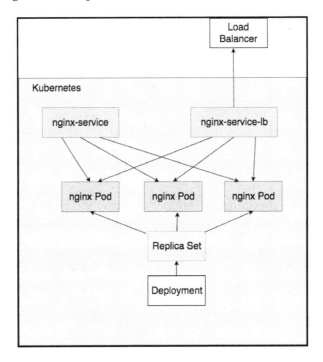

The preceding diagram is the perfect explanation of what we've built in this section. As you can see, the load balancer is outside of Kubernetes, but everything else is inside our cluster as virtual elements of an API.

Other Building Blocks

In the previous sections, you learned the basics needed to deploy applications into Kubernetes successfully. The API objects that we visited are as follows:

- Pod
- ReplicaSet
- Deployment
- Service

In Kubernetes, there are many other building blocks that can be used to build more advanced applications; every few months, the Kubernetes engineers add new elements to improve or add functionality.

One example of these additions is the ReplicaSet that was designed to replace another item called ReplicationController. The main difference between the ReplicationController and the ReplicaSet is that the latter one has a more advance semantics label selection for the Pods that were recently re-engineered in Kubernetes.

As a new product, Kuberentes is constantly changing (in fact, it is possible that by the time that you read this book, the core elements might have changed), so the engineers try to keep the compatibility across different versions so that people are not urged to upgrade in a short period of time.

Other examples of more advanced building blocks are the following:

- DaemonSet
- PetSets
- Jobs and CronJobs
- CronJobs

In order to go in deep to the full stack in Kubernetes, we would need a full book (or more!). Let's visit some of them.

Daemon Sets

Daemon Sets are an API element used to **ensure that a Pod is running in all (or some) nodes**. One of the assumptions in Kubernetes is that the pod should not worry about which node is being run, but that said, there might be a situation where we want to ensure that we run at least one pod on each node for a number of reasons:

- Collect logs
- Check the hardware
- Monitoring

In order to do that, Kubernetes provides an API element called Daemon Set. Through a combination of labels and selectors, we can define something called **affinity**, which can be used to run our pods on certain nodes (we might have specific hardware requirements that only a few nodes are able to provide so that we can use tags and selectors to provide a hint to the pods to relocate to certain nodes).

Daemon Sets have several ways to be contacted, from the DNS through a headless service (a service that works as a load balancer instead of having a cluster IP assigned) to the node IP, but Daemon Sets work best when they are the initiators of the communication: something happens (an event) and a Daemon Set sends an event with information about that event (for example, a node is running low on space).

PetSets

PetSets are an interesting concept within Kubernetes: they are strong named resources whose naming is supposed to stay the same for a long term. As of now, a pod does not have a strong entity within a Kubernetes cluster: you need to create a service in order to locate a pod as they are ephemeral. Kubernetes can reschedule them at any time without prior notice for changing their name, as we have seen before. If you have a deployment running in Kubernetes and kill one of the pods, its name changes from (for example) *pod-xyz* to *pod-abc* in an unpredictable way. so we cannot know which names to use in our application to connect to them beforehand.

When working with a Pet Set, this changes completely. A pet set has an ordinal order, so it is easy to guess the name of the pod. Let's say that we have deployed a Pet Set called mysql, which defines pods running a MySQL server. If we have three replicas, the naming will be as follows:

- `mysql-0`
- `mysql-1`
- `mysql-2`

So, we can bake this knowledge in our application to reach them. This is suboptimal but good enough: we are still coupling services by name (DNS service discovery has this limitation), but it works in all cases and is a sacrifice that is worth paying for because in return, we get a lot of flexibility. The ideal situation in service discovery is where our system does not need to know even the name of the application carrying the work: just throw the message into the ether (the network) and the appropriated server will pick it up and respond accordingly.

Pet Sets have been replaced in later versions of Kubernetes with another item called **Stateful Set.** The Stateful Set is an improvement over the Pet Set mainly in how Kubernetes manages the **master knowledge to avoid a split brain situation**: where two different elements think that they are in control.

Jobs

A **Job** in Kubernetes is basically an element that spawns the defined number of pods and waits for them to finish before completing its life cycle. It is very useful when there is a need to run a one-off task, such as rotating logs or migrating data across databases.

Cron jobs have the same concept as Jobs, but they get triggered by time instead of a one-off process.

Both in combination are very powerful tools to keep any system running. If you think about how we rotate logs without Kubernetes via ssh, it is quite risky: there is no control (by default) over who is doing what, and usually, there is no review process in the ssh operations carried by an individual.

With this approach, it is possible to create a Job and get other engineers to review it before running it for extra safety.

Secrets and configuration management

On Docker in general, as of today, secrets are being passed into containers via environment variables. This is very insecure: first, there is no control over who can access what, and second, environment variables are not designed to act as secrets and a good amount of commercial software (and open source) outputs them into the standard output as part of bootstrapping. Needless to say, that's rather inconvenient.

Kubernetes has solved this problem quite gracefully: instead of passing an environment variable to our container, a volume is mounted with the secret on a file (or several) ready to be consumed.

By default, Kubernetes injects a few secrets related to the cluster into our containers so that they can interact with the API and so on, but it is also possible to create your own secrets.

There are two ways to create secrets:

- Using `kubectl`
- Defining an API element of type secret and using `kubectl` to deploy it

The first way is fairly straightforward. Create a folder called *secrets* in your current work folder and execute the following commands inside it:

```
echo -n "This is a secret" > ./secret1.txt
echo -n "This is another secret" > ./secret2.txt
```

This creates two files with two strings (simple strings as of now). Now it is time to create the secret in Kubernetes using `kubectl`:

```
kubectl create secret generic my-secrets --from-file=./secret1.txt --from-
file=./secret2.txt
```

And that's it. Once we are done, we can query the secrets using `kubectl`:

```
kubectl get secrets
```

This, in my case, returns two secrets:

- A service account token injected by the cluster
- My newly created secret (`my-secrets`)

The second way of creating a secret is by defining it in a `yaml` file and deploying it via `kubectl`. Take a look at the following definition:

```
apiVersion: v1
kind: Secret
metadata:
    name: my-secret-yaml
type: Opaque
data:
    secret1: VGhpcyBpcyBhIHNlY3JldA==
    secret2: VGhpcyBpcyBhbm90aGVyIHNlY3JldA==
```

First, the values for `secret1` and `secret2`, seem to be encrypted, but they are not; they are just encoded in `base64`:

```
echo -n "This is a secret" | base64
echo -n "This is another secret" | base64
```

This will return the values that you can see here. The type of the secret is Opaque, which is the default type of secret, and the rest seems fairly straightforward. Now create the secret with kubectl (save the preceding content in a file called `secret.yml`):

```
kubectl create -f secret.yml
```

And that's it. If you query the secrets again, note that there should be a new one called `my-secret-yaml`. It is also possible to list and see the secrets in the dashboard on the **Secrets** link in the menu on left-hand side.

Now it is time to use them. In order to use the secret, two things need to be done:

- Claim the secret as a volume
- Mount the volume from the secret

Let's take a look at a `Pod` using a secret:

```
{
    "apiVersion": "v1",
    "kind": "Pod",
    "metadata": {
        "name": "test-secrets",
        "namespace": "default"
    },
    "spec": {
        "containers": [{
            "name": "pod-with-secret",
            "image": "nginx",
            "volumeMounts": [{
                "name": "secrets",
                "mountPath": "/secrets",
                "readOnly": true
            }]
        }],
        "volumes": [{
            "name": "secrets",
            "secret": {
                "secretName": "my-secret"
            }
        }]
    }
}
```

So, you have learned a new thing here: `kubectl` also understands JSON. If you don't like YAML, it is possible to write your definitions in JSON without any side-effects.

Now, looking at the JSON file, we can see how first, the secret is declared as a volume and then how the secret is mounted in the path/secrets.

If you want to verify this, just run a command in your container to check it:

```
kubectl exec -it test-secrets ls /secrets
```

This should list the two files that we have created, `secret1.txt` and `secret2.txt`, containing the data that we have also specified.

Kubernetes- moving on

In this chapter, you learned enough to run simple applications in Kubernetes, but even though we cannot claim ourselves to be experts, we got the head start in becoming experts. Kubernetes is a project that evolves at the speed of light, and the best thing that you can do to keep yourself updated is follow the project on GitHub at `https://github.com/kubernetes`.

The Kubernetes community is very responsive with issues raised by the users and are also very keen on getting people to contribute to the source code and documentation.

If you keep working with Kubernetes, some help will be required. The official documentation is quite complete, and even though it feels like it needs a reshuffle sometimes, it is usually enough to keep you going.

The best way that I've found to learn Kubernetes is by experimenting in Minikube (or a test cluster) before jumping into a bigger commitment.

Summary

In this chapter, we looked at a good amount of concepts required to deploy an application on Kubernetes. As mentioned earlier, it is impossible to cover everything abound Kubernetes in a single chapter, but with the amount of knowledge from this chapter, we are going to be able to set up a continuous delivery pipeline in the following chapter in a way that we automate zero downtime deployments without the big bang effect (the big deployment that stops the world), enabling our organization to move faster.

8
Release Management – Continuous Delivery

Release management has been always the boring part of software development. It is the discussion where people from different teams (operations, management, development, and so on) put all the details together to plan how to deploy a new version of one of the apps from the company (or various others).

This is usually a big event that happens at 4 a.m. in the morning, and it is a binary event: we either succeed in releasing the new version or we fail and have to roll back.

Stress and tension are the common denominators in these type of deployments, and above everything else, we are playing against the statistics.

In this chapter, you are going to learn how to create a continuous delivery pipeline and deploy a microservices-based system to update it, keeping all the lights on.

We will specifically cover the following topics:

- Playing against the statistics
- The test system
- Setting up a continuous delivery pipeline for images
- Setting up Jenkins
- Continuous delivery for your application

Playing against the statistics

We have spoken several times about the Big Bang event that a deployment is. This is something thatI always try to avoid when I set up a new system: releases should be smooth events that can be done at any time without effort and you should be able to roll back within minutes with little to no effort.

This might be a gigantic task, but once you provide a solid foundation to your engineers, marvelous things happen: they start being more efficient. If you provide a solid base that will give them confidence that within a few clicks (or commands) that they can return the system to a stable state, you will have removed a big part of the complexity of any software system.

Let's talk about statistics. When we are creating a deployment plan, we are creating a system configured in series: it is a finite list of steps that will result in our system being updated:

- Copy a JAR file into a server
- Stop the old Spring Boot app
- Copy the properties files
- Start the new Spring Boot app

If any of the steps fail, the whole system fails. This is what we call a series system: the failure of any of the components (steps) compromises the full system. Let's assume that every step has a 1% failure ratio. 1% seems quite an acceptable number...until we connect them in a series. From the preceding example, let's assume that we have a deployment with 10 steps. These steps have a 1% of failure rate which is equals to99% of success rate or 0.99 reliability. Connecting them in a series means that the whole reliability of our system can be expressed as follows:

```
(0.99)^10 = 0.9043
```

This means that our system has a 90.43 percent success rate or, in other words, 9.57 percent failure rate. Things have changed dramatically: nearly 1 in every 10 deployments is going to fail, which, by any means, is quite far from the 1 percent of the individual steps that we quoted earlier.

Nearly 10 percent is quite a lot for depending on the systems, and it might be a risk that we are not willing to take, so why don't we work to reduce this risk to an acceptable level? Why don't we shift this risk to a previous step that does not compromise production and we reduce our deployment to a simple switch (on/off) that we can disconnect at any time?

These are two concepts called canary and blue green deployments, and we are going to study how to use them in Kubernetes so that we reduce the risk of our deployments failing, as well as the stress of the **big bang event** that a deployment means in traditional software development.

The test system

In order to articulate a continuous delivery pipeline, we need a system to play with, and after some talks and demos, I have developed one that I tend to use, as it has pretty much no business logic and leaves a lot of space to think about the underlying infrastructure.

I call the system **Chronos**, and as you can guess, its purpose is related to the management of time zones and formats of dates. The system is very simple:

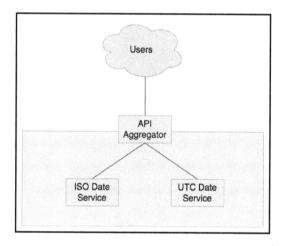

We have three services:

- An API aggregator

- A service that translates a timestamp into a date in ISO format

- A service that translates a timestamp into a date in UTC format

These services work in coordination to translate a timestamp into a date in different formats, but it is also open to extensions as we can aggregate more services to add more capabilities and expose them through the API Aggregator.

Every service will be packed into a different Docker image, deployed as a Deployment in Kubernetes and exposed via Services (externals and internals) to the cluster and to the outer world in the case of the API Aggregator.

ISO date and UTC date services

The ISO date service simply takes a timestamp and returns the equivalent date using the ISO format. Let's take a look at its code:

```
const Hapi = require('hapi')
const server = new Hapi.Server()
const moment = require('moment')

server.connection({port: 3000})

server.route({
  method: 'GET',
  path: '/isodate/{timestamp}',
  handler: (request, reply) => {
    reply({date: moment.unix(request.params.timestamp).toISOString()})
  }
})

server.start((err) => {
  if (err) {
    throw err
  }
  console.log('isodate-service started on port 3000')
})
```

This service itself is very simple: it uses a library called moment and a framework called **hapi** to provide the ISO Date equivalent to a timestamp passed as a URL parameter. The language used to write the service is Node.js, but you don't need to be an expert in the language; you should just be able to read JavaScript. As with every Node.js application, it comes with a `package.json` that is used to describe the project and its dependencies:

```
{
  "name": "isodate-service",
  "version": "1.0.0",
  "description": "ISO Date Service",
  "main": "index.js",
  "scripts": {
    "start": "node index.js"
  },
  "author": "David Gonzalez",
```

```
    "license": "ISC",
    "dependencies": {
      "hapi": "^15.2.0",
      "moment": "^2.15.1"
    }
}
```

Some fields of the `package.json` are customized, but the important parts are the dependencies and the scripts sections.

Now, one important file is left; the Dockerfile:

```
FROM node:latest

RUN mkdir /app/
WORKDIR /app/

COPY . /app/
RUN npm install
EXPOSE 3000

CMD ["npm", "start"]
```

In order to test our service, let's build the Docker image:

docker build . -t iso-date-service

After a few seconds (or a bit more), our image is ready to use. Just run it:

docker run -it -p 3000:3000 iso-date-service

And that's it. In order to test it, use curl to get some results:

curl http://localhost:3000/isodate/1491231233

This will return a JSON with the ISO Date representation of the timestamp passed as a URL parameter, as you can see in your terminal.

The UTC date service is very much the same but with different code and a different interface:

```
const Hapi = require('hapi')
const server = new Hapi.Server()
const moment = require('moment')
server.connection({port: 3001})

server.route({
  method: 'GET',
```

```
    path: '/utcdate/{timestamp}',
    handler:  (request, reply) => {
      let date =
moment.unix(request.params.timestamp).utc().toISOString().substring(0, 19)
      reply({date: date})
    }
})

server.start((err) => {
  if (err) {
    throw err
  }
  console.log('isodate-service started on port 3001')
})
```

As you can see, there are some changes:

- The port is 3001
- The date returned is the UTC date (which is basicallythe ISO Date without timezone information)

We also have a Dockerfile, which is the same as for the ISO Date service, and a package.json, which is as follows:

```
{
  "name": "utcdate-service",
  "version": "1.0.0",
  "description": "UTC Date Service",
  "main": "index.js",
  "scripts": {
    "start": "node index.js"
  },
  "author": "David Gonzalez",
  "license": "ISC",
  "dependencies": {
    "hapi": "^15.2.0",
    "moment": "^2.15.1"
  }
}
```

These are minor changes (just the description and name). In total, you should have these files in the UTC date service:

- Dockerfile (the same as ISO Date Service)
- index.js with the code from earlier
- package.json

If you want to make your life easier, just clone the repository at `git@github.com:dgonzalez/chronos.git` so that you have all the code ready to be executed.

Now in order to test that everything is correct, build the Docker image:

```
docker build . -t utc-date-service
```

And then run it:

```
docker run -it -p 3001:3001 utc-date-service
```

Once it is started, we should have our service listening on port `3001`. You can check this by executing curl, as follows:

```
curl http://localhost:3001/utcdate/853123135
```

This, in a manner similar to ISO Date Service, should return a JSON with the date but in a UTC format in this case.

Aggregator service

The `aggregator` service is the microservice that, as the name indicates, aggregates the other two (or more) services and provides a front API for consumers so that all the logic behind the scenes gets encapsulated. Even though it is not perfect, this is a common pattern because it allows us to play with the idea of circuit breaking as well as manage the errors on a dedicated layer.

In our case, the service is quite simple. First, let's take a look at the code:

```
const Hapi = require('hapi')
const server = new Hapi.Server()
let request = require('request')

server.connection({port: 8080})

server.route({
  method: 'GET',
  path: '/dates/{timestamp}',
  handler:  (req, reply) => {
    const utcEndpoint =
`http://utcdate-service:3001/utcdate/${req.params.timestamp}`
    const isoEndpoint =
`http://isodate-service:3000/isodate/${req.params.timestamp}`
```

```
      request(utcEndpoint, (err, response, utcBody) => {
        if (err) {
          console.log(err)
          return
        }
        request(isoEndpoint, (err, response, isoBody) => {
          if (err) {
            console.log(err)
            return
          }
          reply({
            utcDate: JSON.parse(utcBody).date,
            isoDate: JSON.parse(isoBody).date
          })
        })
      })
    }
  })

  server.start((err) => {
    if (err) {
      throw err
    }
    console.log('aggregator started on port 8080')
  })
```

In order to simplify the understanding of the code, we did not use promises or async/await in it at the cost of having a nested `callback` (which is quite simple to read).

Here are a few points to note from the preceding code:

- We are calling the services by name (`utcdate-service` and `isodate-service`), leveraging the communication to the Kubernetes DNS
- Before returning, `aggregator` service issues a call to the two services and returns a JSON object with the aggregated information

In order to test this service, we would need to create DNS entries (or host entries) pointing to `isodate-service` and `utcdate-service`, which is harder than testing it in Kubernetes, so we will skip the testing for now.

As with any node application, the `aggregator` service needs a `package.json` to install the dependencies and control a few aspects:

```
{
    "name": "aggregator",
    "version": "1.0.0",
    "description": "Aggregator service",
    "main": "index.js",
    "scripts": {
        "start": "node index.js"
    },
    "author": "David Gonzalez",
    "license": "ISC",
    "dependencies": {
        "hapi": "^15.2.0",
        "request": "^2.75.0"
    }
}
```

The `package.json` is very important. The scripts block particularly instruct us on what to do when the `npm start` command is executed by the Docker container based on the image defined in the Dockerfile:

```
FROM node:latest

RUN mkdir /app/
WORKDIR /app/

COPY . /app/
RUN npm install
EXPOSE 3000

CMD ["npm", "start"]
```

By now, you should have three files:

- `index.js`
- `Dockerfile`
- `package.json`

Build the `docker` container with the following command:

```
docker build . -t aggregator
```

Check whether it works as expected:

```
docker run -it -p 8080:8080 aggregator
```

Even though the server won't be able to resolve requests because it does not know how to communicate with `isodate-service` and `utcdate-service`, it should start.

Pushing the images to Google Container Registry

So as of now, we have three images in our local repository:

- `iso-date-service`
- `utc-date-service`
- `aggregator`

These three images live in your computer but unfortunately, our Kubernetes cluster in the GKE won't be able to reach them. The solution for this problem is to push these images into a Docker registry that will be reachable by our cluster. Google Cloud provides us with a Docker registry, which is extremely convenient for using with GKE due to several reasons:

- **Data containment**: The data never leaves the Google network
- **Integration**: Services in GCP can interact with implicit authentication
- **Automation**: This integrates with GitHub and other services so that we can build our images, automatically creating a pipeline of continuous delivery of images.

Before setting up a continuous delivery pipeline with Git, we are going to push the images manually in order to understand how it works. **Google Container Registry (GCR)** is replicated across the globe, so the first thing that you need to do is choose where you want to store your images:

- `us.gcr.io` hosts your images in the United States
- `eu.gcr.io` hosts your images in the European Union
- `asia.gcr.io` hosts your images in Asia

In my case, `eu.gcr.io` is the perfect match. Then, we need our project ID. This can be found by clicking on the project name in the top bar of the console:

In my case, the project ID is `implementing-modern-devops`. Now, the third component is the name of the image that we already have. With these three components, we can build the name for our Docker images URL:

- `eu.gcr.io/isodate-service:1.0`
- `eu.gcr.io/utcdate-service:1.0`
- `eu.gcr.io/aggregator:1.0`

The 1.0 part is the version of our image. If not specified, the default is latest but we are going to version the images for traceability.

Now it is time to tag our images as appropriate. First up is the ISO Date service:

```
docker tag iso-date-service eu.gcr.io/implementing-modern-devops/isodate-
service:1.0
```

Then, there's the UTC date service:

```
docker tag utc-date-service eu.gcr.io/implementing-modern-devops/utcdate-
service:1.0
```

And finally, we have the `aggregator` service:

```
docker tag aggregator eu.gcr.io/implementing-modern-devops/aggregator-
service:1.0
```

This is the mechanism that Docker uses to identify where to push the images: Docker reads the name of our image and identifies the URL to which the image is to be pushed. In this case, as we are using a private registry (Google Container Registry is private), we need to use credentials, but using the `gcloud` command, it becomes quite easy:

```
gcloud docker -- push eu.gcr.io/implementing-modern-devops/aggregator-
service:1.0
```

Now it's time for the `isodate-service`:

```
gcloud docker -- push eu.gcr.io/implementing-modern-devops/isodate-
service:1.0
```

And finally, there's `utcdate-service`:

```
gcloud docker -- push eu.gcr.io/implementing-modern-devops/utcdate-
service:1.0
```

 Be careful; the project ID will change, so customize the command to fit your configuration.

After a bit of time (it can take up to a few minutes to push the three images to GCR), the images should be up in our private instance of the Google Container Registry.

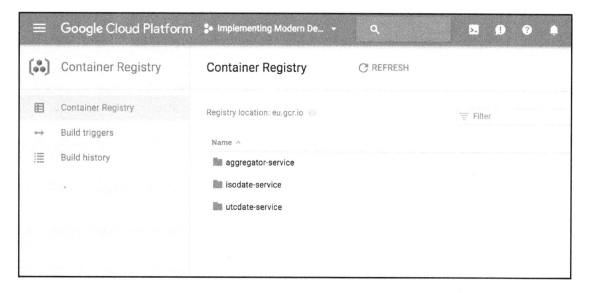

Let's recap what we have done:

- We've built the images locally
- We've tagged the images with the appropriated name so that we can push them to GCR
- We've pushed the images to GCR using `gcloud`

This is fairly straightforward, but it can be tricky if you have not done it before. All our images are sitting in our private container registry, ready to be used.

Setting up a continuous delivery pipeline for images

Now that we have deployed our images to GCR, we need to automate the process so that we minimize the manual intervention. In order to do that, we are going to use the Build Triggers section of our Google Container Registry. In this case, we are going to use GitHub as it is the industry standard for Git repositories management. Create an account at `https://www.github.com` (if you don't have one already) and then create three repositories:

- `aggregator`
- `isodate-service`
- `utcdate-service`

These can be public but, in the future, if you are working with private code, you should either create private repositories (which you need to pay for) or select a different provider, such as the source code repositories in Google Cloud Platform.

The first thing that we need to do is push the code for the three services into the repositories. Github will give you the instructions to that, but basically, the process is as follows:

1. Clone the repository
2. Add the code from the preceding section as appropriate
3. Push the code into the remote repository

My GitHub username is `dgonzalez` and the commands to push the code for the `aggregator` are as follows:

```
git clone git@github.com:dgonzalez/aggregator.git
```

Now copy the code from the `aggregator` into the newly created folder with the `clone` command and execute (inside the `aggregator` folder):

```
git add .
```

Commit the changes:

```
git commit -m 'Initial commit'
```

And then `push` them to the remote repository:

```
git push origin master
```

After these commands, your repository should look like what is shown in the following screenshot:

The commands that we used are quite basic Git commands. You probably know about Git, but if you don't, I would recommend that you follow some tutorials, such as `https://try.github.io/levels/1/challenges/1`.

Now that we have our repository ready, it is time to go back to GCP to set up the **Build triggers** for our pipeline. The first thing that we need to do is go to the triggers section of the Container Registry in Google Cloud Platform:

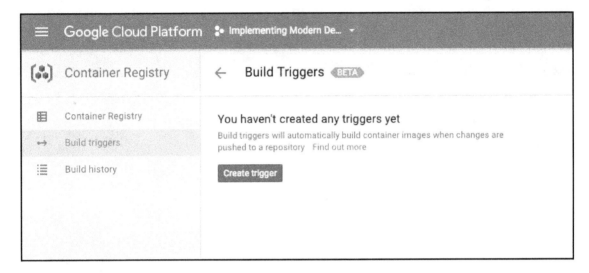

This functionality allows us to create triggers that fire off the build of our images based on events. There are several approaches to triggering strategies. In this case, we are going to build the image based on the creation of new tags. The most common way of doing this is by monitoring changes in the master branch, but I am a big fan of versioning. Think about this: containers are immutable artifacts: Once created, they should not be altered, but what if there is an issue with the code inside the container? The strategy is to branch off from the master and then create what is called a hot-fix build. With tagging, we can do this too but by branching from a tag instead of from the master, which has the following benefits:

- The master can change without firing events
- Tags cannot be accidentally created (so no accidental releases)
- Version is kept in the source code manager instead of in the code
- You can correlate a tag to a build the artifact

That said, it is perfectly valid to use the master as a reference point and other combinations: the important lesson here is to stick to a procedure and make it clear to everyone.

Click on **Create Trigger** and select GitHub. Once you click on **Next**, it will let you select the project from a list; then, click on **Next**again. Now we get presented with a form and a few options:

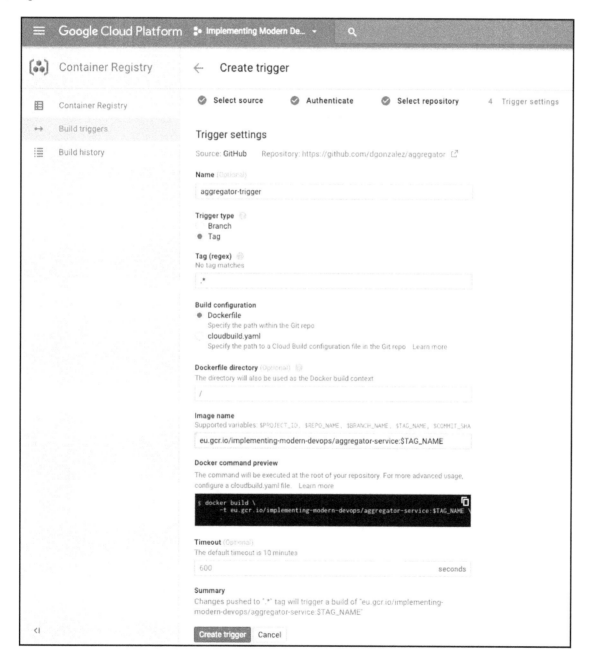

We are going to use the Dockerfile instead of `cloudbuild.yaml` (the latter is GCP-specific) and set the trigger on the tag; the image name has to match the repositories created in the preceding section (remember the `eu.*` name and check the name of the repository as well).

Once created, nothing happens. Our repository has no tags, so nothing has been built. Let's create a tag:

```
git tag -a 1.0 -m "my first tag"
```

This will create a tag, and now we need to push it to the server:

```
git push origin 1.0
```

Now, we go back to GCP Container Registry and check what happened: a new build has been triggered, pushing version 1.0 to the registry for the `aggregator` image:

From now on, if we create a new tag in our repository, GCP is going to build an image for us, which can be correlated to a commit in GitHub so that we can fully trace what is in every environment of our build. It does not get better than this.

This whole build and push could have been done with Jenkins, as you learned in the chapter 4 (continous integration), but I am of the opinion that if someone can take care of your problems for a reasonable price, it'sbetter than solving them yourself and add more moving parts to your already complex system. In this case, the registry, the build pipeline, and the automation are taken care of by Google Cloud Platform.

Setting up Jenkins

In the preceding section, we leveraged the image operations to Google Cloud Platform, but now, we need to manage Kubernetes in a CI/CD fashion from somewhere. In this case, we are going to use Jenkins for this purpose. We have several options here:

- Deploy Jenkins in Kubernetes
- Install Jenkins in baremetal
- Install Jenkins in a container outside of Kubernetes

Lately, Jenkins has become Kubernetes-friendly with a plugin that allows Jenkins to spawn slaves when required in a containerized fashion so that it leverages the provisioning and destruction of hardwareto Kubernetes. This is a more than interesting approach when your cluster is big enough (50+ machines), but when your cluster is small, it may be problematic as it can lead into a noisy neighborhood.

I am a big fan of segregation: CI/CD should be able to talk to your production infrastructure but should not be running in the same hardware for two reasons:

- Resource consumption
- Vulnerabilities

Think about it: a CI/CD software is, by default, vulnerable to attackers as it needs to execute commands through an interface; therefore, you are giving access to the underlying infrastructure to a potential attacker.

My advice: start simple. If the company is small, I would go for Jenkins in a container with a volume mounted and evolve the infrastructure up to a point where your cluster is big enough to accommodate Jenkins without a significant impact; move it into your cluster in a dedicated namespace.

In the chapter 4 (Continuous Integration), we set up Jenkins in a container without making use of any volume, which can be problematic as the configuration might be lost across restarts. Now, we are going to set up Jenkins in bare metal so that we have another way of managing Jenkins.

The first thing that we need to do is create a machine in GCP.

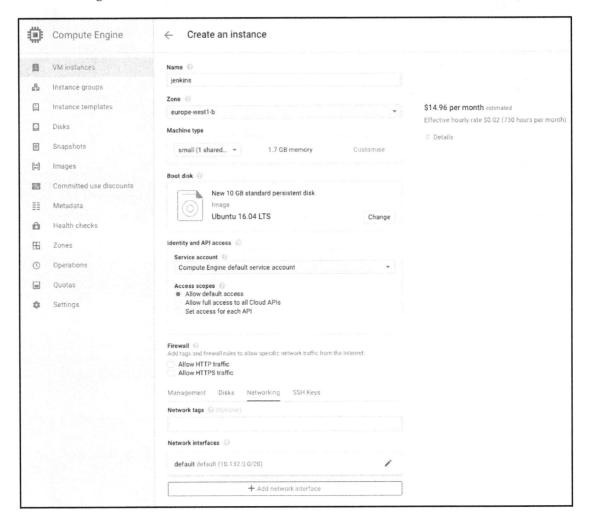

The preceding screenshot is the configuration of my Jenkins machine. A few important aspects are as follows:

- Ubuntu instead of Debian (I selected the latest LTS version of Ubuntu)
- Small instance (we can scale that later on)
- Changes might need to be done to the firewall in order to access Jenkins

Everything else is standard. We are not attaching a static IP to Jenkins as this is just a demo, but you probably want to do that, as you learned earlier, as well as have an entry in the DNS that can have a static reference point for your CI server.

It also would be a good exercise to do this in Terraform as well so that you can manage your infrastructure in an **Infrastructure as code**(**IaC**) fashion.

Once the machine has spun up, it is time to install Jenkins. We are going to follow the official guide, which can be found at`https://wiki.jenkins.io/display/JENKINS/Installing+Jenkins+on+Ubuntu`.

Using the web SSH Terminal from the Google Cloud platform, open a shell to your newly created machine and execute the following commands:

```
wget -q -O - https://pkg.jenkins.io/debian/jenkins-ci.org.key | sudo apt-
key add -
```

Then, add the Jenkins repository:

```
sudo sh -c 'echo deb http://pkg.jenkins.io/debian-stable binary/ >
/etc/apt/sources.list.d/jenkins.list'
```

Then, update the list of packages:

```
sudo apt-get update
```

And finally, install Jenkins:

```
sudo apt-get install jenkins
```

That's it. Once the preceding command is finished, Jenkins should be installed and can be started, stopped, and restarted as a service. To ensure that it is running, execute the following command:

```
sudo service jenkins restart
```

Now if we browse the public IP in our server on port 8080, we get the initial screen for Jenkins.

> You might need to tweak the firewall to allow access to port 8080 on this machine.

This initial screen is familiar, and we need to get the password to initialize Jenkins. This password is in the logs:

```
cat /var/log/jenkins/jenkins.log
```

Enter the password and initialize Jenkins (suggested plugins). This might take a while; meanwhile, we also need to set up the Gcloud SDK. First, switch to the user Jenkins:

```
sudo su jenkins
```

And then just execute the following:

```
curl https://sdk.cloud.google.com | bash
```

Once the installation finishes. you need to open a new shell for the changes to take effect. Do that and install kubectl:

```
gcloud components install kubectl
```

Now that we have theKubectl binary in our system, we need to connect it to a cluster, but first, it's time to create a cluster. As you learned in previous chapters, just create a cluster with three machines of a small size. Once it is created, connect to the cluster from the Jenkins machine, as shown in the previous chapter, but first, run gcloud init to configure a new auth session (option 2) with your account.

Once you are done, make sure that kubectl can talk to your cluster by executing a test command, as follows:

```
kubectl get nodes
```

You should list the three nodes that compound your cluster. Now we need to make kubectl accessible to the user jenkins. Just run the following command:

```
ln -s /root/google-cloud-sdk/bin/kubectl /usr/bin/kubectl
```

Change the owner to Jenkins:

Now, going back to Jenkins, set up the admin user as shown in the following screenshot:

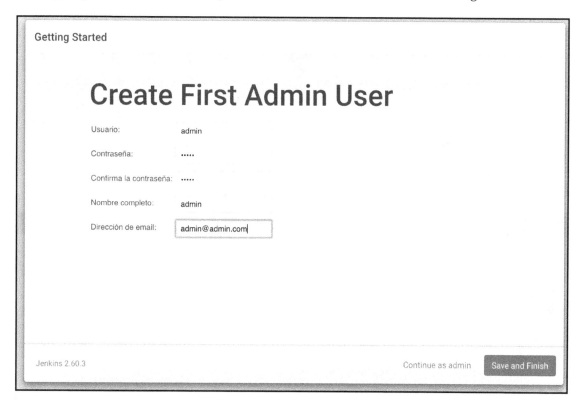

Click on **Save and Finish**, and it's done.

Before we start creating jobs, we need to make the binary kubectl available to the user `jenkins`. Login as root and execute:

```
ln -s /var/lib/jenkins/google-cloud-sdk/bin/kubectl /usr/bin/kubectl
```

This will make sure that the `kubectl` command for `jenkins`points to the SDK installed by the `jenkins` user in the preceding steps.

Now, we have everything:

- Jenkins
- The Google Cloud SDK
- A GKE cluster
- A connection between Jenkins and GKE

Before proceeding, we are going to make sure that everything works as expected. Go to Jenkins and create a new free style project and add a build step with the following command:

```
kubectl get nodes
```

Save the project and run it. The output should be very similar to what is shown in the following screenshot:

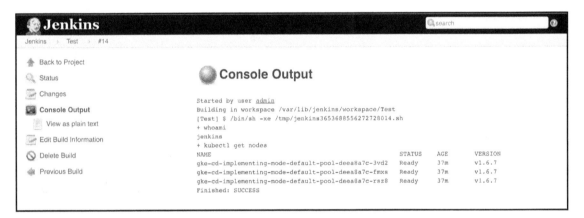

This indicates that we are good to go.

In general, Jenkins and other CI systems should never be exposed over the internet. Never. It only takes a weak password for someone to destroy your system if it is accessible to the public. In this case, as an illustrative example, we have not configured the firewall, but in your company, you should allow access onlyfrom the IP of your office.

Continuous delivery for your application

Up until now, we have set up a few elements:

- A GitHub repository with our code (`aggregator`)
- A continuous delivery pipeline in GCP for our Docker image that gets fired once we tag the code
- A Kubernetes cluster
- Jenkins connected to the preceding cluster

Now we are going to set up the continuous delivery pipeline for our code and the Kubernetes infrastructure. This pipeline is going to be actioned by a Jenkins job, which we will trigger manually.

You might be thinking that all that you have read about **Continuous Delivery** (**CD**)is about transparently shipping code to production without any human intervention, but here we are, with a few events that need manual steps in order to action the build. I have worked in some places where continuous delivery is triggered automatically by changes in the master branch of your repository, and after few incidents, I really believe that a manual trigger is a fair price to pay for having an enormous amount of control over the deployments.

For example, when publishing the image, by creating a tag manually in order to build our image, we are adding a barrier so that no one accidentally commits code to master and publishes a version that might be unstable or, even worse, insecure. Now we are going to do something similar, but the job that releases our code is going to be actioned manually in Jenkins, so by controlling the access to Jenkins, we have an audit trail of who did what, plus we get role-based access control for free. We can assign roles to the people of our team, preventing the most inexperienced developers from creating a mess without supervision but still allowing enough agility to release code in an automated fashion.

The first thing that we need to do is create a repository that we are going to call `aggregator-kubernetes` in GitHub to host all our YAML files with the Kubernetes resources. We will do this for `utcdate-service` and `isodate-service`, but let's do the `aggregator` first.

Once we have created our repository, we need to create our Kubernetes objects to deploy and expose the service. In short, our system is going to look like what is shown in the following diagram:

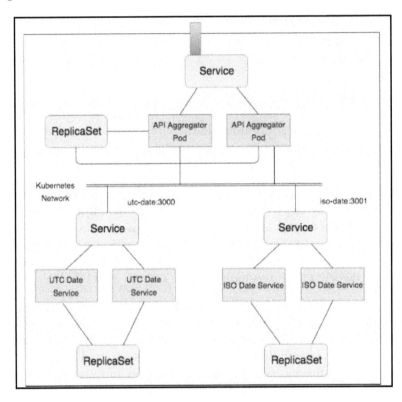

On the above picture, we can see the Kubernetes objects (*ReplicaSet* and *Service*) that we need to create for each application (deployments are omitted). In red, we can see the application itself. For now, we are focusing on the `aggregator`, so we need to create a `ReplicaSet` that is going to be managed by a Deployment and a Service of the`LoadBalancer` that is going to expose our API to the rest of the world through a `gcloud`load balancer.

The first element that we need is our deployment:

```
apiVersion: extensions/v1beta1
kind: Deployment
metadata:
  name: aggregator
spec:
  replicas: 2
  template:
    metadata:
      labels:
        app: aggregator-service
    spec:
      containers:
      - name: aggregator-service
        image: eu.gcr.io/implementing-modern-devops/aggregator-service:1.0
        ports:
        - containerPort: 8080
```

This is nothing that we wouldn't expect. It's a simple deployment object with the image that our automatic build process has created for us (remember, we created a tag with the version 1.0...also remember to customize it to your project). In our new repository, `aggregator-kubernetes`, save this file under a folder called objects with the name `deployment.yaml`. Now it is time to create the service that is going to expose our application:

```
kind: Service
apiVersion: v1
metadata:
  name: aggregator-service
spec:
  ports:
    - port: 80
      targetPort: 8080
  selector:
    app: aggregator-service
  type: LoadBalancer
```

Again, it's very straightforward: a service that exposes anything tagged with app: `aggregator-service` to the outside world via a load balancer in Google cloud. Save it inside the objects folder with the name `service.yaml`. Now it is time to commit the changes and push them to your GitHub repository:

```
git add .
```

And then, execute this:

```
git commit -m 'Initial commit'
```

And finally, look at this:

```
git push origin master
```

By now, you have all the code for the infrastructure of the `aggregator` sitting in your GitHub repository with a layout similar to the following:

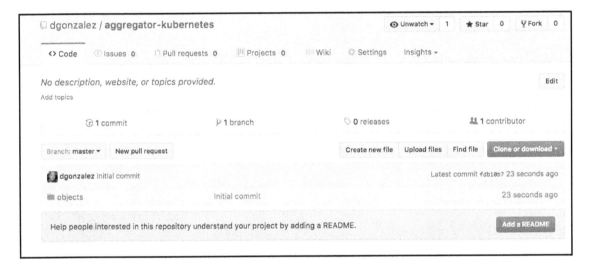

Inside the objects folder, you can find the two YAML files: `deployment.yaml` and `service.yaml`. We can run these files locally with `kubectl` (connecting them to the cluster first) in order to verify that they are working as expected (and I recommend that you do this).

Now it is time to set up a Jenkins job to articulate our build. Create a new freestyle project in Jenkins with the following configuration:

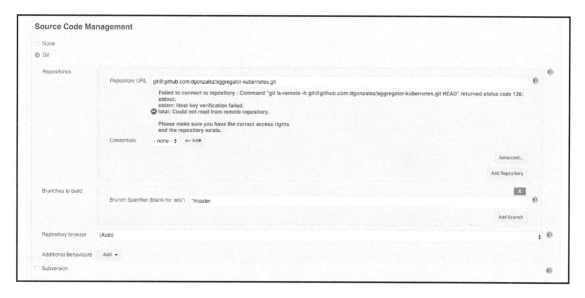

First, look at the GitHub repository. As you can see, it is creating an error, and that's is only because GitHub needs an SSH key to identify the clients. GitHub explains how to generate and configure such keys at https://help.github.com/articles/connecting-to-github-with-ssh/.

Once you have added the credentials with the private key that was generated, the error should be removed (remember, the type of credentials is 'SSH key with username', and your username has to match the one in GitHub).

Here, we can play a lot with Cit options, such as creating a tag on every build in order to trace what is going in your system or even building from tags. We are going to build the master branch: no tags this time.

Now, we are going to add our only build step for this job:

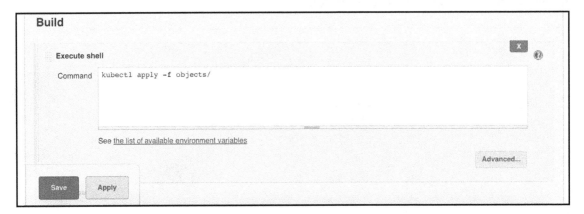

As you learned in previous chapters, with `kubectl apply`, we can pretty much rule the world. In this case, we are adding our folder with the `yamls` as a parameter; therefore, `kubectl` is going to action on Kubernetes with the YAML definitions that we are going to create.

Save the job and run it. Once it finishes, it should be successful with a log similar to the following one:

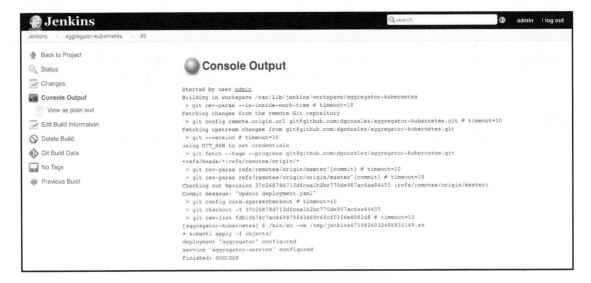

This job might fail a few times as there are many moving parts. By now, you have enough knowledge to troubleshoot the integration of these parts.

That's it. Our Continuous Delivery (CD) pipeline is working. From now on, if we want to make changes to our `aggregator`, we just need to add/modify files to our code repository, tag them with a new version, modify our `aggregator-kubernetes` definitions to point to the new image, and kick off our Jenkins job.

There are two extra steps:

- Create a tag
- Kick off a job manually

This is the price you pay for having a lot of control in our deployment but with a bit of a secret sauce: we are set for a great deployment flexibility, as we are going to see in the next section, but first, you should repeat the same exercise for `utcdate-service` and `isodate-service` so that we have our full system running. If you want to save a lot of time or check whether you are going in the right direction, check out my repository at `https://github.com/dgonzalez/chronos`.

Inside every service, there is a folder called definitions that contains the Kubernetes objects to make everything work.

 Be careful with the name of the services: the aggregator is expecting to be able to resolve `isodate-service` and `utcdate-service` from the DNS, so your Services (Kubernetes objects) should be named accordingly.

Regular release

Now we are all set; if you've completed the deployment of `utcdate-service` and `isodate-service`, a fully working system should be installed on Kubernetes. The way it works is very simple: When you get the URL of the `aggregator` in the `/dates/{timestamp}` path, replacing timestamp with a valid UNIX timestamp, the service will contact `utcdate-service` and `isodate-service` and get the timestamp converted into the UTC and ISO formats. In my case, the load balancer provided by Google Cloud Platform will lead to the URL: `http://104.155.35.237/dates/1111111111`.

It will have the following response:

```
{
    utcDate: "2005-03-18T01:58:31",
    isoDate: "2005-03-18T01:58:31.000Z"
}
```

You can play around with it for a bit, but it is nothing fancy: just a simple demo system that makes microservices and their automation easy to understand. In this case, we are not running any test, but for a continuous delivery pipeline, testing is a must (we will talk about this later).

Now as the title of the section suggests, we are going to create a new version of our application and release it using our continuous delivery pipeline.

Our new version it is going to be very simple but quite illustrative. On the `aggregator`, replace `index.js` with the following code:

```
const Hapi = require('hapi')
const server = new Hapi.Server()
let request = require('request')

server.connection({port: 8080})

server.route({
  method: 'GET',
  path: '/dates/{timestamp}',
  handler: (req, reply) => {
    const utcEndpoint =
`http://utcdate-service:3001/utcdate/${req.params.timestamp}`
    const isoEndpoint =
`http://isodate-service:3000/isodate/${req.params.timestamp}`
    request(utcEndpoint, (err, response, utcBody) => {
      if (err) {
        console.log(err)
        return
      }
      request(isoEndpoint, (err, response, isoBody) => {
      if (err) {
        console.log(err)
        return
      }
      reply({
        utcDate: JSON.parse(utcBody).date,
        isoDate: JSON.parse(isoBody).date,
        raw: req.params.timestamp
        })
      })
    })
```

```
    })
  }
})

server.start((err) => {
  if (err) {
    throw err
  }
  console.log('aggregator started on port 8080')
})
```

In the highlighted part, we have added a new section to the return object that basically returns the raw timestamp. Now it is time to commit the changes, but first, let's follow a good practice. Create a branch:

```
git checkout -b raw-timestap
```

This is going to create a local branch called `raw-timestamp`. Now commit the changes created in the preceding code:

```
git add . && git commit -m 'added raw timestamp'
```

And push the branch to GitHub:

```
git push origin raw-timestamp
```

If we visit the GitHub interfacenow, we'll notice that something has changed:

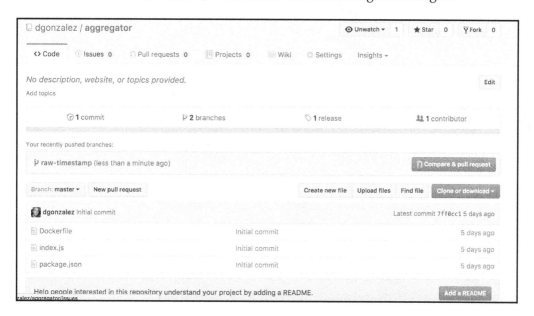

It is suggesting that we create a **Pull requests**. Basically, a pull request is a request to add code to a repository. Click on **Compare & pull request**and then add a description in the new form and click on **Create pull request**. This is the outcome:

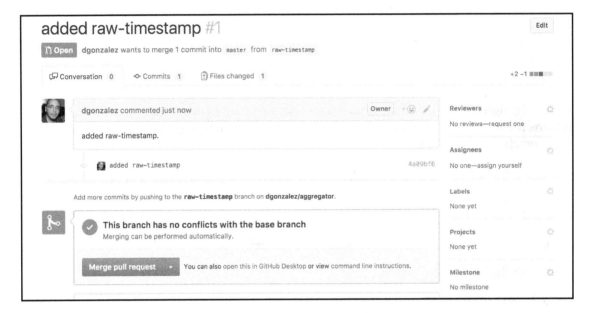

There are three tabs:

- **Conversation**
- **Commits**
- **Files changed**

The first one is a list of comments by the participants. The second tab is the list of commits that they pushed into the server, and the third one is the list of changes in diff style with additions and deletions, where you can drop comments asking for changes or suggesting better ways of doing things. In big projects, the master branch is usually blocked, and the only way to push code into it is via pull requests in order to enforce the review of the code.

Once you are happy, click on **Merge pull request** and merge the code. This pushes the changes into the master branch (needs confirmation).

Now we are ready to create a tag. This can be done via the GitHub interface. If you click on the **release**link (beside the number of contributors above the list of files), it brings you to the releases page:

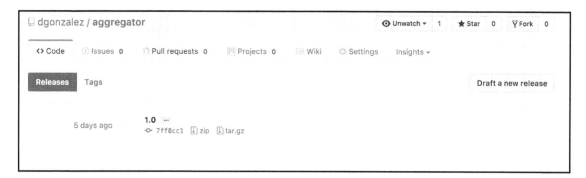

There, you can see the tag that we created earlier from the terminal and a button called **Draft a new release**. Click on it, and it will show a new form:

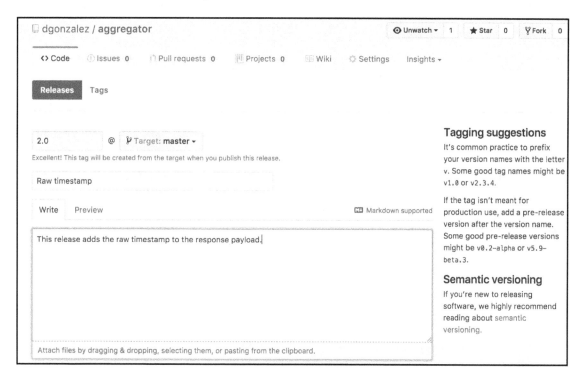

Fill in the details, as shown here, and create the release. This creates a tag that is connected to our container registry in Google Cloud Platform, and by now (it is very quick), a new version of our image should be available:

As you can see, there is a good level of control over what is going into our production buckets (registry and cluster). Now the only step left is to release the new version into Kubernetes. Go back to the repository called `aggregator-kubernetes` (we created it in the preceding section) and change the tag of the image in the `deployment.yaml` file from `eu.gcr.io/implementing-modern-devops/aggregator-service:1.0` to `eu.gcr.io/implementing-modern-devops/aggregator-service:2.0`. Be aware that the project needs to be tailored to your configuration.

Once this is done, commit and push the changes (from `aggregator-kubernetes` folder):

```
git add . && git commit -m 'version 2.0 of aggregator' && git push origin
master
```

Now everything is ready. We are at the edge of the cliff. If we click on **Run** in the job that we created in Jenkins, the new version of the software is going to be deployed in Kubernetes with zero downtime (depending on your configuration, as seen earlier); we have the control. We can decide when is the best time to release, and we have an easy way to roll back: revert the changes and click on **Run** again in Jenkins.

Once you are comfortable with the changes, run the job that we created in Jenkins (in my case, `aggregator-kubernetes`).

If you hit the same URL as earlier (`http://104.155.35.237/dates/1111111111`), the result should have changed a bit:

```
{
    utcDate: "2005-03-18T01:58:31",
    isoDate: "2005-03-18T01:58:31.000Z",
    raw: "1111111111"
}
```

The new version is up. As you can imagine, this is a fairly powerful argument to adopt DevOps: release software transparently to the users with minimal effort (create a tag and run a job in Jenkins).

In the next section, we are going to execute the same deployment but using a technique called blue-green deployment, which consist on release the new version in a private mode running in the production environment in order for us to test the features before making them available to the general public.

Blue-green deployment

In order to execute a blue-green deployment, first, we need to roll back to version 1.0. Edit `deployment.yaml` in `aggregator-kubernetes`, adjust the image to the tag `1.0`, and push the changes to GitHub. Once that is done, run a job called `aggregator-kubernetes`in Jenkins,and there you go; we have rolled back to version 1.0. Leave version 2.0 of the image in the registry as we are going to use it.

A blue-green deployment is a technique used to release software to production that is not visible to the general public, so we can test it before making it available to everyone. Kubernetes makes this extremely simple: the only thing we need to do is duplicate the resourcesin `aggregator-kubernetes` and assign to them different names and tags. For example, this is our `deployment-bluegreen.yaml`:

```
apiVersion: extensions/v1beta1
kind: Deployment
metadata:
  name: aggregator-bluegreen
spec:
  replicas: 2
  template:
    metadata:
      labels:
        app: aggregator-service-2.0
    spec:
      containers:
```

```
  - name: aggregator-service
    image: eu.gcr.io/implementing-modern-devops/aggregator-service:2.0
    ports:
      - containerPort: 8080
```

And this is our `service-bluegreen.yaml`:

```
kind: Service
apiVersion: v1
metadata:
  name: aggregator-service-bluegreen
spec:
  ports:
  - port: 80
    targetPort: 8080
  selector:
    app: aggregator-service-2.0
  type: LoadBalancer
```

As you can see, we have created a vertical slice of our app with a different set of selectors/tags; therefore, our original version is working, but now, we have a new service called `aggregator-service-bluegreen` that serves the new version of our application via a load balancer, which we can check via the Kubernetes interface (using the `kubectl proxy` command, as explained earlier):

Services

Name	Labels	Cluster IP	Internal endpoints	External endpoints	
✓ aggregator-service	-	10.63.248.231	aggregator-service:80 ... aggregator-service:311...	104.155.35.237:80 ⧉	⋮
✓ aggregator-service-blu...	-	10.63.241.255	aggregator-service-blu... aggregator-service-blu...	146.148.17.32:80 ⧉	⋮
✓ isodate-service	-	10.63.244.240	isodate-service:3000 T... isodate-service:0 TCP	-	⋮
✓ kubernetes	component: apiserver provider: kubernetes	10.63.240.1	kubernetes:443 TCP kubernetes:0 TCP	-	⋮
✓ utcdate-service	-	10.63.249.144	utcdate-service:3001 T... utcdate-service:0 TCP	-	⋮

If you play around the two external endpoints, you can see the difference: the new one is returning the raw payload as well as the dates in the ISO format and in UTC timezone (version 2.0), whereas the old one only returns the dates (version 1.0).

We are now in what we call the blue status: we are happy with our release and we are sure that our software works with our production configuration without affecting any of our customers. If there was any problem, no customers would have noticed it. Now it is time to go to the green phase. We have two options here:

- Remove the `aggregator-bluegreen` deployment and all its children (ReplicaSet and pods as well as the `aggregator-service-bluegreen` service) and upgrade our base deployment (`aggregator`)
- Change the labels for the selector in the aggregator service and make it point to the new Pods

In general, I am a big fan of the first option as it keeps things simple, but it is your choice; also it's a good time for experimenting. Changing the selector in the service has an immediate effect, and it is probably the easy route if you are in a hurry.

When working with complex systems, I always try togo over a blue-green deployment phase to remove stress from the team. Think about it: instead of thinking that everything is solid, you are actually verifying that everything works as expected with no surprises, so the psychological factor of the uncertainty is gone at the moment of release.

In the next section, we are going to visit another type of release, which introduces a new pod into the running system so we get to expose it to the users but only to a subset of them, so if something goes wrong, it does not kill the system; it just produces some errors. Before proceeding, make sure that you return your cluster to the original status: just a deployment called `aggregator` with its pods (remove the blue-green deployment).

Canary deployment

There is a story about the name of this type of deployment, which very interesting. Before all the gas detectors, miners used to bring a canary (the bird) into the mines, as they are extremely sensitive to dangerous gases. Everybody was working normally but keeping an eye on the bird. If, for some reason, the bird died, everybody would leave the mine in order to avoid getting poisoned or even killed.

This is exactly what we are going to do: introduce a new version of our software, which will actually produce errors if there is any problem so we only impact a limited number of customers.

Again, this is done via the YAMl files using the selectors that our service is targeting but with a new version of our app. Before continuing, make sure that you have only one deployment called `aggregator` with two pods running the version 1.0 of our app (as shown in the **Regular Release** section).

Now, in `aggregator-kubernetes`, create a file (inside objects folder) with the following content:

```
apiVersion: extensions/v1beta1
kind: Deployment
metadata:
  name: aggregator-canary
spec:
  replicas: 1
  template:
    metadata:
      labels:
        app: aggregator-service
    spec:
      containers:
      - name: aggregator-service
        image: eu.gcr.io/implementing-modern-devops/aggregator-service:2.0
        ports:
        - containerPort: 8080
```

Here's an easy explanation: we are creating a new deployment, with only one Pod, with the same tags that the original deployment pods (`aggregator`) has; therefore, the `aggregator-service` is going to target this pod as well: three in total.

Push the changes to GitHub and run the job `aggregator-kubernetes`, which will apply this configuration to our cluster. Now open the endpoint that we used earlier for testing, in my case, `http://104.155.35.237/dates/1111111111`, and keep refreshing the URL a few times. Approximately, one-third of the requests should come back with the raw timestamp (new version of the app) and two-third should come back without it (version 1.0).

You can verify that everything went well via the Kubernetes dashboard by checking the
`aggregator-service`:

Here, you can see the newly created pod being targeted by our service. I usually leave this
status for a few hours/days (depending on the release), and once I am happy, I remove the
`canary` deployment and apply the configuration to the `aggregator` deployment. You can
play with the number of replicas as well in order to change the percentage of the users that
get the new version or even gradually increasethe number of `canaries` and decrease the
number of regular pods until the application is completely rolled out.

This strategy is followed by big companies such as Google to release new features with a lot
of success. I am a big fan of using it as starting point when the system is big enough (10 +
pods running), but I would be reluctant to do that in a small system as the percentage of
affected requests would be too big (33.3% in the preceding example).

Summary

This chapter was pretty intense: we set up a CD pipeline as well as visited the most common release strategies, which, using Kubernetes, were within the reach of our hand. Everything was automated except a couple of checkpoints that were left on purpose so that we could control what was going in our system (just for peace of mind). This was the climax of the book: even though the examples were basic, they provided you with enough tools to set up something similar in your company in order to get the benefit of working with microservices but padding the operational overhead that they involve as well as facilitating the release of new versions.

In the next chapter, we will learn an important aspect of continuous delivery: monitoring. With the right monitoring in place we can remove a lot of stress from the releases so that our engineers are more confident on being able to catch errors early leading into smoother rollouts and a lower production bug count.

9
Monitoring

Introduction

So far, we have seen a large number of tools that we can use as DevOps engineers in our company to enhance our capabilities. Now we are able to provision servers with Ansible, create Kubernetes clusters on Google Cloud Platform, and set up a delivery pipeline for our microservices. We have also dived deep into how Docker works and how we should organize our company to be a successful delivering software.

In this chapter, we are going to take a look at the **missing piece of the puzzle**: monitoring. Usually overlooked, monitoring is, in my opinion, a key component of a successful DevOps company. Monitoring is the first line of defense against problems. In `Chapter 8`, *Release Management – Continuous Delivery*, we talked about how we should shift our focus toward being able to fix the arising problems rather than spending a huge amount of resources in trying to prevent them:

> *20 percent of your time will create 80 percent of the functionality. The other 20 percent is going to cost you 80 percent of your time.*

This non-written rule dominates the world. With monitoring, we can bend this rule to live comfortably with 20 percent of unknown outcomes as we are able to identify the problems quite quickly.

We will review some of the tools to monitor software, but our focus will be on Stackdriver, as it is the monitoring solution from Google Cloud Platform that, out of the box, provides us with a fairly comprehensive set of tools to deal with the flaws in our systems.

Types of monitoring

In the SRE book from Google, there are two types of monitoring defined:

- BlackBox monitoring
- WhiteBox monitoring

This is generally accepted by everyone, leading to a solid amount of tools that are clearly differentiated around whitebox and blackbox monitoring.

One of the best comparisons I've ever heard on whitebox versus blackbox monitoring is the diagnosis of a bone fracture. When you first go to the doctor, he/she only has access to your blackbox metrics:

- Does the area have any bump?
- Is it painful on movement?

Then, once the initial diagnoses has been pronounced, the next step is getting X-rays from the area. Now we can confirm whether the bone is broken and, if it is, what is the impact in the system. The X-rays are the WhiteBox monitoring that the doctor is using.

Blackbox monitoring

Whitebox monitoring is the type of monitoring that observes a system from outside without having to look into how the system is built. These metrics are the first ones that impact the users and the first external symptoms that something is going wrong in our application or server.

Among the metrics that can be used for blackbox monitoring, we can find the following ones:

- Latency
- Throughput

These two metrics are the holy grail of blackbox monitoring.

The latency is, by definition, how long takes our system to respond. If we are looking at an HTTP server, from the very first time that we sent the request to the time when the server on the other side of the line replies is what we understand as latency. This metric is a fairly interesting one because it is the absolute truth about how the users see our system: the bigger the latency is, the worse the experience they get.

Throughput is extremely related to the latency. Basically, it is the number of requests that our software can serve per time unit, usually per second. This measure is a critical one for capacity planning, and you are discouraged to measure it in real time in a running system, as it pushes a lot of load through the system, which is surely going to affect the response time for live users. In general, throughput is measured at the performance testing stage of our application, which might be tricky:

- The hardware for testing has to match production
- The dataset for the database has to be similar to production

The performance testing step is usually overlooked by many of the companies as it is fairly expensive. That is why preproduction is usually used for capacity testing in order to guess the amount of hardware needed in production. Nowadays, this is less problematic, as with auto scaling groups in the cloud infrastructure, it becomes less of a problem as the infrastructure is going to scale on its own when needed.

As you can see, these metrics are fairly simple to understand, and even though they play a key role in the error response time, they might not be the first indicators of problems.

Whitebox monitoring

Whitebox monitoring, as the name indicates, is the monitoring that needs to know about how the system is built in order to raise alerts on certain events happening inside of our application or infrastructure. These metrics are quite fine-grained (unlike blackbox monitoring), and once we have been alerted, they are the answer to the main questions of a postmortem analysis:

- Where is the problem?
- What is causing the problem?
- Which flows are affected?
- What can we do to avoid this in future?

Among other metrics, these are a fairly interesting set of examples:

- Function execution time
- Errors per time unit
- Requests per time unit
- Memory usage
- CPU usage

- Hard drive usage
- I/O operations per time unit

As you can see, there is an endless number of whitebox metrics to ensure the stability of our system. There are almost too many, so we usually need to pick the right ones in order to avoid the noise.

An important detail here is the fact that when a blackbox monitoring metric gives an abnormal reading, there is always a whitebox metric that can be used to diagnose, but it is not true the other way around. A server can have a spike in the memory usage due to an internal problem without impacting the users.

One of the most important artifacts in whitebox monitoring are the logging files. These files are the ordered chain of events happening in our software, and usually, they are the first line of attack to diagnose problems related to our software. The main problem with log files is the fact that they are stored on production servers and we should not access them on a regular basis just to check the log files as it is a security threat on its own. It only takes an open terminal to a server forgotten by someone to give access rights to the wrong person.

Monitoring third-party tools

Monitoring is usually a good candidate to involve third-party companies. It requires a fair amount of redundancy in the systems in order to keep the monitoring active, which is primordial in order to ensure that we are not blind to what is happening in our system.

Another positive aspect of using third-party apps for monitoring is the fact that they don't live in the same data center, and if they do (usually AWS), their redundancy is enough to ensure stability.

In this section, we are going to take a look at three tools in particular:

- Pingdom
- Logentries
- AppDynamics

That doesn't mean that they are the best or the only tools in the market. There are other interesting alternatives (for example, New Relic instead of AppDynamics) that are worth exploring, but in this case, we are going to focus on Stackdriver, the monitoring solution for Google Cloud Platform, due to a number of factors:

- It integrates very well with Google Cloud Platform

- It has a very interesting free tier
- The alerting systems are one of the most advanced systems you can find in the market

Pingdom

Pingdom is a tool used to measure the latency of our servers from different sides of the world. As you can see, if you have worked in a 24/7 company, latency across the globe varies a lot depending on where our customers are in relation to our data centers. As a matter of curiosity, if our server is in Europe, someone from Australia will have around 2-3 seconds extra on the latency.

Pingdom has servers spread across the globe to monitor how our users see the system and take adequate measures to solve the problem (for example, spawning a new data center closer to them).

You can register in Pingdom for free with a 14-days trial, but you need to enter a credit card (don't worry; they will advise you when your trial is over so you can cancel the plan if you don't want to continue with it).

Take a look at the following screenshot:

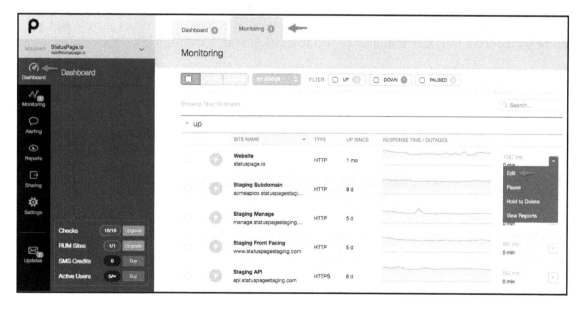

As you can see, after specifying hosts, Pingdom will start issuing requests to the specified URL and measuring the response time from different parts of the world.

Lately, Pingdom has included fairly interesting capabilities: now it can read custom metrics through an endpoint in order to monitor an endless amount of data:

- Free space on the disks
- Used amount of RAM
- Stock levels (yes, you can send any number of items you have left in your warehouse to Pingdom)

In general, I have used Pingdom quite successfully in the past to measure the latency in my servers and improve the experience of the users by distributing the data centers strategically across the globe to mitigate this problem. One of the most interesting insights that Pingdom (and similar tools) can give you is that your site might be down due to network splits on the internet or failures in some DNS servers (in the latter case, it is not really down but Pingdom and users won't be able to reach it).

Logentries

Logentries is one of these companies that makes your life much easier when dealing with a large number of logs. It basically solves one problem that was an impediment for few years: it aggregates all the logs from your system in a common place with access controls and a more than decent interface that allows you to quickly search through big datasets.

Creating an account is free, and it provides 30 days of usage with some limits that are more than enough for testing and evaluation.

Go to `https://logentries.com/` and create an account. Once you are logged in, the first screen should be similar to what is shown in the following screenshot:

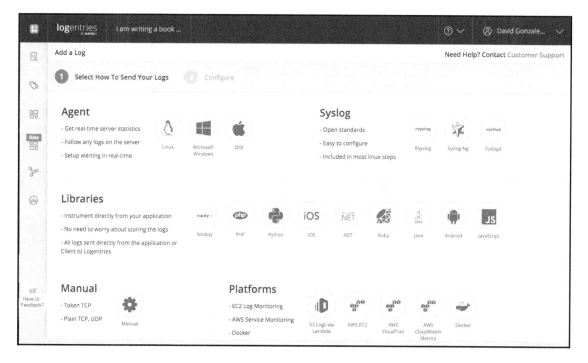

As you can see, there are explanations for how to configure the log aggregation in an endless number of platforms: you can monitor from systems to libraries going through a number of platforms (AWS, Docker, and so on).

Agents are usually a good choice for two reasons:

- They do not create coupling in your application (the agent reads the log files and sends them to the Logentries servers)
- They push the complexity to a third-party software

But there are also other interesting options, such as manual log aggregation. In this case, we are going to demonstrate how to use a custom logger to send logs from a very simple Node.js application to Logentries. Create a folder called `logentries` and execute the following command:

```
npm init
```

This assumes that Node.js is installed on your system, so if it is not, download any version of Node.js from `https://nodejs.org/en/` and install it.

Now we need to install the Logentries library for Node.js. Logentries provides support for a number of platforms, but support for Node.js is particularly good. Execute the following command:

```
npm install --save le_node
```

Once it is finished, we should have the required library installed. Now it is time to create a simple Node.js program to demonstrate how it works, but first, we need to create a service token. On the following screen, click on **Manual** and fill in the form, as follows:

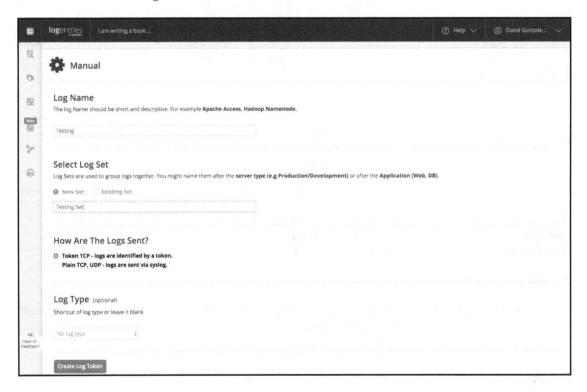

Logentries is able to understand many different types of logs, but it really shines on JSON logs. We don't need to specify any type of logs for it to catch them, so leave this option empty and give a name to the log and the set. Once you click on **Create Log Token**, the token should be displayed after the button. Save it for later; you are going to need it.

Now if we go to the main dashboard, we should be able to see our log set called **Testing Set**:

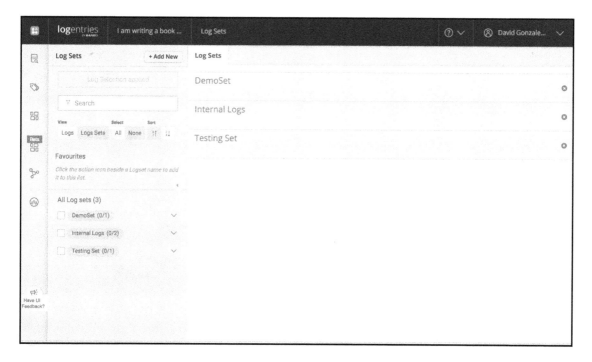

Now it is time to send some data:

```
const Logger = require('le_node')
const logger = new Logger({token: '5bffdd28-fb7d-46b6-857a-c3a7dfed5410'})

logger.info('this is a test message')
logger.err('this is an error message')
logger.log('debug', {message: 'This is a json debug message', json: true})
```

This script is enough to send data to Logentries. Be aware that the token specified has to be replaced by the token obtained in the previous step. Save it as index.js and execute it a few times:

```
node index.js
```

Once you have executed it a few times, head back to Logentries and open **Test log** inside **Testing Set**:

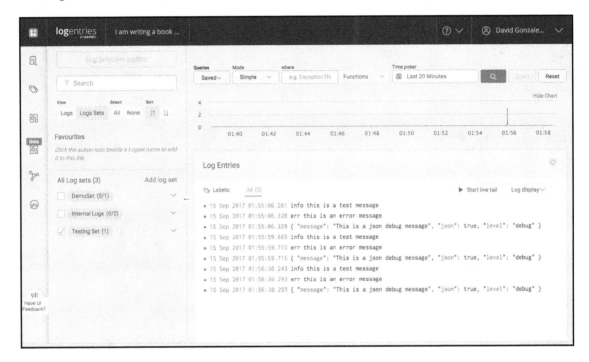

Now you can see our logs in Logentries being aggregated. There are some interesting things in Logentries that have been improving with time:

- The UI is quite slick
- The search mechanisms are very powerful
- Logentries is able to live stream the logs in real time (more or less)

Regarding search mechanisms, Logentries has developed something called **LEQL**, which is basically a language designed by Logentries to search for certain events using JSON fields or just plain text searching. You can find more information about it at `https://docs.logentries.com/v1.0/docs/search/`.

The other interesting feature is the live tailing of the logs. Let's test that feature. Create another file in the project called `livetail.js` and add the following code:

```
const Logger = require('le_node')

const logger = new Logger({token: '5bffdd28-fb7d-46b6-857a-b3a7dfed5410'})

setInterval(() => {
  logger.info(`This is my timed log on ${Date.now()}`)
}, 500)
```

It does not need explanation: a function that gets executed every 500 milliseconds and sends a log line to Logentries.

Execute the script:

node livetail.js

It might look like nothing is happening, but things are actually happening. Go back to Logentries and click on the **Start live tail** button:

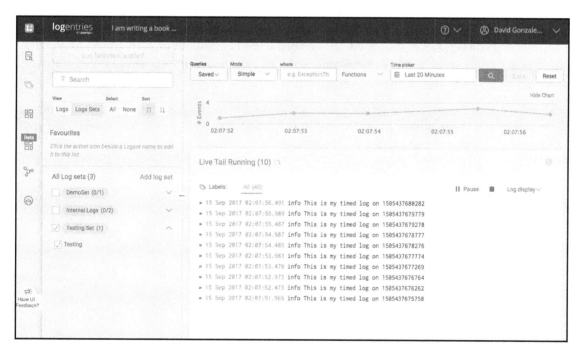

After a couple of seconds (or less), the logs will start flowing. This can be done on any log file that is stored in Logentries, and it is a fairly interesting mechanism to debug problems in our servers.

Logentries is also able to send alerts to a certain email. You can configure it to alert your team on the following:

- Exceptions
- Patterns
- Lack of logs
- Increased activity

This alert is usually the first indicator of problems on a system, so if you want an early response to errors, the best practice is to try to reduce the noise up to a point where alerts are not missed and the false positives are reduced to a minimum.

AppDynamics

AppDynamics was the king for a while (as it was the only real option on monitoring). It is a very curated software that allows you to explore what is going on in your software and servers: exceptions, requests per time unit, and CPU usage are among many other metrics that AppDynamics can capture for us.

It also captures interactions with the third-party endpoints: if our software is consuming a third-party API, AppDynamics will know about it and display the calls in a dashboard similar to the next screenshot:

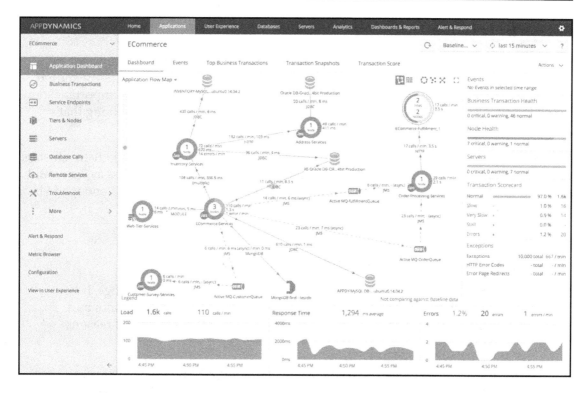

AppDynamics is quite advanced regarding proactive measures. One of these measures is automated actions, such as restarting a Tomcat server or reloading a service running on the server on certain events. For example, if we deploy a new version of our Java application that is having a problem with the PermGen space (this is not the case anymore in Java 8+), it is usually very tricky to fix as the problem comes from many classes loaded by the JVM and only manifests a few hours after the deployment. In some cases, we can instruct AppDynamics to restart the application when the usage reaches 80 percent and more of the assigned total so that instead of crashing badly and not being able to serve to any customers, we only have a few dropouts every few hour getting an air balloon to act and fix the problem.

AppDynamics works with what is known an agent model. An application needs to be installed on your server (for example, Tomcat) in order to collect metrics that are sent to a centralized server to process and create the pertinent dashboards and trigger the workflows. The interesting part of AppDynamics is that if you don't feel comfortable sending data to a third-party (which is usually a security requirement for companies handling high-profile data), they provide an on-premises version of the dashboard.

Stackdriver

Up until now, we have visited a set of tools from different third-parties but now we are going to take a look at Stackdriver. Stackdriver was a cloud monitoring solution acquired by Google and integrated (not fully) into Google Cloud Platform. This is an important step for GCP, as being able to provide an integrated monitoring solution is something that's pretty much mandatory nowadays.

With Stackdriver, we are not only able to monitor applications, but also Kubernetes clusters or even standalone VMs. As we will see, the integration is not yet as seamless as we would desire (it might be completed by the time you are reading this), but it is good enough to be considered a big player in the market.

Monitoring applications

Stackdriver can monitor standalone applications by capturing metrics and logs. It has support for major platforms and libraries, so our technology choices should not be a concern. In this case, we are going to create a Node.js application for several reasons:

- It is easy to understand
- The official examples are well documented for the Node.js version
- Node.js is increasingly becoming a big platform for enterprise and startups

The first thing we need to do is write a small Node.js application. Create a new folder and execute this command:

```
npm init
```

Follow the instructions on the screen and you should now have `package.json` in the folder that you just created. Now it is time to install the dependencies:

```
npm install --save @google-cloud/logging-bunyan @google-cloud/trace-agent
express bunyan
```

We are going to use four libraries:

- **express**: To handle the HTTP requests
- **bunyan**: To log our application activity

The two libraries from Google are for interacting with Stackdriver:

- **logging-bunyan**: This will send the logs from bunyan to Stackdriver
- **trace-agent**: This will trace the requests through our application

Now let's create a simple application:

```
require('@google-cloud/trace-agent').start()
const express = require('express')
const bunyan = require('bunyan')
const LoggingBunyan = require('@google-cloud/logging-bunyan')
const loggingBunyan = LoggingBunyan()

const log = bunyan.createLogger({
 name: "stackdriver",
 streams: [
 {stream: process.stdout},
 loggingBunyan.stream()
 ],
 level: 'info'
})

const app = express()

app.get('/', (req, res) => {
 log.info(`request from ${req.connection.remoteAddress}`)
 res.send('Hello World!')
})

app.listen(3000, () => {
 console.log('Listening in port 3000')
})
```

Now it is time to explain what the interesting parts of the code do:

- The first line enables the tracing for Stackdriver. It is very important that this line happen before anything else; otherwise, the tracing won't work. We'll see how amazing the tracing is.
- In order to let Stackdriver collect logs, we need to add a stream to the bunyan logger, as shown in the code.

Everything else is quite normal: an `Express.js` Node.js application that has a handler for the URL/replying with the classic Hello World.

There is one thing missing: there are no credentials to access the remote APIs. This is done on purpose as Google Cloud Platform has a very sophisticated system for handling credentials: basically, it will be handled for you.

Now, it is time to deploy our application. First, create a VM in Google Cloud Platform, as we have seen a few times in the previous chapters. A small one will suffice, but make sure that you allow HTTP traffic. Debian Stretch is a good choice as an operating system.

Once the machine is up, install Node.js, as shown in `http://nodejs.org`.

Now we need to copy the code into our newly created machine. The best solution is to create a GitHub repository or use mine: `https://github.com/dgonzalez/stackdriver`.

By cloning it in our VM (don't forget to install Git first via `apt`), we just need to install the dependencies with the following command:

```
npm install
```

And we are good to go. Just run the application with the following command:

```
node index.js
```

Now go to the external IP of the machine (shown in Google Compute Engine) on port `3000`. In my case, this is `http://35.195.151.10:3000/`.

Once we have done it, we should see Hello World in the browser and something similar to the following in the logs of our app:

```
Listening in port 3000
{"name":"stackdriver","hostname":"instance-3","pid":4722,"level":30,"msg":"
request from ::ffff:46.7.23.229","time":"2017-09-18T01:50:41.483Z","v":0}
```

If there are no errors, everything worked. In order to verify this, go to `http://console.cloud.google.com` and open the **Logging** section of Stackdriver.

Stackdriver is a different system from Google Cloud Platform; it might ask you to log in using a Google account.

Once you are there, you should see something similar to what is shown in the following screenshot:

Be aware that you have to select the section on the logs, in my case, GCE VM Instance, Instance-3.

This is exactly the log from your app uploaded to Google Cloud Platform with a bunch of very interesting information. You can play around by having different handlers for other URLs and different logging events, but the result is the same: all your logs will be aggregated here.

Now we can do this with Trace as well. Open the trace section of Google Cloud Platform under Stackdriver.

The screen should look similar to what is shown in the following screenshot (select the traces list option):

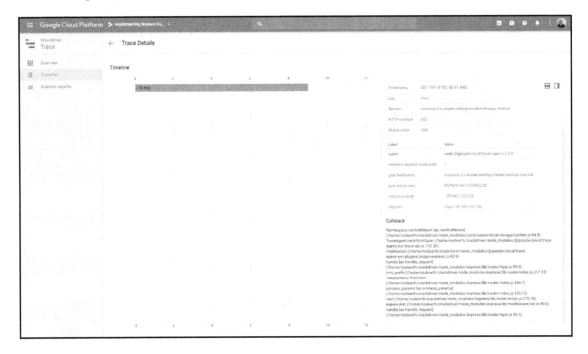

As you can see, there is a lot of useful information:

- The call stack
- Duration
- Start and finish time

You can also play around, issue multiple calls, and get familiar yourself with how it works. Now we are going to modify our program to call a third-party API and see how Stackdriver is able to trace it:

```
require('@google-cloud/trace-agent').start()

const express = require('express')
const bunyan = require('bunyan')
const LoggingBunyan = require('@google-cloud/logging-bunyan')
const request = require('request')

const loggingBunyan = LoggingBunyan()

const URL = "https://www.googleapis.com/discovery/v1/apis"

const log = bunyan.createLogger({
 name: "stackdriver",
 streams: [
 {stream: process.stdout},
 loggingBunyan.stream()
 ],
 level: 'info'
})

const app = express()

app.get('/', (req, res) => {
 log.info(`request from ${req.connection.remoteAddress}`)
 res.send('Hello World!')
})
app.get('/discovery', (req, res) => {
 request(URL, (error, response, body) => {
   return res.send(body)
 })
})
app.listen(3000, () => {
 console.log('Listening in port 3000')
})
```

Now we are listing all the available APIs on Google by executing an HTTP GET into the `https://www.googleapis.com/discovery/v1/apis` URL. Redeploy it into your VM in Google Cloud Platform and go to the endpoint/discovery of your VM. A big JSON payload will be presented on your screen, but the interesting part is happening under the hood. Go back to Stackdriver in the **Trace list** section, and you'll see that there is a new trace being captured:

Here, you can see how our program contacted the remote API and that it took 68 seconds to reply.

Getting this type of information in real time is very powerful--if customers are getting a very large response time, we can immediately see what is happening inside of our application pretty much real-time.

Monitoring Kubernetes clusters

Kubernetes covers 99 percent of the needs for any software company, but one part where it does not really shine is in embedded monitoring, leaving a space to be filled by third-parties. The main problem with Kubernetes comes from Docker: containers are ephemeral, so a common practice is to dump the logs into the standard output/error and use *syslogd* to gather them in a centralized location.

With Kubernetes, we have an added problem: the orchestrator on top of Docker needs to know how to fetch logs in order to make them available via the API or dashboard, so it is possible for the user to access them when required. But then there is another problem. Usually, logs are rotated on the basis of time and archived in order to avoid a log sprawl that can consume all the free space in our servers, preventing the application (and the OS) from functioning normally.

The best solution is to use an external system to aggregate logs and events inside the cluster so that we push the complexity to the side, allowing Kubernetes to focus on what it does best: orchestrate containers.

In this case, in order to integrate our cluster with Stackdriver in Google Cloud Platform, the only thing that we need to do is mark the two checkboxes in the cluster creation screen:

This will enable the monitoring across the different nodes in our cluster and improve the way in which we tackle problems happening in our applications. Click on **Create** and allow the cluster to be provisioned (might take a few seconds or even minutes). It does not need to be a big cluster; just use the small size for the machines, and two VMs will be enough. In fairness, we will probably need to reduce the size during the load testing in order to speed up the alerting part.

> As we've seen in the previous section, with GKE monitoring active, Kubernetes also sends the logs to the Logging capabilities of Stackdriver, so you don't need to connect to the nodes to fetch the logs.

Once it is created, we are going to add monitoring from Stackdriver. The first thing that we need to do is open **Monitoring** in the Stackdriver section of Google Cloud Platform. This will open a new site, the original Stackdriver site, which looks very similar to what is shown in the following screenshot:

Even though the UI might be a bit confusing in the beginning, after a bit of usage, it becomes clear that it is really hard to pack the huge amount of functionality that Stackdriver offers in a better UI. By default, we can see some metrics about our cluster (the bottom-right section of the image), but they are not very useful: we don't want to have someone looking at the metrics the full day in order to raise alerts. Let's automate it. The first thing that we need to do is create a group. A group is basically a set of resources that work together, in this case, our cluster. Click on **Groups** and create a new one:

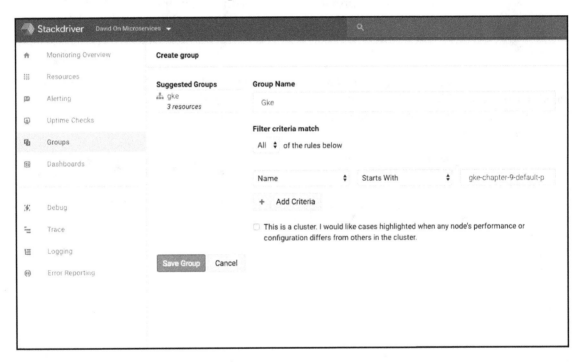

By default, Stackdriver will suggest groupings to you. In this case, in the suggested **Groups** section, we can see that Stackdriver has suggested our cluster. It is possible to add more sophisticated criteria, but in this case, matching the start of the name of our machines will work as the GKE names them according to some criteria, including the name of the cluster in the very beginning.

Create a group (call it GKE, the default suggested name). Once the group is created, you can navigate to it and see different metrics such as CPU or even configure them, adding others such as disk I/O and similar. Get yourself familiar with the dashboard:

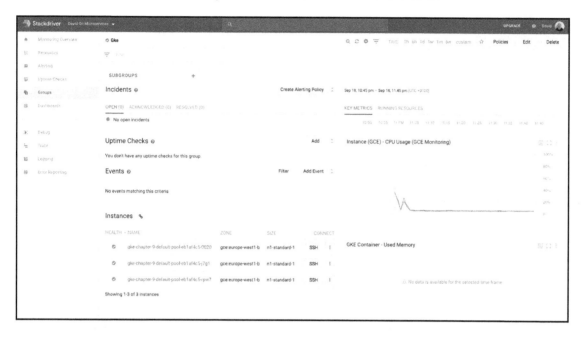

In my case, I have added a metric for capturing the used memory in the cluster. Even though this amount of available data is quite interesting, there is an even more powerful tool: the alerting policies.

The alerting policies are criteria in which we should get alerted: high memory usage, low disk space, or high CPU utilization, among others, are events that we want to know about in order to take actions as soon as possible. The beauty of the alerting policies is that if we configure them as appropriated, we enter a state that I call the *autopilot* mode: we don't need to worry about the performance of the system unless we get alerted, which drastically reduces the number of people required to operate a system.

Let's create an alerting policy by clicking on the **Create Alerting Policy** button:

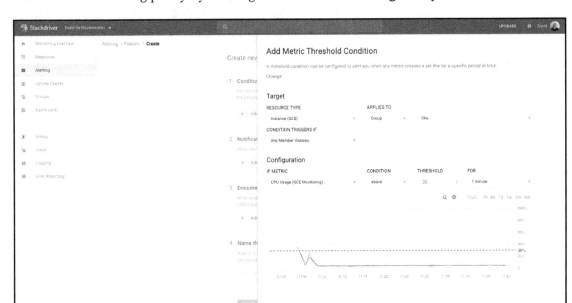

As shown in the preceding screen, we need to select a metric. We are going to use the type Metric Threshold as it is included in the basic package of Stackdriver, so we don't need to upgrade to a Premium subscription. Our alert is going to be raised if any of the members of our cluster has a CPU usage of more than 30 percent for one minute.

The next step is to configure the notification. In the basic package, only email is included, but it is sufficient to test how the system works. Stackdriver also allows you to include text to be sent across with the notification. Just enter something like `Test alert` alongside your email and save the alert policy with the name of your choice.

As you can see, creating alerts is very simple in Stackdriver. This is a very simplistic example, but once you have set up your cluster, the next step is to set up the acceptable set of metrics where it should operate normally and get alerted if any of them is violated.

Now it is time to set off the alarm to see what happens. In order to do that, we need to overload the cluster with several replicas of the same image, and we are going to use a tool called Apache benchmark to generate a load on the system:

```
kubectl run my-nginx --image=nginx --replicas=7 --port=80
```

And now expose the deployment called `my-nginx`:

```
kubectl expose my-nginx --type=LoadBalancer
```

Be aware that you first need to configure `kubectl` to point to your cluster, as we've seen in previous chapters.

Once nginx is deployed, it is time to stress it out:

```
ab -k -c 350 -n 4000000 http://130.211.65.42/
```

The `ab` tool is a very powerful benchmark tool called Apache Benchmark. We are going to create 350 concurrent consumers, and they will issue 4 million requests in total. It might be possible that you need to reduce the size of your cluster in order to stress the CPU: if you reduce the size while the benchmark is running, Kubernetes will need to reschedule containers to reorganize the resources, adding more load to the system.

> I would recommend that you further explore Apache Benchmark, as it is very useful for load testing.

Once the CPU has gone beyond the threshold for any of our nodes for over a minute, we should receive an alert by email, and it should be displayed in the Stackdriver interface:

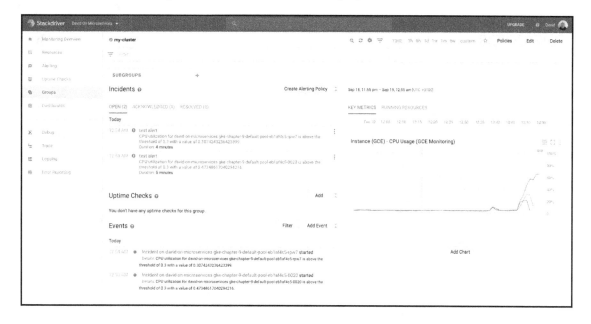

In this case, I have received two alerts as two of the nodes went beyond the limits. These alerts follow a workflow. You can acknowledge them if the rule is still broken and they will go to resolved once they are acknowledged and the condition has disappeared. In this case, if you stop Apache Benchmark and acknowledge the raised alerts, they will go straight into the resolved state.

In the Premium version, there are more advanced policies, such as Slack messages or SMS, which allows your team to set up a rota for acknowledging incidents and managing the actions.

Summary

This is the final chapter of the book. Through the entire book, we visited the most important tools used by DevOps engineers, with a strong focus on the Google Cloud Platform. In this chapter, we experimented with what, in my opinion, is a very important aspect of any system: monitoring. I am of the opinion that monitoring is the best way to tackle problems once they have hit your production systems, which, no matter how much effort you put in it, will eventually happen.

What is next?

This book did not go particularly in deep into any subject. This is intended. This book is meant to plant the seed of a big tree: the culture of DevOps, hoping that you have enough information to keep growing your knowledge of DevOps tools and processes.

Keeping yourself up to date with the latest tools is a full-time job on its own, but it's very necessary if you want to be on the top of the wave. My opinion is that we are very lucky to be able to participate in the rise and shine of the DevOps culture, and the future is bright. Automation and better languages (Golang, Kotlin, Node.js, and so on) will allow us to reduce human intervention, improving the overall resilience of our systems.

If you look five years back and compare it with what it is there in the market today, can you imagine how our jobs are going to be in 15 years?

If you want to follow up about any question or check what I am working on nowadays, you can always get in touch with me in LinkedIn:

- `https://www.linkedin.com/in/david-gonzalez-microservices/`

Index